HATH GOD SAID?

WHO IS RIGHT -
GOD OR THE LIBERALS?

— By —

UURAS SAARNIVAARA, Th.D., Ph.D.

WIPF & STOCK · Eugene, Oregon

Wipf and Stock Publishers
199 W 8th Ave, Suite 3
Eugene, OR 97401

Hath God Said?
Who is Right - God or the Liberals?
By Saarnivaara, Uuras
Copyright©1968 by Saarnivaara, Uuras
ISBN 13: 978-1-55635-885-2
Publication date 3/6/2008
Previously published by Osterhus, 1968

CONTENTS

	Page
FOR ORIENTATION	9
I. WHO TELLS WHAT THE TRUTH IS?	12
1. Traditionalistic View	13
2. Liberal or Subjectivistic Position	13

Mysticism, Rationalism, Schleiermacher, Ritschl, Kant, 13; Theory of evolution, 14.

   3. Bible-believing Evangelical Position 15

The original Christian view. Thirty-nine Articles of the Anglican Church. Westminster Confession, 15; Lutheran Confessions, 16; Martin Luther: Inerrancy of Scripture; Scripture and secular authors, 16; Copyists' errors, "Difficult passages," 18; Consistency of Scripture, 19; "Lowly and trivial things." 19; Main purpose of the Bible, 20; "Urging Christ against Scripture," 20; Perspicuity, Authority, 21; Liberal views of Luther's attitude toward the Bible, 22.

II. TEACHINGS OF CHRIST AND HIS APOSTLES ON THE
    SCRIPTURES 26
   1. Teaching of Christ 26

Statements of Scripture, Liberal views, 26; Testimonies of Himself, 27; His statements on the Old Testament, 27; Machen's statement on the liberal position, 29; Burrows as a representative of liberal criticism, 30; Consequences of liberal criticism, 31; The Christian position, 31.

   2. The Apostles' Attitude toward the Old Testament and Their
      Own Writings 32

III. INSPIRATION OF THE BIBLE 36

Liberal and Bible-believing positions, 36; William Hordern, 38; Gerhard Forde, 43; Editor of The Lutheran, 44; Teaching of Scripture, 45; Theories of inspiration, 46; The divine and human "natures" of Christ and the Bible, 46.

IV. INTERPRETATION OF SCRIPTURE 48

Liberal-critical method and its value, 48; Luther's principles of interpretation; Necessity of faith and enlightenment of the Spirit; Context; Interpretation of Scripture by itself, 50; Perspicuity of Scripture and its literal sense, 52; Figurative interpretations and Zwingli's alloeosis, 53; Neo-Orthodox and Butlmannian methods, 54; "Golden Rule of Interpretation,"

56; Nature and consequences of Neo-Orthodox and other liberal symbolical and mythical interpretations, 56.

V. WHO WROTE THE "BOOKS OF MOSES" 58
  1. Liberal Theory of the Origin of the Pentateuch 58
    Spinoza, Astruc, Graf and Wellhausen, 58; Wellhausen's method and assertions, 59; The Graf-Wellhausen JEDP-theory, 62; Present situation: Liberal double-talk, 65; Recent Sunday School material of the United Church of Canada, Lutheran Church in America and The American Lutheran Church, 65; "Intellectual respectability," 67.

  2. Implications of Liberal Criticism 68
    OT passages branded as forgeries and lies, 68; Statements of Jesus branded as mistakes or lies, 70; Statements of apostles declared as erroneous, 72; Note: Origin of some New Testament books, 73.

  3. Critique of Liberal Arguments 74
    The divine names, 74; Time of Deuteronomy, 77; Time of the Levitical law, 80; Passages used against the Mosaic authorship of the Pentateuch, 83; The so-called "doublets," 86.

  4. Inner Testimony of the Pentateuch 88
    The Tabernacle and its worship, 89; Instrument music and singing, 90; Jerusalem and its priesthood, 90; Destruction of Canaanites and Amalekites, 90; The name "Lord of hosts," 91; The Samaritan Pentateuch, 92.

  5. Tablets of Tell-el-Amarna and Testimony of Archeology 93

  6. Final Conclusions 95
    Real sources: family records, 95; Segal and Külling, 97; Additional facts, 98; Note: Opposing liberal theories, 99.

VI. INTERPRETATION OF BIBLICAL PROPHECIES 101
  1. Liberal Criticism of Prophetical Books 101
    Oral tradition, schools of prophets, repeated revisions, lack of headings, redactorial work, results. Refutation of the liberal claims.

  2. Liberal and Biblical Views of Prophecy 105
    Attitude toward supernatural, 106; "Situation" in prophecies, 106; Examples of the liberal procedure, 108; The four deceptive liberal methods, 112; Biblical teaching of prophecy and the liberals' attitude toward it, 113; Anonymity, 115; Fulfilled predictions and the so-called prophetical perfect, 115; Original intention, later understanding and "adjustments," 117.

VII. UNITY OF ISAIAH 120
   1. Liberal Splitting of Isaiah 120
   2. Cyrus and the "Servant of the Lord" 123
      Liberal views on Is. 40-66, 123; Various views on the "Servant," 124; Conservative view, 125; The Cyrus prophecies, 126; The "Servant Songs," 127; Modern Sunday School material, 130; Either—or, 132.
   3. Historical Facts that Support the Unity of Isaiah 133
      Headings, Manuscripts, History, Jerusalem existing, 133; Ecclesiasticus, NT references and quotations, 134; Note: Differences in style and theories of multiple authorship, 135.

VIII. AUTHORSHIP AND RELIABILITY OF THE BOOK OF DANIEL 137
   1. Criticism of Porphyry 138
      Porphyry's book Against the Christians, 138; Daniel's world-empire prophecies, 139.
   2. Modern Liberal Criticism 140
   3. What is the Truth? 142
      Languages of the book of Daniel, 142; Historical facts, 144; Daniel's place in the OT canon, 148; Reliability of Daniel's prophecies, 151 ("Little horns" in Dan. 7 and 8, 152; The 70 year-week prophecy, 153; The 3.5 years, 1290 and 1335 days, 159; The ten toes and ten horns, 159; Antiochus IV and the Antichrist, 160).
   4. Proofs of the Authenticity of Daniel 161

IX. "DIFFICULT PASSAGES" OF THE BIBLE 164
   1. The Genesis Account of Creation 166
      The "firmament" and waters under and above it, 166; The two parts of the creation account, 167; Creation of light, sun and moon, 167; Structure of the univesre, 168; Origin of the universe and the laws of thermodynamics and morpholysis, 170; Origin of species, 172; Origin of man, 174; Age of the world, 177; Age of mankind, 181.
   2. Fall into Sin and the Serpent 182
   3. The "NEPHILIM" of Genesis 6 185
   4. Animals in the Ark. The Great Flood 186
   5. Differences in Names and Numbers 188
   6. Abraham's Age and Place of Calling 192
   7. The Israelites' Stay in Egypt. Confirmation of the Covenant ... 193

8. Marriages of Brothers and Sisters 194
9. Was Isaac Abraham's Only Son? 195
10. Number of Jacob's Family and Their Burial Places 196
11. Horses of Egypt and Passage through Edom 198
12. Daughter of Jephthah and the Course of His Life 198
13. Last Phases of King Saul's Life 200
14. Did Absalom have Sons? 201
15. Who Moved David to Number Israel? Price for the Threshing floor 201
16. Contents of the Ark of the Covenant 202
17. Removal of High Places by Asa. Relations between Asa and Baasha 203
18. Service Age of Levites 204
19. Dates of Kings. Elisha and Ben-hadad 204
    Note: Chronology of the Kings of Israel and Judah 206
20. Standing Still of Sun and Moon. Returning of Shadow in Sun Dial. Hare that Chews Cud. Jonah in the Belly of a Whale 209
21. Genealogies of Jesus and His Virgin Birth 212
22. Cyrenius the Governor. Accounts of Jesus' Infancy 214
23. Beginning of Jesus' Public Ministry 216
24. Temptations of Jesus 218
25. Use of Wine in Prov. 31 and in the Wedding of Cana 219
26. Centurion and His Servant 221
27. Ahimelech and Abiathar. "Zechariah Son of Barachiah" 221
28. Names of Some Apostles 224
29. Supplies to Be Taken for Missionary Journey 224
30. The Unrighteous Steward 224
31. Violence to God's Kingdom and Its Coming 227
32. Was Jesus Mistaken as to the Time of His Second Coming? 230
33. Did Paul Expect Christ's Second Coming in His Lifetime? 236
34. Blind Men Near Jericho 239
35. Peter's Denials and the Crowings of the Cock 239
36. Judas Iscariot's Betrayal and Death. Aceldama 240
37. How Long Was Jesus in Grave? 242
38. Inscription of the Cross 243
39. Thieves on the Cross 244
40. Times of the Last Supper and Crucifixion 244

41. Events after Jesus' Resurrection 247
42. When Did the Disciples Receive the Holy Spirit? 253
43. Infilling with the Spirit and Speaking in Tongues 253
44. Reports of Paul's Conversion 259
45. Does God "Repent"? 259
46. Election and Responsibility. Eternal Security and Backsliding 261
47. Attitude toward Enemies 263
48. Does God Originate Evil? 265
49. Peace and Conflict 266
50. Paul and James 267
51. Law of Love, False Teachers, and the Christian Unity 269

X. SOME FAULTY TRANSLATIONS 275
    Judges 15:19: Spring at Lehi 275
    2 Kings 6:25: Price of "dove's dung" 275
    2 Kings 23:29: Pharaoh Neco and king of Assyria 276
    Psalm 2:11: "Kiss the Son," or, "kiss his feet"? 276
    Proverbs 8:22-25: "Possessed" or "created"? 276
    Ecclesiastes 3:19-21: The fate of men and beasts 277
    Hebrews 9:4: Altar of incense or censer? 278

CONCLUSION (Prayer) 279

SCRIPTURE INDEX 282

AUTHOR, NAME AND SUBJECT INDEX 286

FOR ORIENTATION

Ezekiel saw in Mesopotamia, the land of two rivers, a vision of the double river of life that issued from the temple of God. It brought life wherever it went (ch. 47).

Grace and truth are the two main constituents in the divine river of life. These two, grace and truth, cannot be separated. If one of them is removed or lost, the other also is forfeited.

Satan is a great imitator of God. He, too, has cast out of his mouth a flood or river (Rev. 12:15f.) which is twofold: Divine truth is replaced in it by human errors and heresies, and in the place of God's saving and sanctifying grace are church ceremonies and human achievements.

Paul wrote to Timothy:

> "But continue thou in what thou hast learned and hast been assured of, knowing from whom thou hast learned them; and that from a child thou hast known the holy Scriptures, which are able to make thee wise for salvation through faith in Christ Jesus. All Scripture is given by inspiration of God and is profitable for teaching, for reproof, for correction, for instruction in righteousness..." (2 Tim. 3:14ff.).

The Apostle states here three important truths:

1. In the matter of truth, the decisive thing is **from whom** one has learned it. It must be learned from persons whom God has authorized to serve as His messengers and ambassadors of His revelation.

2. All **Scripture** is the sure and divinely authoritative word of truth.

3. All Scripture, the whole Bible, is given **by inspiration of God,** and this is the reason why it is trustworthy, the divine Word of Truth.

The powers of darkness are trying to lead men away

from all these three aspects of truth. They are striving to deprive them (1) of reliance on the authenticity of the books of the Bible, namely, that they were written by the men of God to whom Scripture itself ascribes them, (2) of assurance of their reliability and authority, and (3) of true and real salvation and new life through faith in Christ.

When Satan approached the first men in Paradise in the shape of a serpent, his very first question intended to make God's word doubtful: "Yea, hath God said... ?" Gen. 3:1). The crafty enemy was saying: "Has God really said so . . . ?" The purpose of Satan was to destroy from Eve's heart faith in God's word and obedience to it.

The same question is being sounded in our time by the agents of Satan almost all over the world, and even throughout almost all Christendom, and it is being done in ever more deceptive forms.

The greatest tragedy of our time is that large sections of Christendom have followed the delusive voices that have made God's Word doubtful: The so-called Christian churches have to a large extent abandoned faith in the reliability of the Bible and its divine authority. The result is that Christendom is divided into two factions which are separated from each other by an impassable gulf. The following words of **The Christian Century,** Jan. 1924, are now even more true than they were then:

> "Christianity according to fundamentalism [Bible-believing Protestantism*] is one religion and Christianity according to Modernism another. . . . There is a clash as profound and grim as between Christianity and Confucianism [Chinese pagan philosophical religion]. The God of the fundamentalist is one God, and the God of the Modernist is another" (Quoted from Herman J. Otten's book BAAL OR GOD, New Haven, Mo., 1965, p. v).

---

* Robert Jenson, Luther College, Decorah, Iowa, gives a wholly distorted description of fundamentalism: "Fundamentalism is a notable murder of faith because it intellectualizes it; it makes of faith a brute-force assent: 'I will believe . . .'" **(Theological Perspectives,** Luther College Press, Deorah, Iowa, 1963, p. 11). In reality, fundamentalism in general means evangelistic Bible-believing Protestantism.

Dr. David Hedegard, a Swedish Lutheran theologian, writes in his book ECUMENISM AND THE BIBLE (second revised ed. 1964, The Banner of Truth Trust, 78b Chiltern St., London, W 1) about the same: Protestant Modernism "is actually a new religion, as far from authentic Christianity as is Buddhism or Mohammedanism ... it is new faith, a new religion" (p. 38).

The foundation of Modernism is its liberal critical study of the Bible, which has destroyed faith in its reliability from the hearts of most theologians, pastors, and church leaders of our time. These liberal students of the Bible claim that their study of the Scriptures is "scientific," and that it is this kind of "factual" research that has rendered faith in the reliability of the Bible impossible.

We admit that real well-substantiated facts must be honored whoever may bring them forth—even if this is done by the liberals, who, according to the conviction of Bible-believers, study the Bible with an unchristian attitude of heart and mind. It is never right to try to defend the Bible by concealing or disregarding the facts.

The present book has been written from a Bible-believing point of view, with the conviction that Scripture is right in what it says of itself. But at the same time it looks for the facts—trying to find out whether biblical, historical, etc., facts confirm the truth of the Scriptures or lend support to the ancient question of the serpent, "Hath God said?"

I. WHO TELLS WHAT THE TRUTH IS?

The statement is often heard, that it does not matter WHO says what the truth is. This does not, however, apply to Christianity. In it the decisive thing is WHO says the final word concerning what is true and false and what is right and wrong, in other words, WHO is the **supreme authority**.

Three different authorities have been set forth in the Christian Church: (1) holy Scripture, (2) the tradition and official teaching of the Church, and (3) Christian intelligence, reason.

According to these three different views, the final authority from which there is no appeal, is either (1) the Bible interpreted by itself, or (2) the Bible interpreted and supplemented by church tradition and teaching office, or (3) the Bible examined and interpreted by means of human reason and scientific study.

These three views are usually called (1) Bible-believing, or conservative, or evangelical, (2) traditionalistic, and (3) modernistic, or liberal-subjectivistic.

Confessional Protestants who hold to the principles of the 16th century Reformation represent the first, the Roman and Greek Catholics the second, and the liberal* or modernistic Protestants the third.

This division cuts across the old Protestant denominations, as well as many of the younger churches. In recent times the Roman Catholic Church also has became divided into the conservative and liberal factions.

---

* Carl Fr. Wisloff, prof. of Church History in the Free Theological Seminary (Menighetsfakultet) of Oslo, Norway, says to the point: "... liberal is a theologian who does not yield to Scripture in matters of faith, and who does not ... trust what it says is true ..." **(Raamatun Ystävä,** Helsinki, Finland, No. 9, 1961).

1. Traditionalistic View

The Roman and Greek Catholic Churches and "Romanizing" (or "high church") Protestants hold that the Bible is not clear and understandable in itself, neither is it sufficient to interpret itself. It must be interpreted in the light of the traditions of the Church and by its teaching office. The Church's tradition is also God-given, and its teaching office is guided by the Holy Spirit. Human reason has no right to criticize and judge the Bible or the tradition, but only accept, defend and apply them. The decisive thing, therefore, is not what the Bible says, but what the church says it means, and what the tradition says.

2. Liberal or Subjectivistic Position

In the course of the history of the Christian Church, the subjectivistic-liberal view on authority has appeared in many variations. In **Mysticism** it values man's own insights and experiences, the real or supposed revelations of the Spirit, etc., as the decisive instance. In **Rationalism** it relies on man's understanding, reason, scientific study, etc., as the ultimate instance of authority. In many cases it has appeared as various combinations of these two.

The two German theologians **F. E. D. Schleiermacher** (1768-1834) and **Albrecht Ritschl** (1822-89) have influenced the so-called Neo-Protestant theology perhaps more than any others. Following them, this theology has taken for its starting point the theory of knowledge (epistemology) of the philosopher **Immanuel Kant** (Koenigsberg, Germany, 1724-1804). According to it, our knowledge is bound to this material world, sense observations and thinking on that basis. Since we have no sense experience of God and the invisible world, we have no real knowledge of them. We can have mere "practical postulates" on the world beyond. Religion, Christianity included, can therefore be studied only as a human psychological, social and historical phenomenon. The Kantian theory of knowledge discards the possibility of real revelation by God—and it is on this that true Christian faith and theology bases its knowledge of God and His world.

In applying the Kantian principle to the Bible, the Neo-Protestant theology has—more or less consistently—treated it as a mere piece of human religious literature. The **theory of evolution** has been, since the latter part of the 19th century, coupled with the Kantian axiom. The theologians who follow this trend think that, in order to be "scientific," they must study the Bible with an "open mind" and without the "prejudice" that what it says of itself is true. In addition to "internal criticism," they measure and judge the Bible by what they learn from secular historical, scientific, psychological and other sources. When they do so, their reason, conscience and feeling perceive what in the Bible is right and what wrong and—perhaps—also what in it is God's word and what not.

Protestant liberal subjectivists usually admit that the Bible is a product of profound religious insight, and even that God has been with its authors (which admission, of course, is inconsistent to the Kantian axiom). In writing its books, they have been inspired, and their writings are inspiring to read. This inspiration, however, has not been of the sort that it would have guaranteed the full reliability and truthfulness of their writings, so that they would be God's word in their every part. The Bible is uneven, as all human products are. In numerous instances, one part of it contradicts another part. Some of its passages contain antiquated views which are unacceptable in the light of modern knowledge.

The Bible's essential message is to be disentangled from its obsolete trappings in order that it would be relevant to modern man. It must be re-formulated in the light of the knowledge of our time and restated in modern terms. Human reason must measure and judge both the Scriptures and church traditions, sifting out the wheat from among the chaff, and bringing it into line with the thought-forms and needs of the people of today. The work of the Holy Spirit as Bible-interpreter is sometimes identified with this activity of reason, conscience and feeling. **Faith** means to the representatives of this trend fidelity to one's own religious and other convictions, which he has formed by means

HATH GOD SAID? 15

of the described factors. The final authority which gives the ultimate verdict on all issues of faith and life, truth and right, is not the Bible, but human reason and feeling.*

3. Bible-believing Evangelical Position

The original stand of the Christian Church, as we see it from the New Testament writings, was that Scripture is, such as it is (or more accurately, as it was in the original autographs), the completely dependable and authoritative Word of God. A person who wants to come to the knowledge of the divine truth must see and hear what the Bible says, for it is God who speaks in it.

The Scriptures contain all that the Church and individual Christian needs for salvation and guidance in life and activity. It also gives the principles and rules for its own interpretation. It does not, therefore, need for its exposition and supplementation either church tradition or human reason. It rather demands that it must have the right to evaluate and judge both of these. The words and views of men—both of the Church as a whole and individuals—must be proved and judged by God's Word.

The Protestant or Evangelical churches that were born of the 16th century Reformation set forth this faith in their "Confessions." We take a few examples.

The Thirty-nine Articles (1562) of the Anglican Church declare:

> "Holy Scripture containeth all things necessary to salvation; so that whatever is not read therein, nor may be proved thereby, is not to be required of any man that it should be believed as an article of the Faith, or to be thought requisite or necessary to salvation" (Art. 6).

The **Westminster Confession,** drawn by the Westmin-

---

* In the Roman Church, Pope Pius XII issued in 1943 his bull **Divino alffante Spiritu,** by which he opened the door for a liberal Bible study in his church. Roman Catholic liberals practice a critical Bible study of the same type as the Protestant liberals (See Otten, op. cit., pp. 156 ff.).

ster Assembly, 1643-48, which is the most important confession of English speaking Calvinistic churches, states:

"The whole counsel of God, concerning all things necessary for His own glory, man's salvation, faith, and life, is either expressly set down in Scripture, or by good and necessary consequence may be deduced from Scripture; unto which nothing at any time is to be added, whether by new revelations of the Spirit or traditions of men. Nevertheless we acknowledge the inward illumination of the Spirit of God to be necessary for the saving understanding of such things as are revealed in the word; and that there are some circumstances concerning the worship of God, and government of the Church, common to human actions and societies, which are to be ordered by the light of nature and Christian prudence, according to the general rules of the word, which are always to be observed" (1:6).

The **Formula of Concord,** one of the Lutheran Confessions (1577), declares:

"We believe, teach and confess that the prophetic and apostolic writings of the Old and New Testaments are the only rule and norm according to which all doctrines and teachers alike must be appraised and judged, as it is written in Ps. 119:105, 'Thy word is a lamp to my feet and a light to my path.' . . . Holy Scripture remains the only judge, rule and norm according to which . . . all doctrines should and must be understood and judged as good or evil, right or wrong" (Preface).

Martin Luther affirmed again and again his faith in the inerrancy and supreme authority of the canonical books of the Bible. Liberal Lutherans have repeatedly tried to find support for their own view from Luther. His real convictions are seen from what he himself says, e.g. in the following statements:

"The Holy Scriptures have been spoken by the Holy Spirit" (St. Louis ed., abbr. SL., 3:1896).

"So, then, the entire Scripture is assigned to the Holy Spirit" (SL, 3:1890).

"But if they take exception and say . . . Peter, Paul, and even Christ, were men—when you hear people of this stamp who are so blinded and hardened as to deny that what Christ and the apostles spoke and wrote is God's word, or doubt it, then be silent and speak no more with them, and let them go" (Weimar ed., Abbr. WA., 12:362).

Luther says again and again that since the Bible was written by the inspiration and guidance of the Holy Spirit it cannot err:

> "The Scriptures cannot err" (SL, 19:1073).
> "For it is certain that the Scriptures do not lie" (SL, 1:713f.).
> "Scripture has never erred" (SL, 15:1481).

Men, even the most enlightened Christians, err and make mistakes, but the apostles, being led by the Spirit of God, did not err:

> "We are not all apostles who were sent by a firm decree of God to us as infallible teachers (infallibiles doctores). Hence they cannot err, but we can, and we may be deceived in our faith, since we lack such a decree of God" (SL, 3:785).

The same applies, according to Luther, to the prophets who wrote biblical books:

> "A prophet is one who gets his understanding directly from God, into whose mouth the Holy Spirit puts the right words.... For instance, in Mt. 23 those are called 'wise' who derive their doctrine from the prophets, for God speaks through men, and not without means. But prophets are those who have their doctrine from God without means" (SL, 3:785).

Luther says in this statement that the prophets have received directly from God both the "right words" and "their doctrine."

The "fathers" of the Church should be believed only so far as they speak in accord with the Scriptures: "One should not trust the holy fathers and the Church unless it is certain that they have the word of God." If they speak something that is "beyond and aside from God's word," they speak it "according to their own reason, without the Holy Spirit." "That is why St. Augustine ... laid down the fixed axiom that holy Scripture alone is to be considered inerrant" (WA, 34, I:347).

Whenever Luther observed conflicts between the information given by the Bible and that found in the works of secular authors, he held that it was the Bible that was to be trusted:

> "I make use of secular writers in such a manner that I am not forced to contradict Scripture. For I believe that the God of truth speaks in the Bible, but in the histories good people display their diligence and fidelity according to their ability (but only as men), or at least their copyists have perchance made mistakes" (SL, 14:491).

Luther was aware that there also were copyists' errors in the biblical text. In certain cases when he was not able to harmonize some biblical passages he assumed that there was a copyist's error in the text, and that there was no discrepancy in the original text. Later discoveries of older and more reliable manuscripts have shown that Luther usually was right in assuming a copyist's error in such a case. E.g. in Acts 13:19f. Luther observed a discrepancy with the OT chronology and assumed that it was due "to the fault of a copyist." His guess of the nature of the error in this case did not hit the mark, but he was right in assuming that the difficulty was due to a copyist's error. Another such case was I Cor. 10:9 when compared with Nu. 14:22 (WA, 64:66). Recent versions which base their translations on corrected texts do not contain any difficulty in either of these cases.

Luther realized that not all the "difficulties" in the biblical text were due to mistakes in copying. But he never charged the Bible with error. He believed that the Holy Spirit, who was the real Author of the Bible, had for some reason given certain passages a form that seems to us obscure. When we meet such a passage in Scripture, we must confess our "ignorance, as is fitting; for the Holy Spirit is the only One who knows and understands everything." Luther said this in dealing with a difficulty in the chronology of the life of Abraham. He explained that the Spirit of God had given this passage as it is in order that Christians would not be able to calculate the time of the end of the world, but would "continually exercise their faith and fear of God" (SL, 1:721f.). In speaking of another difficult passage (Mt. 24), Luther says that the Holy Spirit should not be blamed for "mixing things." "The fault is ours, who have not understood the language..." (SL, 14:1418).

Luther had the conviction that (in its original text) the Bible cannot contain real discrepancies. The Holy Spirit, its true Author, cannot contradict Himself. "We are certain that the Holy Spirit cannot oppose and contradict himself" (ist nicht wider sich selbst, WA, 54:66).

The differences between the various accounts of the same events or statements, e.g. in the Gospel records, are, according to Luther, due to the express guidance of the Holy Spirit, who has His own designs in such things. In speaking of the various reports of the institution of the Lord's Supper, Luther says: "The Holy Spirit arranged it so that no evangelist agrees with the other in using the same words" (SL, 19:1104).

In a word, Luther had the conviction that "Scripture does not contradict itself nor any one article of faith, even though to our mind a contradiction and inconsistency may exist" (WA, 34, II:385).

Because of this, all true Bible interpretation is "harmonistic." Scripture must never be explained so that one passage contradicts another, for "the Bible agrees with itself everywhere" (SL, 3:18). "It is impossible that Scripture would contradict itself" (SL, 9:356).

Luther believed that even the "trivial" and "lowly" things in the Bible were written by the inspiration of God. He warned "every pious Christian" of being led astray to assume that "the high Majesty of God" would not be concerned with the lowly things of human life, and that such passages would be in the Bible without His will (SL, 14:3). Luther says another time: "God takes pleasure in describing such lowly things [as e.g. Jacob's domestic life] to show and testify that He does not despise or abhor the household, nor is far away from a pious husband and from wife and children" (SL, 2:537ff.).

Luther saw wholesome teachings even in the Biblical accounts of shameful events. On the narrative of Judah and Tamar in Gen. 38 Luther said: "The Holy Spirit is wonderfully diligent in narrating this shameful, adulterous history; ... What induced the most pure mouth of the Holy Spirit to condescend to such low, despised things . . . ?" He answers this question by pointing out how full of teaching, reproof, admonition and comfort are even the passages of this sort for God's people in all ages (SL, 2:1200ff.).

Luther emphasizes that the **main purpose of Scripture** is to lead men to repentance and salvation through faith in Christ:

> "The whole Bible does nothing else than to give one an understanding of what he was, what he is now, and what behooves him. . . . It lets him know that he is completely undone. Secondly, it tells what God is, . . . and especially the mercy of Christ. It leads him to know Him, and it conducts us through His incarnation from earth to heaven" (WA, 48:272).

Since Christ and salvation in Him is the heart and center of Scripture, "men must study and search it ... [in order to] learn that He, **He,** Son of Mary, is the One who is able to give eternal life to all who come to Him and believe in Him. The one who wants to read the Bible in the right way and for his benefit should therefore see to it that he finds Christ in it; then he finds eternal life without fail" (WA, 51:4).

Liberal "Lutherans" have often appealed to Luther's statement: "If our opponents urge Scripture, we urge Christ against Scripture" (WA, 39, 1:47).

These words are usually taken, without regard to their context, to support the liberal idea that one can use Christ (whatever view he may have of Him) for refuting what the Bible says. In its context the quoted word of Luther means nothing of this sort. Luther speaks here against the Catholics who, in opposing the Evangelical doctrine of justification by grace, appealed to such biblical statements as:

"Thou shalt keep the commandments" (Dt. 8:6).

"Thou shalt love the Lord thy God" (Mt. 22:37). "This do, and thou shalt live" (Lk. 10:28). Etc.

When these passages were used to support the Catholic view that works were necessary for justification before God, Luther "urged Christ against [such misuse of] Scripture": He showed how the good works that were required in these passages always presupposed Christ, His saving grace and faith in Him; for only after having received salvation in Christ and having become a new creature through faith in Him, and having Christ in his heart, a person is able to love, to keep God's commandments and do good works—though even then weakly and defectively. This is seen from the words of Christ: "Apart from me ye can do nothing" (Jn. 15:5).

Luther says prior to the quoted statement on "urging Christ against Scripture": "Scripture is to be understood as testifying for Christ, not against Him; it must therefore either be understood as referring to Him, or not to be considered true Scripture" (WA, 39, I:47).

Luther means: If a person takes certain words from the Bible and uses them in a manner that is in conflict with its actual teachings (as the Catholics did with the quoted passages), they are not true Scripture (in the sense then used), although the words are from it.

Luther believed—as did the entire Reformation movement—in the perspicuity of the Bible: It is a **clear and plain book** for all who use it for the purpose God has given it, seeking from it Christ and salvation in Him. It is, however, obscure and difficult to understand for those who use it with some other purpose. "It is clear enough so far as truths necessary for salvation are concerned, and it is obscure enough for souls given to prying into things" (WA, 8:99).

The fact that the Bible is to many people obscure is due to the darkness of their hearts and minds. It is not the fault of the Holy Writ. "Let miserable men, therefore,"

Luther says, "cease to ascribe, with blasphemous perverseness, the darkness and obscurity of their hearts to the brilliantly clear Scriptures of God" (WA, 18:609).

The **authority of Scripture** means that the Church and every Christian, yea, every man, is duty bound to believe and obey it as God's Word. The Church has no right to teach anything contrary to this Word and independently of it:

> "Every pious Christian knows that the Church cannot decree or regulate anything independently of the Bible. He who, nevertheless, does so belongs to the nominal church only, as Christ says in Jn. 10:27, 'My sheep hear my voice.' They do not hear the voice of the stranger but flee him... Something is not God's word because the Church says it, but the Church is where the word of God is spoken.... Therefore, things that are ordained without the word of God are not ordinations of the Church, but of Satan's synagogue which goes under the name of the Church" (WA, 8:49).

Every Christian has the right, and even the duty, to test and judge teachers and doctrines in the light of God's written Word:

> "Bishops, the Pope, the learned . . . have the right to teach; but the sheep [believers] are to judge whether they are teaching what Christ says, or what a stranger says" (WA, 11:409).

On the basis of this biblical principle, Luther says:

> "I want ... to be subject to this inviolable rule of the apostle: 'Prove all things, hold to that which is good' (I Thess. 5:21).... We are, therefore, of necessity obligated to flee for refuge to the solid rock of the divine Scriptures and not to ... believe anything ... without this authority" (WA, 2:446f.).

> "We should ... let Scripture rule and master us, and we should not be masters ourselves according to our mad heads, setting ourselves above the Scriptures" (WA, 47:367).

These teachings and convictions of Luther were the common property of the entire Evangelical Reformation.

Liberal Views of Luther's Attitude Toward the Bible

Liberal theologians and churchmen have again and again asserted that Luther did not believe in the inerrancy and absolute authority of Scripture. As a representative of this liberal conception, the editor of THE LUTHERAN, official organ of the Lutheran Church in America, LCA, asserted in the Feb. 24, 1965, issue of the said paper that Luther was "very free in his criticism of the Bible." To support their view, the liberals have often appealed to Luther's statement on the epistle of James as a "straw epistle" when compared with the epistles of Paul and Peter (SL, 14:91).

Conservative theologians have repeatedly shown that Luther expressed critical remarks only concerning certain books that in the Ancient Church belonged to the "Antilegomena" ("Gainsaid") books, whose canonicity was doubted or disputed by a part of the Church. Luther followed here the Ancient Church and did not regard the "Antilegomena" books as fully canonical and as belonging to the actual Bible (many Bible-believing Protestants of our time have the same view, e.g. conservative Missouri Synod Lutherans). Fr. Pieper, the Missouri Synod dogmatician, writes: "Even the weakest mind can see without much reflection how foolish it is to conclude from an adverse verdict of Luther on a book which he did not regard as canonical that he held liberal views on the inspiration of those books which he regarded as canonical: just the opposite ought to be concluded" (**Christian Dogmatics** I:292).

Liberals have also appealed to Luther's words in his preface to W. Link's **Annotations to the Five Books of Moses**, where he says that "some hay, straw and stubble slipped in at times (into the writings) of these good and faithful teachers" (SL, 14:150). Fr. Pieper (**op. cit.,** p. 288) is obviously right in writing on these words of Luther: "It is utterly impossible to refer Luther's words to the 'Biblical authors,' that is, to the Prophets insofar as they wrote the Bible of the Old Testament. Luther is rather speaking of those periods in the lives of the prophets when they were not moved as infallible organs of the Holy Spirit to write the Holy Scriptures, but when outside the state of [this kind of] inspiration they, just like other people, made the Scriptures of the Old Testament the object of their study and, in doing this, entered 'in a book' the good thoughts the Holy Spirit awakened in them during this study. To this study and this writing, which took place when they were not inspired to write the Holy Scriptures, refer Luther's words: 'Though some hay, straw, and wood [stubble] slipped in at times, etc.' What Luther teaches is that the Prophets of the Old Testament did not always infallibly speak and write God's word, but only at times, temporarily, namely, when inspired by the Holy Ghost. Read his remarks on Gen. 44:18: 'The theologians have a common proverb: 'The Holy Ghost did not always touch the hearts of the Prophets.' "

This view is based on what the O.T. itself says: It has several references to books written by prophets which did not become parts of the Bible. Such are e.g. the lives of David and Solomon by Nathan (1 Chr. 24:29; 2 Chr. 9:29), the Acts of David by Gad (1 Chr. 29:29), and the Acts of Uzziah by Isaiah (2 Chr. 26:22), which obviously belong to the group of the books by prophets to which Luther refers in the quoted statement. This is the only possible explanation of his quoted words, for otherwise he would contradict himself. We have given a number of his statements in which he consistently speaks of the infallibility of the canonical books of the Bible.

A number of studies have been published on Luther's attitude toward the Bible. One of the best is M. Reu's **Luther and the Scriptures** (Columbus, Ohio, 1944). The two most recent studies are those by the American Jaroslav Pelikan, **Luther the Expositor,** and by the Danish E. Thestrup Pedersen, **Luther som skriftfortolker** (L. as Bible interpreter), both in 1959. Having been influenced by the Barthian (Neo-Orthodox) theology, Pelikan asserts that after Immanuel Kant the conception of Scripture held by Lutheran Orthodoxy is impossible, for Kant destroyed the epistemological (theory-of-knowledge) foundation on which Orthodoxy built. This means: The Lutheran Orthodoxy, which had the same view of the Bible as Luther had, built on divine revelation and the divinely inspired Bible, believing that on its basis and through it Christians have real knowledge of God. The Kantian theory of knowledge denies the possibility and reality of divine revelation and inspiration, and the Neo-Protestant theology (Neo-Orthodox, Lundensian, etc.) that accepts it—when consistent—naturally cannot accept Luther's view of Scripture as the inspired record of divine revelation. But the Kantian axiom, being agnostic, cannot be accepted by any **Christian** theologian, and no theologian who accepts it is Christian.

Luther says (WA,1:507) that theologians whose "bellies are distended with the husks of those swine, the philosophers," do not have the proper reverence for the Bible. These words apply to the Neo-Protestant theologians: Their "bellies have been distended with the husks" of Kant (or Heidegger, as are the Bultmannians), and this is the reason why they are not able to "swallow" the Scriptures' own teaching that it is the inspired record of God's revelation and as such wholly true and dependable.

Dr. Pedersen shows in the above mentioned book that "Luther can directly identify the word of the Bible with God's word . . . [It is] the Holy Spirit's infallible word . . . The entire contents of the Bible, even the human things, have theological significance" (p. 200).*

---

* In his review of the two books B. W. Teigen (**Lutheran News,** Feb. 24, 1964, p. 7) remarks that Pedersen's work is a real research of original sources, whereas Pelikan builds largely on second-hand sources.

Ewald M. Plass, **What Luther Says I** (St. Louis, 1959) gives a large selection (pp. 61-109) of quotations from Luther concerning the Bible.

II. TEACHINGS OF CHRIST AND HIS APOSTLES ON THE SCRIPTURES

According to the Bible-believing evangelical view, the teachings of Christ and His apostles decide the question of the dependability and authority of the Bible, and not the opinions of churches or theologians.

1. Teaching of Christ

Jesus Christ is, according to the testimony of the NT, the Son of God, "the true God and eternal life" (1 Jh. 5:20), "who is over all, God, blessed for ever" (Rom. 9:5).* "All the treasures of wisdom and knowledge" are hid in Him (Col. 2:3). He was sinless, and no deceit or lie was ever found in His mouth (2 Cor. 5:2; Heb. 4:15; 7:26; I Pet. 2: 22). This implies that He is wholly and absolutely reliable and inerrant in all that He says.

The liberal critics deny the dependability and authority of Christ in His statements on the OT books. They explain that He either adapted Himself to the views of His contemporaries on these matters, without caring to correct them, or that He "emptied Himself" (Phil. 2:7; the KJV translation of this passage is a "paraphrase," not a literal translation: "emptied himself" is the literal meaning) in such a manner that He was ignorant on the true authors and the reliability of OT books and followed in these questions the current views of His time.

It is not at all true that Jesus just followed the views current in His time. He spoke often against the views of

---

* The Revised Standard Version translates this passage in the text: "... is the Christ. God who is over all be blessed for ever." This is a plainly false translation (obviously a liberal-inspired one) of the words: **ho Cristos kata sarka, ho on epi panton Theos eulogetos eis tous aionas.** The RSV, however, has the correct translation in the footnote: "Christ, who is God over all, blessed for ever."

the scribes (theologians of that time), Pharisees, etc., rejecting and refuting their conceptions and teachings. But He never said a word against the conviction of Israel that the OT was God's word, wholly inerrant and the absolute authority. On the contrary, He confirmed this faith in plain words. He himself spoke consistently of the OT Scriptures as God's Word and divine truth, referring to them again and again with the words, "It is written." According to Him, the teachings of Scripture have an absolute divine authority, and there is no appeal from them. True, the OT law ceased to be in force after the coming of the new covenant, but it was God's law for the old covenant people.

Jesus spoke of Himself again and again as God's Son and of His teachings as God's own Word. We take some of His statements:

". . . the Father who sent me beareth witness to me . . . and I speak to the world what I have heard from him . . . I do nothing of myself; but as my Father hath taught me, I speak these things . . . He who is of God heareth God's words" (Jh. 8:18, 26, 28, 47).

"I have not spoken of myself; but the Father who sent me he gave me a commandment what I should say and what I should speak" (Jh. 12:49).

"The word which ye hear is not mine, but the Father's who sent me. . . . I have given them the words thou [Father] gavest me; and they have received them" (Jh. 14:24; 17:8).

On this basis Jesus said of his own words: "Heaven and earth will pass away, but my words will not pass away" (Mk. 13:31).

All these statements of Jesus apply to everything that he said, also to his words on the Old Testament. But the liberals deny their truth with regard to a number of His words, thus making Him either ignorant (who knew much less than these modern liberals) or a liar (whereas the liberals claim to speak the truth).

When Jesus spoke of the "Law" (Heb. TORAH—the Pentateuch, i. e. the Five Books of Moses) as being from Moses, He did not merely follow the Jewish opinion and use the current Jewish term, as the liberals claim. He followed here the teachings and the terminology of the OT, for it spoke from Joshua on of the Pentateuch as the book or Law of Moses (e.g. Josh. 1:7; 8:31; I Ki. 2:3; 2 Ki. 21:8; 1 Chr. 15:15; Ezra 6:18). According to the emphatic words of Jesus, this fivefold book, commonly called the Law, was wholly reliable: "For verily I say to you, till heaven and earth pass away, one jot or one tittle shall in no way pass from the Law, till all is fulfilled" (Mt. 5:18).

Jesus said to people who did not know and obey the Scriptures: "Do ye not therefore err, because ye know not the Scriptures, neither the power of God" (Mk. 12:24). His words meant: Only by knowing, believing and obeying the Scriptures and trusting in and experiencing the power of God one could come to the knowledge of the truth and avoid error and going astray.

When there were dissensions concerning religion and truth, Jesus repeatedly asked: "Have ye not read . . . ?" (Mt. 12:3, 5; 19:4; 16:42). His question showed that what was read in the Scriptures was final: it was the divine truth that decided the issue, and this truth was in the Scriptures.

The foundation of Christianity is the person, teaching and work of Jesus Christ. "For other foundation can no man lay than that is laid, which is Jesus Christ" (I Cor. 3:11). Our knowledge of His person and the meaning of His work is mainly based on what He Himself said of them.

According to Christ's own statements, His Messiahship and work was at every point based on the OT, being the fulfillment of its Law and Prophets. The Gospel records, particularly that of Matthew, state again and again: ". . . that it might be fulfilled what was spoken (written) by . . ." In speaking of Himself and His work as a fulfilment of the OT, Christ always referred to it as God's infallible Word. He said of "Moses" (=the Pentateuch) to the people of His time: "If ye believed Moses, ye would believe me; for he wrote of me. But if ye believe not his writings, how will ye believe my words?" (Jh. 5:46f.).

This statement implied that Christ ascribed equal

authority to the writings of Moses, his Five Books, as to His own teachings: both were God's word, and one must be believed like the other (of course, He, as person, was much higher than Moses, and the revelation given by Him was higher than that given through Moses). Those who do not believe the writings of Moses, the Pentateuch, to be God's Word, but regard them as forgeries (as the liberals do), do not believe Christ's words either.

The liberals have frequently said that the Christian faith is not faith in a book but in Christ. This assertion implies that it does not make much difference whether one believes the teachings of the Bible or not, as long as he believes in Jesus Christ.

In reality it is impossible to believe in Christ as the divine-human Savior and Lord, and to do so in a personal way, without believing in the Bible as God's word, for Christ is the Christ of the Bible, and the Bible is Christ's Bible. Those who deny what Christ says of the full reliability of the Scriptures make Him either a liar or ignorant, and a person who regards Christ as less honest or as less knowing as he is himself hardly can believe in Him as his Savior and Lord—he rather wants to be Christ's "savior" from His errors of His ignorance!

J. Gresham Machen has said to the point:

"The impression is sometimes produced that the modern liberal substitutes for the authority of the Bible the authority of Christ. . . . he regards himself as being the true Christian because, rejecting the rest of the Bible, he depends on Jesus alone . . .

"As a matter of fact, however, the modern liberal does not hold fast even to the authority of Jesus. Certainly he does not accept the words of Jesus as they are recorded in the Gospels. For among the recorded words of Jesus are found those things which are most abhorrent to the modern liberal . . . Evidently, therefore, those words of Jesus which are to be regarded as authoritative . . . must first be selected from the mass of the recorded words by a critical process . . . , and the suspicion often arises that the critic is retaining as genuine words of the historical Jesus only those words which conform to his preconceived ideas. But even after the sifting process has been completed, the liberal scholar is still unable to accept as authoritative all the sayings of Jesus; he must finally admit that even the 'historical' Jesus . . . said some things that are untrue . . . It is not Jesus, then, who is the real authority, but the modern principle by which the selection within Jesus' recorded teachings has been made . . .

"It is no wonder, then, that liberalism is totally different from Christianity, for the foundation is different. Christianity is founded upon the Bible. It bases upon the Bible both its thinking and its life. Liberalism on the other hand is founded upon the shifting emotions of sinful men" (op. cit., pp. 76-79).

Machen's words apply both to the older liberalism and its newer forms. (Neo-Orthodoxy and others).*

We are confronted here by a great choice: If Jesus truly was God's Son and all that the NT teaches Him to be, and if He spoke only what the Father gave Him to speak, all His words must be absolute truth and the final supreme authority from which there is no appeal. This includes His statements on the OT books, their writers and their reliability.

If we reject faith in the absolute truth of all that Christ said, we reject Him as God's Son and Christ, the Savior and Lord. The liberals do this on the basis of their own authority, or the authority of their liberal teachers. In so doing they place human opinions and the authority of men above that of Christ, thus "denying our only Master and Lord, Jesus Christ" (Jude 4).

To those who reject Christ and the truth He spoke, apply the words of Scripture: "Every spirit that confesseth not Jesus is not of God; and this is the spirit of antichrist" (I Jn. 4:3).

---

* Millar Burrows, a key translator of the National Council of Churches Revised Standard Version of the Bible states frankly the subjectivistic position of the liberals: "We have abandoned the position that because anything is in the Bible it must be true" ("The Bible in the Theological Curriculum," **The Journal of Religion**, Oct., 1953, pp. 384f.). Burrows holds that "we cannot take the Bible as a whole and in every part as stating with divine authority what we must believe and do," and that "what is ultimately authoritative for us is that which commands the assent of

our best judgment, accepted as the witness of the Spirit within us" (**Ibid.**, p. 50). Thus, the liberals' own best judgment, their reason and feeling, is their final arbiter that decides what is true and false, right and wrong. Burrows explains that the Bible account of the flood of Noah's time "is not history but myth," and so are the accounts of the creation and fall; Moses was probably a polytheist, the book of Micah probably a forgery, etc., (**Ibid.**, pp. 45-47, 57, 68, 113-119, 123, 128, 265; according to Otten, **op. cit.**, pp. 144f.). We surumise what "spirit" leads to views of this sort!

The assertion of some liberals is that in speaking of the inerrancy and authority of the OT, Jesus adapted Himself to the views of His hearers in order to induce them to accept more readily what He Himself had to say. This assertion makes of Jesus a representative of "Jesuit morality," according to which even lie and deceit may be used if the purpose is good. The liberals who set forth this view in reality charge Jesus with willful deception and hypocrisy.

Those liberals who explain that Jesus "emptied Himself" in such a manner that He did not know the truth concerning the authors and the quality of the OT books disregard the fact that He spoke of the OT in the same manner after His resurrection, as the risen and glorified Lord who no longer was subject to human limitations. During the forty days between His resurrection and ascension He instructed His disciples particularly concerning the fulfillment of the OT prophecies in Himself. In doing so, He reminded them of what He had spoken to them previously: "These are the words that I spoke to you while I was yet with you, that all things must needs be fulfilled, which are written in the law of Moses, and the prophets, and the psalms, concerning me. Then he opened their understanding that they might understand the Scriptures; and he said to them, Thus it is written, that Christ should suffer, and rise again from the dead on the third day . . ." (Lk. 24:44ff.).

The conception of the Apostolic Church on the OT, as we find it in the Acts, the Epistles, and Revelation, was mainly based on the teachings of the **risen** Christ and His "opening their understanding" to perceive the true meaning of the OT Scriptures. The Holy Spirit continued this work, leading the apostles and through them the Primitive Church "into all the truth" (Jh. 16:13). This implied the truth concerning the OT.

The liberal theory that Jesus "emptied Himself" of His divinity in such a manner that He was liable to make errors and be subject to the misconceptions and prejudices of His time both in the "days of His flesh" and after His resurrection leads to the downfall of the entire Christian faith. If this liberal theory is true, we have no certainty that anything that He said was true. Maybe He erred in everything? Or who can say with any certainty which of His sayings were true and which false? In that case Albert Schweitzer was right in holding that Christ's life and work was a great fiasco, an illusion and failure that had its final collapse in His death!

If the liberals' claim is true that they are able to distinguish truth from error in the teachings of Jesus, then we should put more reliance on them than on Christ, and they would have a higher authority than He had. But who would care or dare to be a Christian on such a basis?

The Christ of the Bible is the final and absolute authority of all Christians. He says: "My sheep hear my voice . . . and they follow me" (Jn. 10:27). Those who do not hear, believe and obey His voice are not His disciples. His true followers do not want to hear the voice of strangers, whether they are liberals or traditionalists (Roman Catholics and others). They are determined to listen only to what He says—either personally in the Gospels or through His apostles—and that is final to them.

Our fate in time and eternity depends on our attitude toward Christ and His words, as He says: "He who rejecteth me, and receiveth not my sayings, hath one that judgeth him: the word that I spoke will judge him in the last day" (Jh. 12:48).

2. The Apostles' Attitude toward the Old Testament and Their Own Writings

The apostles were Christ's special authorized messengers, representatives, and mediators of the revelation given by Him. As such they proclaimed and taught what their Sender and Master gave them in charge, as He said: "As the Father hath sent me, even so I send you" (Jh. 20:21). In His "high priestly prayer" Jesus said to the Father: "I have given them the words which thou gavest me; and they have received them . . . Sanctify them in the truth; thy word is truth" (Jh. 17:7f., 17).

Christ's words concerning the OT belonged to the words that He gave to His apostles. His statement, "Thy word is truth," referred both to the OT words of God and His words, for, as we read in Heb. 1:1, God has "in these last days spoken to us in his Son."

Following Christ, the apostles repeatedly appealed to the OT, and they always spoke of it as the fully reliable and authoritative word of God. Paul writes: "Whatever things were written aforetime were written for our instruction, that through steadfastness and through the comfort of the Scriptures we might have hope" (Rom. 15:4). The reason why the OT writings are divine and authoritative is that "all scripture [is] inspired by God . . ." (2 Tim. 3:16), and "no prophecy was ever brought by the will of men, but men spoke from God, being moved by the Holy Spirit" (2 Pet. 1:21).

Paul expressed the faith of the entire Apostolic Church when he said:: "I worship the God of our fathers, believing all that is according to the law and what is written in the prophets" (Acts 24:14).

The apostles taught concerning **their own words** that these were God's Word, just as was the OT and the teaching of Jesus. Paul wrote of the Word proclaimed by him: "Ye received from us the word of the message (Gr. hearing) . . ., not as word of men but, as it is in truth, the word of God" (I Thess. 2:13). These words are in the first epistle that Paul ever wrote (at least as far as we have them in the NT), and not a later developed view. When 2 Pet. 3:15f. place the epistles of Paul alongside "the other scriptures," this is not a later view, as the liberals think, but the one prevalent from the first apostolic epistle on.

According to I Cor. 2:13, not only the thoughts of the apostles' message, but also their words were given by the Holy Spirit: "We speak, not in words which man's wisdom teacheth, but which the Spirit teacheth." Because of this, the apostolic teaching has divine authority, and no change is permitted to be made in it: "Though . . . an angel from heaven would preach you any gospel other than that which we preached to you, let him be accursed" (Gal. 1:8).

The apostles expected Christians to be obedient to their teachings and commandments, for they had given them as ambassadors of Christ. Paul writes in 2 Thess. 3:4, 6: "That ye both do and will do what we command . . . Now we command you . . . in the name of our Lord Jesus Christ . . ."

No one was permitted, not even in the name of (pretended) prophecy or spirituality, to teach or do anything contrary to the apostolic word, since it was the Lord's own word: "If any man thinketh himself to be a prophet, or spiritual," Paul wrote, "let him take knowledge of these things which I write to you, that they are the commandment of the Lord. But if any man is ignorant, he is not acknowledged" (**agnoeitai**, or, let him be ignorant, **agnoeito**, I Cor. 14:37f; both readings are attested about equally well).

The liberals assert that the Bible-believers commit a logical fallacy of reasoning in circles when they hold that the Bible is inerrant and absolutely authoritative God's word **because it says so itself.**

The Pharisees charged Jesus with the very same "logical fallacy": "Thou bearest witness to thyself; thy witness is not true." Jesus answered to them: "Even if I bear witness to myself, my witness is true . . . Ye judge after the flesh" (Jh. 8:13ff.).

This applies to Scripture as well: Even though it testifies to itself, its testimony is true, for it is the Holy Spirit, yea, God who bears this witness. Among men, one witness is not enough, but at least two are needed. But this does not apply to God: The testimony of His Spirit, or His Son, is sufficient alone. When He says something in His Word, He does not need a confirmation from men—and least of all from liberal theologians! To require such a confirmation is blasphemy, making God a liar.

The liberals are guilty of blasphemy when they say that trusting in the testimony of God in His Word is "logical fallacy." This assertion of the liberals is due to the fact that they "judge after the flesh," just as the Pharisees did. And "the mind of the flesh is enmity against God; for it is not subject to the law of God, neither indeed can it be" (Rom. 8:7).

Those who deny the absolute reliability and authority of Christ deny His lordship. Since He is the Lord and Head of the Church, His words, and the words of His authorized apostles, are the supreme, absolute and only rule and norm of the teaching, faith and practice of the Christian Church and its every member, as the Confessions of the Protestant Churches state.

III. INSPIRATION OF THE BIBLE

Bible-believing evangelicals and liberals (modernists) have wholly opposite starting points in their study of the Scriptures.

The Bible-believers launch out with the conviction of faith that the Holy Writ is to be taken for what it (particularly in the statements of Christ and His apostles) itself claims to be.

The liberals start with the principle (axiom) of unbelief —which they falsely call "scientific"—that the Bible should be studied in the same manner as any other ancient piece or collection of literature—without the faith that Christ and His apostles are right in what they say of it. The results of their critical study decide whether the statements of Christ and His apostles are right or not. In their view, the question whether Christ is reliable or not is to be decided by men, namely, the liberal critics.

In taking this attitude, the liberals forget—or are unwilling to admit—that they are mere men, and that their understanding is darkened by sin. They are in various ways bound and led astray by their sinful inclinations, habits of thinking, the training that they have received, their liberal tradition, the philosophical school(s) by which they have been influenced, etc. Because of all this they are not able to pursue their study of the Bible in a truly objective, impartial and factual manner.* Paul's words apply to them:

> "The natural (Gr. psychical, unspiritual) man receiveth not the things of the Spirit of God; for they are foolishness to him, and he cannot know them, because they are spiritually judged (or, discerned)" (1 Cor. 2:14).

---

* James I. Packer, "Contemporary Views of Revelation," in **Revelation and the Bible**, edited by Carl F. H. Henry (Baker, Grand Rapids,
(Continued on the following page)

HATH GOD SAID?

The basic issue that divides theologians, pastors and church people into two opposing camps is not any particular theory of inspiration, as the liberals usually claim. They assert that the Bible-believers (often called "fundamentalists"—for they want to stand on the foundation—Lat. fundamentum—of God's infallible Word) hold to an antiquated 16th century theory of verbal inspiration, which is wholly unacceptable in our "scientific" age. Frequently they charge Bible-believers with a mechanical dictation-theory, according to which God "dictated" the words of the Bible, and its writers merely wrote down what God said to them. They also hold it against the Bible-believers that they believe in the Bible as containing a consistent divine revelation whose different parts are in good harmony with one another.*

Mich., 1958), p. 99, writes to the point: "The mid-twentieth century . . . , bitterly aware of the power of propaganda and brain-washing, and the control that non-rational factors can have over our thinking, is tempted to despair of gaining objective knowledge of anything . . ." The liberals of various shades, unfortunately, have failed to learn this lesson so as to return to a trust in the dependability and authority of God's Word. Packer shows how inconsistent are those who in the described despair require of the Church a reasoned assurance of divine truth. Most miserable are those theologians who have lost trust both in the Bible and in themselves: "When modern theology tells us that we can trust neither the Bible nor ourselves, it condemns us to this fate [namely, to "be left to drift on a sea of speculations and doubts forever"] without hope of reprieve."

* Mikko Juva, professor of Church History at the Lutheran Theological Department of the University of Helsinki, Finland (who also was the host leader of the general assembly of the Lutheran World Federation held in Helsinki in 1963), wrote in 1957 (Ylioppilaslehti/Student paper/No. 38): Such a "fundamentalistic view of the Scriptures," "according to which the Bible is a doctrinal whole, whose aim is to provide material for the construction of a Christian doctrinal system" is "alien both to the Lutheran Reformation and the Primitive Church." Juva rejects the Bible-believing position that "all the books of the Bible should be regarded as equally 'true' or corresponding to the . . . historical reality which it records." The Bible-believers ("fundamentalists") certainly believe that the Bible is true in all its parts, and that it is a doctrinal whole. But hardly any "fundamentalist" holds that its aim is to provide material for the con-
(Continued on the following page)

It is true that Bible-believers see the Bible as a consistent whole, whose different parts (in their original autographs) are in full harmony. But the charge that they would hold to a mechanical dictation-theory is a wholly false accusation.

We give some modern examples of the liberal views.

William Hordern, at the present time a pastor of the American Lutheran Church (TALC), has for years been a spokesman for the "New Reformation Theology," alias Neo-Orthodoxy, the trend that has had its origin in Karl Barth. He explains in his book **The Case for a New Reformation Theology** (Westminster Press, 1959) that holding to the infallibility of the Scriptures "tends to lead to idolatry of the Bible." He declares: "Just because we believe that God is revealed through the Bible, it becomes more necessary to be critical of the Bible. We must be careful to separate the wheat from the chaff precisely because we believe that from the wheat is formed the bread of life" (p. 86).

The liberals have taken upon themselves the role of "threshing-machines" that separate the "wheat" from the "chaff" in the Scriptures—even in the teachings of Jesus. But how can we ever know what in the Bible really is "wheat" and what "chaff," as the liberals disagree among themselves at almost every point in this respect?

The liberals are leading the Church into the "shifting sands" of human opinions and whims.

Hordern uses a queer sort of reasoning in deriding the Bible-believers' faith in the inerrancy of the Scriptures:

struction of a Christian doctrinal system. True, a Christian doctrinal system can and must be constructed on the basis of the Bible, but its aim is not that, but to lead to repentance, faith in Christ and to the obedience of faith. — It is in general characteristic of the liberals that they do not read theological works written by Bible-believers but study onesidedly books of liberals, in which false pictures are given of the teachings of the conservatives.

"An objective revelation is not inerrant until it is inerrantly received ... If there is to be inerrant revelation of propositions, the hearer would have to be as inerrant as the speaker ... to claim that God spoke without error ... is meaningless to us men who are fallible hearers, for we can never know infallibly that we understand correctly the infallible revelation" (ibid., pp. 59f.).

The liberals, particularly the Neo-Orthodox, reject the possibility of a propositional revelation of truth. According to a dictionary definition, "proposition" is "an expression in which the predicate affirms or denies something about the subject." Denial of a propositional truth, then, means that, according to the liberals, it is impossible to state in plain words and understandable sentences what is true and what false. Truth cannot be expressed in human language so that something definite and sure is stated. In practice this means that no one can say what is true and what false, what right and what wrong. Pontius Pilate was in this sense a true scientific Neo-Orthodox when he asked, "What is truth?", and turned away without caring to listen to what Jesus had to say. He had said the previous night in the presence of His apostles: "Thy word is truth." Pilate did not believe this, and the modern liberals are modern "Pilates" in this respect. In denying that there can be any "propositional truth," they reject the statement of Jesus, "Thy word is truth."

Hordern's quoted statement means in practice: If e.g. a pastor's sermon is misunderstood by some of his hearers, it cannot be a true presentation of the Gospel. Misunderstanding on the part of some of his hearers renders the sermon erroneous.

Luther had an opposite view on this question. He emphasized that the Word of God is true and valid in itself whether men believe it or not, just as the sacraments are true and valid in themselves, if administered according to the institution of Christ, whether men use them aright or not. Only the personal blessing depends on the right attitude of the heart, on faith, not the objective truth and validity of the Word and the Sacrament. Luther writes in his **Large Catechism (IV:52-60):**

> "Those are arrogant and stupid spirits who draw this conclusion: Where faith is not right, neither can baptism be right. This is the same as if I should draw the conclusion: If I do not believe, Christ is nothing. Or else: If I am not obedient, father, mother and the temporal government are nothing. My beloved, you should rather say: Baptism is something and right for the very reason that it has been taken in a wrong manner. For were the baptism not right in itself, it could not be misused. Therefore it is said, ... Misuse does not do away with the substance but confirms it."

Luther's words apply to God's Word in general. We think of Jesus' parable of the sower: many grains of the seed sown fell into places where they did not grow or at least bring forth mature fruit. But this did not make the seed wrong. If Hordern—and the liberals of like mind—would be consistent they should conclude: if the seed—Jesus means the proclaimed Word—does not grow and bring forth mature fruit, the fault is in the seed. According to Jesus, the fault is in the ground on which the seed falls.

The Bible, and biblical preaching and teaching, does not become erroneous by the fact that many people do not believe it or fail to understand it. It is right in itself, objectively; the fault is in men who read or listen to it in a wrong way.

In rejecting the old conviction of historical Christianity that God has given His revelation and truth in understandable language and in statements that have a definite meaning, that is, propositional truth, Hordern writes:

> "God's Word never consists of black marks on the pages of a book called the Bible; God's Word is the living Word which speaks through the Bible and to which man must respond by saying yes or no" (ibid., p. 62).

If the words written in the Bible in "black marks" are not God's Words, how can God speak through them? And how can a person respond by "yes" or "no" if there are no propositions, that is, if nothing is really said in terms that have a definite meaning and can be understood?

In denying the possibility of propositional divine revelation and truth the Neo-Orthodox have made void the Formal

Principle of the Reformation: for if truth cannot be expressed in propositions, understandable sentences that have a definite meaning, the Bible cannot be the supreme and only rule and norm of faith. In that case we cannot have any norm and rule of faith and practice at all, since truth cannot be expressed in meaningful sentences. The "living word" of Hordern and the Neo-Orthodox is not the divinely inspired Word of the Bible and its proclamation and teaching in the Church. It must be some hazy feelings and sentiments and fancies of these theologians—of which no one can say what they mean.

The Neo-Orthodox trend to which Hordern belongs is renown for its singular proficiency in double-talking and for its ability of making everything so hazy and ambiguous that nobody knows what is the truth. Theirs is a modern "pilateship" that claims to be "scientific theology"!

The Neo-Orthodox denial of propositional truth is basically agnosticism, and agnosticism is just another name for atheism. In other words, it is a modern echo of the first word of the old serpent: "Hath God said ... ?"

Hordern and his Neo-Orthodox company do not only destroy the Formal Principle of the Reformation. They are doing a similar destructive work with regard to its Material Principle, which is the fundamental evangelical doctrine that a sinner is justified by grace alone, for Christ's sake, through faith, without his own good works and merits; love, obedience and good works are fruits of justifying faith, worked by the Holy Spirit who dwells in the believer's heart. In other words, the Material Principle is the biblical way of salvation rediscovered by Luther and the Reformation.

The "New Reformation" of Neo-Orthodoxy that Hordern represents turns things upside down in the matter of salvation. Hordern writes:

> "A Church that centers man's attention on the question, 'Are you saved?' has betrayed the Reformation and has betrayed Christ. When God's grace really grips us. we lose all concern about

whether we have been saved. 'For whosoever will save his life shall lose it' " (ibid., p. 152).*

If Hordern and the Neo-Orthodox are right, the three thousand people who on the Pentecost were pricked in their hearts and asked, what they should do to be saved, and the Philippian jailer who fell down before Paul and Silas, asking, "Sirs, what must I do to be saved?", were not gripped by the grace of God but by some misleading spirit. If Hordern or somebody else of like mind would have been a counsellor at these occasions, he would have said: Poor people, you are badly mistaken! Don't be concerned about your salvation! Put off the whole question. God has not gripped you. When His grace grips you, you become entirely unconcerned about your salvation!

In the statement that Hordern quotes Jesus speaks of a sinner's attempt to save his natural carnal life. Hordern applies it to the convicted sinner's concern about his salvation from sin.

Truly: "If therefore the light that is in thee is darkness, how great is the darkness!" (Mt. 6:23).

Hordern and the Neo-Orthodox rejoice on "salvation" but on a different salvation from the one on which the Reformers and God's people in general rejoice. After stating that the "New Reformation Theology" "accepts wholeheartedly the findings of biblical criticism," Hordern goes on to say:

> "We are thankful that, having been shown the human finite nature of the Bible, we are saved from an idolatry of the book" (ibid., p. 74).

Salvation from honoring the Bible as God's dependable and authoritative Word! Truly: this is the "salvation" that

---

* Hordern, however, also speaks of knowing God in the sense of having fellowship with Him, in which his life is renewed, redeemed, saved (ibid., pp. 63f.). This is a typical example of Neo-Orthodox double-talk: they affirm and deny the same things. Who can know what they mean?

the devil likes to give all men! The Bible-believers leave the liberals to thank their own lord and master for this sort of salvation. They themselves long for a fuller salvation from the slowness of their heart to believe all that is written in the Bible—a sin that inheres in our flesh and of which Christ rebukes (Lk. 24:25).

Another example of the modern liberals' attitude toward the Bible and its inspiration is what we find in the book **Theological Perspectives. A Discussion of Contemporary Issues in Lutheran Theology** (Luther College Press, Decorah, Iowa). The book contains public lectures by six Luther College (TALC) professors in the fall of 1962. In answering the question, What is the Word of God? the book explains:

> "First, . . . Christ, the Word Incarnate . . . Second, the Bible . . . Thirdly, the preaching on Sunday morning . . . There is qualitatively no difference between the inspiration of the Bible and the inspiration of the preaching of the Church . . . The question, therefore, of whether or not there may be human errors of one sort or another in Scripture is of no particular importance. Just as the pastor on Sunday morning may make errors of one sort or another in preaching and still preach the Word, so also with Scripture" (pp. 64f., Gerhard Forde).

The old biblical and Reformation doctrine of the uniqueness of the inspiration of Scripture is here wholly thrown overboard. The writers of the Holy Writ are said to have been "inspired" in the same manner as any pastor is "inspired" in his preaching and teaching. Liberal clergymen—and especially they—are also included here, for the liberals (to whom Forde belongs) do not acknowledge the preaching of Bible-believers as truly "relevant" for the people of our time and therefore truly "inspired."

In the view of G. Forde, all the various ideas set forth by modernistic clergymen are just as "inspired" as the words of Moses, Isaiah, Paul, Peter—and even of Christ Himself!

If so, why not set the Bible aside and replace it with a collection of the writings and sermons of the liberals?—they would be, in their view, more "up-to-date" than the "antiquated" Bible!

One more example of the liberal attitude toward the Bible is what the editor of THE LUTHERAN, official organ of the Lutheran Church in America (LCA) wrote in the Feb. 24, 1965 issue of the said paper, in the article already quoted:

> "Protestants in the time soon after the Reformation toned down Luther's teaching. They said the word of God is the Bible. It's the infallible book and everything in it is most certainly true. — So Protestants also had an authority, just as the Catholics did. For Roman Catholics the authority was the church and for Protestants it was the Bible. — This was an odd development which would have greatly disturbed Luther."

The words imply that, according to the assertion of the writer, Luther and the other reformers did not acknowledge the authority of the Bible or any authority. They wanted to shake off all authority and give each pastor and church member full freedom to believe and teach what they wished. In other words, according to the editor of THE LUTHERAN, Luther and the Reformers were complete religious and doctrinal anarchists! If this view is right, at the time of the Reformation there was no such thing as the Formal Principle, and Luther would have been "greatly disturbed" by the "odd development" which led the church that used his name to accept the declaration in the **Formula of Concord,** quoted before, which states:

> ". . . the prophetic and apostolic writings of the Old and New Testaments are the only rule and norm according to which all doctrines and teachers alike must be appraised and judged . . ."

The modernists seem to be "rewriting" the history of Protestantism!

The sad fact is that the words of the editor of THE LUTHERAN—though, of course, historically "upside down" —are a reflection of the common modernistic view, which is rebellion against the authority of God's Word and a consequent doctrinal anarchy. The necessary result is that the

Protestantism of our time is for the most part in the process of complete doctrinal disintegration. The final result will be submission to the authority of the Pope—the Antichrist ruling in the city of seven mountains (Rev. 17:9).

Modernism is the great apostasy that, according to 2 Thess. 2:3, is to take place before the second coming of Christ. Already now the words of Paul in this connection are becoming true:

> "Because they received not the love of the truth, that they might be saved . . . , God will send them strong delusion, that they would believe a lie; that they all might be judged who believed not the truth, but had pleasure in unrighteousness" (vv. 10-12).

Bible-believing Protestantism opposes the liberal trend in its various forms and holds to the old biblical Reformation position of the inspiration and authority of the Bible. It may be briefly stated as follows:

The inspiration of the Bible means that, as it declares itself, it is "inspired by God" (Gr. **theopneustos,** God-breathed, 2 Tim. 3:16). Its writers, "moved by the Holy Spirit, spoke from God" (2 Pet. 1:21). They did this in such a manner that the Word that came about in this way is "truth in its entirety" (Ps. 119:160; the Hb. word ROSH means head, sum total, the whole), and that "every word of God is pure" (Prov. 130:5). Because of this, "Scripture cannot be broken" (Jh. 10:35) in any part. "One jot or one tittle will not pass from the Law" (the Five Books of Moses, Mt. 5:18). Christ's words, "Thy word is truth" (Jh. 17:17), apply therefore to the whole Bible. Consequently we must, with Paul, "believe everything that is in accordance with the law, and that is written in the prophets" (Acts 24:14), and the whole Bible, for its words have not been spoken and written "in words taught by human wisdom, but in those taught by the Spirit" (I Cor. 2:13).

The inspiration of the Bible is the activity of God which has led the revelation and its recording in the Bible in such a manner that all that it says of itself is true, whatever means He may have used in it. The Holy Writ itself mentions in this respect God's (and Christ's) direct speaking (the word "dictation" applies to such parts of the Bible), visions, dreams, revelations and words through angels, seeing with eyes and hearing with ears, study of documents, inquiring of eyewitnesses, etc.

The Bible does not teach that God has set aside the personality, position, character and gifts of the men He has used. He has not employed them mechanically. Rather, He used them as they were, but He did it in such a manner that the result was the Bible that is true in its entirety.

Theologians have set forth various theories of the quality of the inspiration of the Bible. Some have proposed "person inspiration," others a "thought or idea inspiration," and some a "word (verbal) inspiration."

Bible-believers refuse to participate in this sort of discussion. They are determined not to go "beyond what is written" (1 Cor. 4:6) and construct human theories of inspiration. They want to abide in simple faith by the statements of Scripture itself on this question and to take them in their simple literal sense.

Liberals have sometimes paralleled Scripture with Christ's two natures: As He was true God and true man in the same person in such a manner that His human nature remained truly human and His divine nature truly divine, and that the two natures were not commingled, so the Bible also is at the same time both divine and human. As the Son of God took the form of servant, having the human nature with its frailties, so God's revelation and Word is in the Bible in a frail human servant form.

Liberals (the Neo-Orthodox included) have charged Bible-believers with a docetic or monophysitic error concerning the Bible. **Docetism** means the view that Christ had only an apparent human nature, not a real one. **Monophysitism** has the conception that Christ divine nature "swallowed up" His human nature in such a manner that He really had only one nature, the divine. Hordern writes of this:

"The conservatives followed a path similar to that of the Docetics and denied the true humanity of the Bible ... as many pay lip service to the humanity of Jesus and then deny it in practice, so the conservative position often denies the true humanity of the Biblical writings. God so overwhelmed the humanity of the writers that the normal tendency to err was erased" (**Op. cit.**, p. 66).

According to the Scriptures (and the ancient Christian Creeds, the Nicean and Athanasian), Christ was, to be sure, true and complete man as to His human nature. This did not, however, imply sinfulness and liability to err, for sin and error did not belong to human nature such as God originally created it. The invincible tendency to sin and go astray entered the human nature in the fall. Christ's human nature was pure and sinless, as was the nature of men prior to the fall. He "knew no sin" (2 Cor. 5:21). He was, to be sure, tempted, "yet without sin" (Heb. 4:15), "nor was any deceit found in his mouth" (I Pet. 2:22). As God-Man, "all the treasures of wisdom and knowledge are hidden in him" (Col. 2:3).

The liberal view of the Bible implies that the human side of the Bible contains historical errors, faulty views, conflicting teachings, myths, legends, literary forgeries, falsifications, etc. When Christ's human nature is paralleled or said to correspond to the human side of the Bible, the unavoidable conclusion is that He too was liable to err, and that His teachings are true only in part. This is what the liberals actually assert of Christ: His statements concerning the OT are largely false.

Our conclusion is that the biblical Christian doctrine of the two natures of Christ is parallel with the Bible-believing position of the divine and human sides of the Bibles, whereas the liberal view is in a clear conflict with it.

IV. INTERPRETATION OF SCRIPTURE

The liberal critics usually call their interpretation of the Bible "historical" and "scientific." They claim to use objective scientific methods in their work for finding out who were the writers of the various books, at what times and circumstances they were written, whether they are reliable, etc. They charge Bible-believers with disregard of historical facts, holding to traditional Jewish views, etc.

The extreme liberals regard the Bible as a collection of Hebrew religious literary products, just as the people of India have their Vedas, the Moslems their Koran, etc. Others admit that Scripture is a record or witness of God's revelatory activity, however, an imperfect and faulty human one. In either case the liberals—some of them more consistently, others less—want to be "scientific" in the sense that they limit themselves to the human and historical elements of the Bible. When they deal with its religious aspects, they treat them as testimonies of men's religious experiences and ideas, not as divine revelation-truths, as the Bible-believers do.

This kind of limitation, however, is not truly scientific. Scientific investigations should not beforehand decide to rule out the possibility of certain factors and facts, but it should all the time be open to all facts and factors. The Kantian epistemological axiom that our knowledge is limited to the material world which can be studied through sense perception does not fit into Christian theology, and even in general it is an arbitrary principle of unbelief. We ask: by what authority (besides that of Kant) are the facts and factors that are discovered by senses regarded as the only legitimate ones? A refusal to consider all the facts renders research unscientific and leads to a failure from the outset.*

---

* Cp. Edward J. Young, **An Introduction to the Old Testament**, Grand Rapids, Mich., 1963, pp. 27f.

Liberals say that a scientific theologian studies the Bible with a neutral attitude, as any other literary product should be studied. This so-called "neutral" attitude is, in reality, however, far from being neutral, for it starts with the preconceived notion that the Bible's own claims of its divine origin and reliability are not true, and that men are justified and able to judge divine revelation, even the question whether Christ, the Son of God, has spoken truth or not. The liberals reject beforehand the statement of Scripture that its prophecies (in a wide sense of the word, the whole Bible is prophetical) are not of any man's private (own human) interpretation (2 Pet. 1:20), and that "a natural man does not accept the things of the Spirit of God..., and he cannot understand them, because they are spiritually appraised" (discerned, judged, I Cor. 2:14).

Instead of being neutral and objective, the liberal attitude is basically hostile toward the Bible and the divine revelation that it records, since it beforehand rejects its own claim to be true. A hostile attitude is not neutral and objective.

If a historian who claims to be scientific has a hostile attitude toward the nation whose history he studies, it is impossible that the results of his study could be objective. His hostility distorts and colors practically everything.

One must have at least a sympathetic attitude toward the object of his study in order that he would be able to understand it aright.

In a truly scientific study, the material that is studied must determine the findings, and not some outside factors that are hostile to this material. In the study of the Bible, this means that the student must be determined by and fulfill the Bible's own requirement: he must himself live by faith in the world of God of which this Book speaks. As it was written by the inspiration of God, it must also be interpreted by the inspiration of God, under the enlightenment and guidance of His Spirit. This inspiration is not, of course, the same as the primary revelation-inspiration that produced the Bible, but the secondary inspiration through which the true meaning of the inspired Word opens to the student. This is possible only if he himself has experienced the salvation and life of which the Scriptures speak, and if he pursues his study as a member of the communion of saints, the family of God, not "privately." God's people are dependent on one another in their understanding of the Bible, just as they are in their entire Christian life. Luther says to the point:

> "No human being sees one iota of Scripture unless he has the Spirit of God. All men have a darkened heart, so that even if they know how to tell and set forth all that the Bible contains, yet they are unable to feel and truly know it . . . For the Spirit is needed for the understanding of the Bible as a whole and its every part" (WA, 18:609).
>
> Therefore, "your first task is to begin to pray . . . that . . . He would . . . graciously grant you the true understanding of the words. For there is but one Master of the divine words, namely, their Author, as He says, 'They shall all be taught by God' (Jh. 6: 45). You must, therefore, completely despair of your own industry and ability and rely solely on the inspiration of the Spirit" (WA, Briefe, 1:133).
>
> "The Holy Bible wants to be dealt with in fear and humility, and one can get into its meaning better by studying it with pious prayer than with keenness of intellect. It is therefore impossible for those who rely on their bare ingenuity (**nudo ingenio**) and rush into the Bible with dirty feet, like pigs, as though Scripture were a sort of human knowledge, not to harm themselves and others, whom they instruct. So utterly they fail to understand it" (WA, 1:507).

The Bible is a complex unity which is made up of narratives, laws, promises, sermons, doctrinal parts, instructions for conduct, proverbs, parables, etc. The right exposition of all this material involves the setting of its different parts into their relations both to the whole and to one another. Scripture does not present the word of God in the form of a theological system, but it can be set forth in that form and, indeed, must be, in order that it could be properly grasped as a whole.

Luther sets forth the common view of the entire Bible-believing Protestantism when he emphasizes that every Bible passage must be understood in its context:

> 'It will not do to tear a statement out of its context and then urge it (**drauf pochen**, use it as a strong proof). One must consider the meaning of the entire text, the relation of its thoughts to one another" (**wie er an einander hängt**, WA, 18:69).

Scripture must be used to interpret itself. The passages that speak of the same or related things must be brought together to explain and supplement one another. Luther says:

> The Bible "wants to interpret itself by comparison of passages from everywhere . . . And the safest of all the ways to search for the meaning of Scripture is to strive for it by a comparison of passages" (WA, 14:556).

This method can, however, be misused. Luther cautions against the coupling of passages which do not really belong together:

> "It is not enough to cite a different passage without the slightest regard to whether it proves the same point or something else. No mistake is more easily and commonly made in dealing with the Bible than bringing together Scripture passages that are different, as though they were identical" (WA, 18:728).

This error is often done because of external similarities, such as the use of the same word, etc. An example of this is the manner in which Hordern uses (in the statement quoted before) the words of Jesus on saving one's life: Just because the word "save" is used, Hordern assumes that Jesus speaks here of salvation from sin, while He really means just the opposite. Another example is the rather common liberal identification of the "little horn" of Dan. 7:8, 20ff. with the "little horn" of Dan. 8:9ff. merely because a somewhat similar expression is employed (though in the original text different words for "little" are used). In reality they are entirely different: the "little horn" of Dan. 8:9ff. belonged to the **fourth** beast-phase (being the Syrian king Antiochus IV Epiphanes in the second century B. C.), whereas the "little horn" of Dan. 7:8, 20ff. belongs to the **sixth** beast-phase, being the last ungodly world power of the present age, to be destroyed at the second coming of Christ. (On this more in the chapter on Daniel).

One of the main reasons why the Catholic Church wants to have the tradition and teaching office of the Church alongside the Bible is that it regards Scripture in itself so obscure and difficult to understand that these are necessary for its proper interpretation. The entire Reformation movement (with the possible exception of the "Fanatics") was unanimous in its conviction that the Bible is so clear and plain that any Spirit-enlightened believer can understand it so far as he needs it for his own faith, Christian walk and testimony. Luther expressed this Protestant conviction as follows:

> "No clearer book has been written than the Holy Bible . . . It is a horrible . . . crime against Scripture and all Christendom to say that the Bible is dark and not so clear that everybody may understand it in order to teach and prove his faith" (WA, 8:236).

The Scriptures are clear if its words mean what they say. Otherwise no one can be sure of its meaning. Luther rejected in 1516-17 the figurative allegorical method practiced in the Roman Church and demanded a literal interpretation of its text.* He said:

> "The Christian reader should devote his first effort to searching what is called the literal sense. It alone is the entire substance of faith and Christian theology; it alone holds its own in tribulation and temptation and gains victory over the gates of hell and triumphs to the praise and glory of God. But allegory is often uncertain and unreliable and very unsafe as a prop of faith, since it frequently depends on human conjecture and opinion. If anyone leans on it, he is leaning on the reed of Egypt" (WA, 14:560; Luther refers here to Is. 36:6).

Luther based his demand that the Bible must be taken in its literal sense on the fact that it has been written by the inspiration of God. He said on this:

---

* On the Catholic allegorical method and this change in Luther's view, see U. Saarnivaara, **Luther Discovers the Gospel** (Concordia, St. Louis, Mo., 1951), pp. 89, 118. On the allegorical method in general, see Ernest F. Kevan, "The Principles of Interpretation," in **Revelation and the Bible,** edited by Carl F. H. Henry (Baker, Grand Rapids, Mich., 1958), pp. 289ff.

"The Holy Spirit is the plainest Writer and Speaker in heaven and on earth. His words can therefore have no more than one sense, and it is the most obvious sense. This we call the literal or natural sense . . . It is . . . surer and safer to abide by the words in their simple sense" (WA, 23:92).

Luther was severe against those who interpreted the Scriptures figuratively, to mean something else from the simple meaning of the text, without any real warranty in it:

"It is the manner of all who evade arguments by means of figurative language, arrogantly holding the text itself in contempt and having for their aim merely to pick out a certain term and twisting and crucifying it on the cross of their own opinion, with utter disregard of the circumstances, of the preceding and following context, and of the intent and purpose of the writer" (WA, 18:713).

Luther demands:

"Whoever is so bold as to give the words of Scripture a meaning that differs from the sense that their simple sound confers is obliged to prove his explanation from the text before him or from the article of faith" (WA, 23:92).

"Neither a conclusion or a figure of speech should be admitted in any place of the Bible, unless evident contextual circumstances or the absurdity of anything obviously militating against an article of faith requires it. On the contrary, we must everywhere adhere to the simple, pure and natural meaning of the words. This accords with the rules of grammar and the usage of speech which God has given men" (WA, 18:700).

Ulrich Zwingli, a Swiss reformer (d. 1531), invented a method of figurative Bible interpretation which he called **alloeosis** (Greek **allos**=other). According to it, the Bible can say one thing and mean something else. Applying this principle to Christ's words in the institution of Holy Communion, Zwingli explained: True, Christ said, "This is my body," "This is my blood," but He meant, This signifies my body, my blood. Likewise Christ, to be sure, said to His disciples: "Whose soever sins ye forgive, they are forgiven to them" (Jh. 20:23), but He meant: Whose soever sins the Holy Spirit forgives, they are forgiven to them. By means of his **alloeosis** Zwingli got around in these (and many other) cases the simple literal meaning of Scripture. He denied that Christ's body and blood are given (of course, in a supernatural and spiritual manner, not in a natural and material sense: Christ's body and blood are no longer material) in Holy Communion in and with bread and wine, and he denied that forgiveness of sins is imparted to penitent sinners through the Gospel proclaimed in the Church—each one must seek for it directly in prayer from the Holy Spirit.

Luther opposed the Zwinglian **alloeosis**, for it made everything in the Bible uncertain. If its text does not mean what it says, who can ever know with any certainty what it means? Luther declared:

> "Beware, beware, I say, of that alloeosis. It is the devil's mask; for from it is born such a Christ, according to whom I would not wish to a Christian" (WA, 26:319).

Luther meant: The Christ of the **alloeosis** does not really mean what He says, and therefore no one knows what He means, and Christians would be forced to build their faith on guesses in this respect. Such a "Christ" would be so obscure and enigmatic that the Church would have no sure foundation for its faith, but would be left to the fancies of men. Luther wrote:

> "If every one is allowed to invent conclusions and figures of speech according to his own whim, nothing could be determined and proved to a certainty concerning any article of faith . . . We must avoid as the most deadly poison all figurative language that the Bible itself does not force us to find in a passage" (WA, 18:700f.).

Luther's words show that he was well aware of the fact that the Bible uses in many cases figurative language (e.g. in parables and types), but he emphasizes that when it does so it makes this plain itself. At any rate, if figurative interpretation is used when the Bible itself does not indicate it, it should be done only in application and in harmony with doctrines based on passages that are taken literally.

In the period of the Reformation, **Zwingli** developed his **alloeosis** interpretation in Zurich Swizerland. Zwingli's most important coworker **Oecolampasius** lived in **Basel**. In

HATH GOD SAID? 55

our time, Karl Barth, the chief "father" of the modern Neo-Orthodox trend, was born (1886) in Basel and served there as professor of theology from 1935 till his retirement in the late 1950's. Emil Brunner, the second most important "father" of Neo-Orthodoxy, was born (1889) in Zurich and served there as professor for several decades till his retirement (he died in 1966). The Neo-Orthodox interpretation of the revelation-events of the Bible as "myths" is a modern form of alloeosis. Another modern form of it is the "demythologizing" interpretation of Rudolf Bultmann (born 1884), who served as professor in Marburg from 1921 till his retirement in the early 1960's. It was in Marburg that Zwingli defended his alloeosis interpretation in his colloquy with Luther in 1529. Although Bultmann wants to uncover the "existential" religious thoughts of the NT from their "mythological" clothing, in reality his interpretation also is a modern figurative method which puts into the biblical text meanings that are different from its simple literal sense.

Luther and all true Protestants of the 16th century who took seriously the divine inspiration and authority of the Bible opposed the Zwinglian alloeosis, just as they opposed the Roman Catholic allegorical interpretation. All Bible-believing Protestants likewise oppose the modern forms of alloeosis, both the Neo-Orthodox and Bultmannian. Luther's warnings against symbolical interpretations and his demands to hold to the simple meaning of the biblical text are needed in our time more than ever before:

> "No violence should be done to the words of God . . . ; but as far as possible we should retain them in their simplest meaning and take them in their grammatical and literal sense, unless an obvious circumstance plainly forbids it" (WA, 6:509).
> "We must not commit sacrilege against the word of God and without the warrant of any express passage of Scripture give a word a meaning that differs from its natural sense" (WA, 11:434).

In harmony with these principles, held by the entire great Reformation of the 16th century, Bible-believing evangelicals hold to the following "Golden Rule of Interpretation":

When the plain sense of Scripture makes common sense, seek no other sense; therefore, take every word in its primary, ordinary, usual, literal meaning, unless the facts of the immediate context, studied in the light of related passages and axiomatic and fundamental truths, indicate clearly otherwise.

The great outcry against this "literalism" of Bible-believers comes from liberal circles which want to have freedom to interpret certain events recorded in the Bible as myths or parables, that is, as nonfactual symbols of spiritual experiences or states. There are many who would explain the narrative of the Fall in Gen. 3 as a symbol revealing the state of man today and the conflicting forces that are struggling in him, but they regard it as false if treated as a record of what has actually happened in history.* The biblical statements concerning Christ's conception of the Holy Spirit and His virgin birth are explained to be mere symbolical expressions of the thought of His superhuman nature. Many other examples could be cited.

By this type of interpretations the Neo-Orthodox and others want to cover up their denial that these things have really taken place in history, or, then, to say that it is unimportant whether they have actually happened or not; these stories contain valuable religious thoughts, and that's the only thing that matters.

If this method of thinking would be applied to other fields of human life, its representatives would be regarded as mentally deranged: One should say that it is unimportant

---

* An example of this type of interpretation is the manner in which Robert J. Marshall deals with the Genesis account of creation and the fall in the LCA book THE MIGHTY ACTS OF GOD (1964), pp. 25-34. Adam is for him a symbol of "Everyman," the snake and tree are symbols of forces struggling in human life, etc. See also Otten, **op. cit.**, pp. 189-195. E. F. Kevan writes of the Alexandrian allegorical method: "Sheer allegorism of the Alexandrian kind introduces nothing but chaos into speech and destroys all objectivity of truth: it is "fantasy unlimited.' . . . it . . . became an arbitrary instrument for making the Old Testament say whatever the expositor wished" (C. F. Henry, **op. cit.**, p. 191). The same applies to the modern forms of symbolical interpretation.

whether the thing on the table is real bread or not; the only thing that matters is that it suggests the valuable thought that eating of bread nourishes. Or else: It is unimportant whether the airplane by which one plans to travel from America to Europe actually exists and carries passengers; the only thing that matters is the valuable idea that one may travel by air from America to Europe.

Bible-believers want to have real revelation facts and a real salvation. They oppose the modern symbolical interpretations because they want to preserve Christianity from becoming something unreal and illusionary, and the Bible from losing its reality as God's Word and its real authority.*

Bible-believers do not reject the use of reason in Bible interpretation. They merely want to follow the teaching of Scripture that human reason and thinking must in all things be subjected to the obedience of Christ (2 Cor. 10:5). They want therefore to interpret the Bible in trust in and obedience to what Christ, and Scripture in general, says of it. Human reason works aright only when it wholeheartedly confesses the lordship of Christ and operates under the guidance of the Holy Spirit, subject to God's Word, the Bible.

One of the tasks of Spirit-enlightened and Spirit-led reason is to apply the biblical truth to the problems, life and activity of modern men. In doing so, it must all the time be faithful to the truth of God's Word, without changing it in the least to something other than it is.**

---

* On Neo-Orthodoxy, see e.g. Otten, op. cit., pp. 17-22, 309ff.; Cornelius Van Til, **Christianity and Barthianism** (Grand Rapids, 1962); Langdon Gilkey, "Neo-Orthodoxy," in **Handbook of Christian Theology** (New York, 1960); Carl F. H. Henry, **op. cit.**, see Subject Index, "Neo-orthodoxy," and Author Index, "Barth, Karl," "Brunner, Emil." Ch. C. Ryrie, **Neo-Orthodoxy. What It Is and What It Does** (Moody Press, Chicago, 1964).

** One of the best books that deal with the questions discussed thus far is J. I. Packer's **'Fundamentalism' and the Word of God** (IVF, London, 1963; in U. S. A., Eerdmans, Grand Rapids, Mich., 1963). The writer has drawn many of the leading thoughts from this book of Packer.

V. WHO WROTE THE "BOOKS OF MOSES"

One of the main tenets of modern liberal critical Bible study is that the first section of the OT, the Pentateuch, called by the Bible itself the "law of Moses" (Mal. 4:4), "book of Moses" (Mk. 12:26), or simply "the Law" (Heb. TORAH=teaching, law), was not written by Moses, and that Christ and His apostles, as well as the writers of many OT books before them, were in error in speaking of it as such. It was the end-product of a series of conglomerations of forgeries, prepared long times after Moses, the critics claim.

1. Liberal Theory of the Origin of the Pentateuch

We let the renowned American Jewish author Herman Wouk, a thorough student of the OT criticism and possibly—as he himself says—the last man on earth to read through Julius Wellhausen's **Prolegomena to the History of Ancient Israel** (1875, Engl. by Meridian Publ.), on which the critical view is mainly based, and to check all his textual references in the OT Hebrew. Wouk writes (**This Is My God**, Doubleday & Co., 1961, pp. 312-316):

"So far as I know, the general theory of modern Bible criticism was first set down by Spinoza, in his **Tractate on Theology and Politics**, though he owed much to Hobbes.... Spinoza's idea in nutshell was that the Bible after all was literature, a book like any other book, though perhaps greater than most.... Rational scrutiny of the text would show the truth about its authors, and the facts of its origin. He outlined all the paraphernalia of what we now call the Higher Criticism: variations of style, repeated passages, ... oddities of grammar and vocabulary, and so forth. He leaned much on an orthodox Hebrew commentator of great stature, Ibn Ezra, often taking the difficulties pointed out by Ibn Ezra and putting new corrosive interpretations on them.

"This gate that Spinoza opened in 1670 was at first a

passage to nothing but trouble... But within a century Voltaire went crashing through the opening and bulldozed a broad path. After Voltaire, rational analysis of the Bible was any man's game, and the run was on.

"The distinction of first proposing forgery as an important motive in the composition of Scripture belongs, I believe, to a German theologian named de Wette, who in 1806 published a scathing attack on the reliability of the Book of Chronicles. But the forgery theory of Scripture documents will always be linked with the name of another German, a history professor named Julius Wellhausen, who extended the range of de Wette's forgers to cover practically all Scripture. The Torah of Moses, in particular, Wellhausen argued, was multilayered fake from the first word to the last.

"... The general idea of the Wellhausen theory, derived for the most part from Astruc, de Wette, and Graf, was that the Old Testament had been in large measure doctored, phonied, or badly counterfeited by priestly canonizers under Ezra in the time of the Second Temple. They pretended to fix a canon of Israel's existing sacred books. They really performed a work of massive manufacture with one end in view: to shore up their own claims to power and money. Their main aim was to perpetuate a single falsehood: that Moses had legislated, and Solomon put in effect, central worship at one sanctuary: the Tabernacle, and later the First Temple. Wellhausen said there had never been a tabernacle. The description in Leviticus, full of antique words and details, was a forgery like the pseudo-antique poems of Chatterton and Ossian. The account of central worship at Solomon's temple in the history books was also a mass of priests' inventions.

"Starting from this premise, Wellhausen reared a new evolutionary vision of Israel's history. There had been no revelation at Sinai. Moses was not the fountainhead of the faith. The Hebrew religion grew out of a crude anthropomorphic polytheism. Moses, if he existed at all, thought himself the votary of a local thunder god or mountain god, possibly a real piece of sacred stone ('Our Rock whose ways are perfect'). Gradually in Canaan the Prophets evolved a more purified faith; but this was hopelessly distorted and falsified by the forgers.

"To maintain this novel view, Wellhausen in 1875 published his **Prolegomena to the History of Ancient Israel**, a panoramic work in almost five hundred pages of close print, with perhaps five thousand textual references to the Old Testament. He traversed the Hebrew Scriptures from the first word of Genesis to the last word of Chronicles, expounding his thesis by chapter and verse. For a generation and more the **Prolegomena** took the field of Bible criticism and held it. Most Bible critics went down before it like ninepins.

"... Wellhausen starts by announcing his grand theme: the forging priests, the non-existent tabernacle, and the phony doctrine of central worship. Then he plunges into his main task: getting the Bible to retell its story according to Wellhausen, in its own words.

"His method is simple, but the working out in detail is grandiose. Whatever passages of Scripture support his thesis, or at least do not oppose it, are authentic. Wherever the text contradicts him, the verses are spurious. His attack on each verse that does not support him is violent. He shows bad grammar, or internal inconsistency, or corrupt vocabulary, or jerkiness of continuity, every time. There is no passage he cannot explain away or annihilate. If he has to change the plain meaning of Hebrew words he does that too. He calls this 'conjectural emendation.'

"Early in the game he seems to realize that he will not quite be able to shout down one haunting question: how is it after all that hundreds and hundreds of Bible verses refute his theory in plain words? Wellhausen answers this challenge by unveiling an extraordinary hypothetical figure, the Interpolater, a sort of master forger. Seeing across a span of twenty-three centuries, this man (or men) obviously anticipated the Wellhausen theory, and went through all the Holy Scripture carefully inserting passages that refute it!

"With the discovery of the Interpolater, Wellhausen's difficulties were at an end. As a tool of controversial logic this figure is wonderful. Sections of the Bible that appear to contradict Wellhausen are not only shorn of their genuineness, they turn around to become arguments in his favor. Wellhausen, of course, does not name the Interpolater. He does not even personify him as a single figure. He merely summons an interpolater, perhaps once on every other page, to do his duty. When all else fails Wellhausen—grammar, continuity, divine names, or outright falsifying of the plain sense of the Hebrew—he works an interpolater.

"This odd spook in priest's clothing is really the key to the **Prolegomena**. It is, of course, quite possible that over thousands of years interpolations crept into the Hebrew holy books. But when a historian finds in a long-stable text dozens and scores and hundreds of verses that directly contradict his pet theory about the text, and reaches the conclusion that this state of things proves a clairvoyant interpolater's hand, his work seems to cross the red line into the curious literature of systematized delusion.

The puzzle today is how such a work ever captured, even for a few decades, a serious scholastic field. But the history of science shows that any vigorously asserted hypothesis can have a good run, in the absence of solid facts. The main thing, probably, was that in 1875 evolution was in the air. The battles over Darwin were still being fought, but it was obvious who was going to win. A theory that imposed evolution on Old Testament religion radiated chic and excitement, even though it stood the Bible on its head. Wellhausen's job of documentation, shrill and twisted though it was, lacking any scientific precision, nevertheless was overpowering in its sheer mass of minute scholarly detail. His construction lasted, with increasing shakiness, until the 1930's. It still lingers to some extent in popular culture, which does not turn on a dime. Serious Bible scholarship has dropped it."

However, the main tenets of the Wellhausenian theory are still being taught in most theological seminaries and theological departments of universities. In 1964-5, a new heyday dawned to this theory when most great Protestant churches in the U.S.A. and Canada published Sunday School material which set forth the essentials of this theory in a popular form, and so it started to determine the church people's view of the origin of biblical books and the history of Israel from childhood on.

We turn to the main details of the "documentary theory."

The French J. Astruc suggested in 1753 A. D. that in writing Genesis, Moses used two source documents: One of them told that the name YAHWEH (Jehovah) was used of God from the time of Seth, Adam's third son (Gen. 4:26) on, whereas the other one related that this name was not known until God revealed it to Moses in appearing to him in the burning bush (Ex. 3:13ff).

Astruc still believed that Moses was the writer of the Pentateuch. Liberal criticism, however, soon rejected this view. It was carried on and developed by H. Hupfeld (1853), K. H. Graf (in the 1860's) and Julius Wellhausen (in the 1870's; he died in 1918). Graf proposed that the ceremonial law of the Pentateuch, the so-called "Priestly Code" ("P", most of Leviticus, altogether about 1/3 of the Pentateuch) was not composed by Moses at Sinai, as the Bible itself reports, but was written in its final form after the Exile (which ended 537 B. C.) by Ezra and his fellows, in the 450's and 440's B.C. Deuteronomy ("D"), which according to its own report was written by Moses on the plains of Moab (except, of course, its last chapter that tells of his death), was, according to Graf, composed by some priests in Jerusalem nearly 800 years after Moses, in the time of king Josiah (640-608 B. C.). The reform that he effected in Jerusalem and Judah in 621 B. C. was done, so Graf asserted, according to this book, not in accord with the ordinances of the other parts of the Pentateuch. Only the "Jehovistic" legislation of the "Book of the Covenant" in Ex. 20:22-23:33 was earlier than the Deuteronomy. Graf revised his theory on account of the criticism that he met, and in its final form

HATH GOD SAID?

the order of the composition and combining of the various forged documents that made up the Pentateuch was as follows:

J (ehovist), the document that reported that the name YAHWEH was used from Seth (Gen. 4:26) on.

E (lohist), the document that reported that the name YAHWEH was not known until God revealed it to Moses (Ex. 3:13ff., 6:3), the name ELOHIM, EL SHADDAI, etc., being used prior to that.

D (euteronomy), written in the time of Josiah in the 600's B.C.

P (riestly Code), largely containing ceremonial laws, written in the time of Ezra, ab. 460-440 B.C.

Wellhausen brought the hypothesis of Graf to dominance among the critics. He explained that, after the earlier documents "J" and "E" had been combined, the author of "D" united that book with his own and revised the whole. The "P" was largely the work of Ezra.

In dating the various documents, Wellhausen followed, in the main, two principles: First, he held that real predictive prophecy is impossible. The passages that contain fulfilled predictions have been written at the time or after the "predicted" events have taken place.* Second, he held that the development of the history of Israel must have

---

* Millar Burrows writes from the liberal critical point of view: "For many events, to be sure, we have ... evidence of their occurrence in addition to the biblical record, but unless the statement that they have been predicted is accepted on the authority of the Bible itself, there is nothing to prove that the supposed prediction was not written after the event took place" (**An Outline of Biblical Theology**, 1946, pp. 17f. Quoted from Otten's **op. cit.**, p. 176). Liberal scholars in general follow at this point the Wellhausenian axiom of unbelief: real foretelling of future events has not been possible. This axiom, in turn, has its source in the liberal denial of the supernatural element in the Bible and of real divine revelation. It has no other foundation.

followed the three-phase theory of the philosopher Hegel. Instead of having been an effect of divine revelation, the religion of Abraham and the other patriarchs was an expression of their natural religious impulses. The period from the patriarchs to the reform of king Josiah in 621 B.C. was the **thesis** phase. In this time sacrifices were offered at different places, and similar idols were permitted as were owned by surrounding nations. The second phase, that of **antithesis,** was from Josiah's reform to the Exile (605-537/6 B.C.). In this period sacrifices were lawfully offered only in the central sanctuary of Jerusalem and only by the Levitical priests, and no idols were allowed. The third phase, that of **synthesis,** came after the Exile, in the period of Ezra. Then the ceremonial laws were carefully gathered, edited and codified, and only the Levitical priests were allowed to perform sacrifices and other ceremonies ordained in this law ("P"). The three stages of the composition of the Pentateuch corresponded to the three phases of the religious history of Israel: "JE" was the first, the **thesis,** "D" was the second, the **antithesis,** and "P" was the third, the **synthesis.**

Later critics have modified this "newer documentary hypothesis" which holds that the Pentateuch was born by a series of forgeries and revisions and their combinations. Some critics have divided the various documents into two or more documents ("J1", "J2", "E1", "E2", etc.), or proposed other variants of the theory. The hypotheses are almost as manifold as the liberal scholars. It is hard to find two critics who accept each other's views. They agree only on one thing, namely, that the Pentateuch is a product of a series of later forgeries, and that Christ was in error in ascribing it to Moses.**

** For a more detailed account of the history of Pentateuch criticism, see e.g. Edw. J. Young, **An Introduction to the Old Testament** (1963), pp. 113-164 (conservative), Robert H. Pfeiffer, **Old Testament Introduction** (1941), pp. 8-12, 29-104 (liberal).

Present Situation

H. Wouk may be right in his statement that serious scholarship has dropped the Wellhausenian documentary hypothesis on the origin of the Pentateuch. But most theological professors and their followers are obviously not representatives of serious scholarship since, as we have pointed out, a new "heyday" began in 1964 in the history of this hypothesis. Then the various great American and Canadian Protestant churches introduced its teaching to their Sunday and Church Schools. In that year the liberals also accomplished the "feat" of managing to have the LIFE magazine publish a well prepared and luxuriously illustrated Christmas issue that set forth basically the Wellhausenian view (though in a somewhat modified and modernized form) for the "illumination" of its millions of readers.

In most cases theological seminaries which at first and even for decades have opposed the liberal view of the Bible have finally succumbed to it—and a sad fact is that the same catastrophic process has started even in some formerly Bible-believing and evangelistic Bible schools (for instance, the Lutheran Bible Institute, LBI, of Minneapolis). The usual course of events has been that they have started to take teachers who have done their graduate work "at the feet" of liberal scholars, and the number of such teachers has gradually increased, until they have become dominated by them. Liberal Bible criticism and Neo-Orthordoxy have in recent times worked hand in hand in "modernizing" church related colleges and theological seminaries.

The earlier method of liberal theological professors was to say to their students something like Martin Lloyd Jones describes in his book, **The Basis of Christian Unity,** "Now this is the real truth in this matter as discovered by scholarship; but do not preach it yet, the people are not in position to receive it. You must introduce this carefully and slowly." The liberals have obviously decided that the time of this sort of caution and doublemindedness is over, and the critical view of the Bible must be publicly taught in churches. But as they have realized that it is difficult to change the minds of older people, they have decided to start it in Sunday Schools. Children are not aware that what they are being taught concerning the origin and quality of biblical books are satanic lies. They take these teachings in simple faith, and so the congregations are gradually trained from "down up" to follow the liberal way of thinking and thus to lose their trust in the Bible as God's truth and divine authority. The liberals have for years complained about the "gap between the pew and the pulpit." They have decided to remove this gap between the liberal pulpit and Bible-believing pew by starting to train the pew toward liberalism in Sunday Schools, then in youth work, etc.

One of the most potent factors in the "modernization" or "liberalization" of the churches have been their mergers. There was much liberalism in the churches (Presbyterian, Methodist, and Congregational) that were united in 1925 and formed the United Church of Canada. But since the merger, liberalism has rapidly become dominant in it. According to its new Sunday School curriculum, the first 11 chapters of the Bible are myths; the virgin birth of Jesus is a myth; the visit of the magi is a myth—these things never happened, but the stories symbolize certain religious truths. When the Curriculum was criticized for its liberal Bible criticism, the organ of the United Church, the **United Church Observer** (December 15, 1964, Dr. A. J. Davidson) admitted that "the charge is a true one. The New Curriculum is firmly undergirded by modern biblical criticism." But it added that the liberal critical approach has been dominant in the United Church since its establishment in 1925," and that "it has been the basis of instruction given in all our theological colleges." Dr. Davidson also admitted that theological liberalism "is the principal approach of the churches which are associated with the World Council of Churches" (Quoted from **Christian Beacon**, Jan. 7, 1965).

The reason why church mergers lead to a faster modernization of churches is that the leadership of these churches is predominantly liberal, and the larger churches formed by mergers have stronger centralization of power. The administrative, theological and spiritual pressure on pastors and congregations is so much greater than in smaller churches that most of them do not dare to say anything or at least to do anything.

Another example of the tremendous speed-up of liberalization of churches subsequent to mergers are the Lutheran Church in America (LCA) and The American Lutheran Church (TALC) both formed by a merger of four church bodies between 1960 and 1963. Only a few years after the merger both denominations, comprising altogether about six million people, published in 1964 Sunday School handbooks that set forth the critical view (of the Wellhausen type) of the Bible. The title of the LCA book was THE MIGHTY ACTS OF GOD (in the following abbr. TMA), being accompanied by a TEACHER'S GUIDE (abbr. TG) and filmstrip with script (TMA and TG prepared by Dr. Robert J. Marshall; the books were published by the Lutheran Church Press, Philadelphia, Pa.). The TALC book had the title THE BIBLE: BOOK OF FAITH (Augsburg Publishing House, Minneapolis, Minn.). The book is intended to be a "resource book" in the TALC's Leadership Edcation Series, and it has been prepared by ten TALC professors. C. Richard Evenson, the editor of the book, writes in its Introduction that it "brings the help from scholars whom the church has called to lead its theological thought and to prepare future pastors. In this book we can 'listen in' on the seminary classroom and be instructed by our theological professors on the nature and purpose and central message of the Bible."

All these books set forth a modified form of the Graf-Wellhausuen theory of the biblical books. According to them, the Pentateuch was composed of the documents called "J," "E," "D," and "P," written about 900-850, 750, 630 and 450 B. C., respectively, and finally put together and revised in the time of Ezra about 460-430 B.C. The LCA book goes somewhat further in the path of liberal criticism than the TALC book, but the basic views are the same.

Trying to set forth "by smooth and fair speech" (Rom. 16:18) the critical assumption that a number of biblical books are later forgeries, Marshall writes: "In antiquity a disciple often wrote in the name of his teacher" (TMA, p. 124). Thus, the men who later wrote and edited the books of which the Pentateuch was finally composed, put their writings in Moses' name, writing them as if the Lord had given revelations and instructions to and through Moses, although they were actually composed by men who lived hundreds of years later.

Of Gen. 1-11 Marshall says that these chapters do not contain "so much historical events," and that there are "outmoded elements" in them. In order to understand the Genesis story of creation, 1:1-2:4a, the creation myths of Babylonia are "invaluable" to us, for this story "probably harks back to the parallel creation stories of ancient [pagan and idolatrous] Babylonia" (TMA, p. 29; TG, pp. 27, 29, 36; on the "Babylonian Genesis," see e.g. Otten, op. cit., pp. 206f. and its literature references). The story of the Fall in Gen. 3 is not historical, but the serpent and tree are symbols of the basic nature of man (TMA, pp. 32ff.). The implication of this explanation is that man's "basic nature" was sinful before the Fall, and that God had created man as a mixture of good and evil.

Marshall (as well a sthe TALC book THE BIBLE: BOOK OF FAITH) holds that the biblical chronology with regard to the exodus from Egypt is wrong, that is, not in keeping with the facts. According to 1 Ki. 6:1, the exodus took place 480 years before the building of the temple of Solomon (which started in 967 B.C.), that is, in 1447 B.C. Marshall tells that it took place about 200 years later (TMA, pp. 6f., 44, 163; TG, 16, 21, 41f.; **The Bible: Book of Faith,** p. 36). Archeological excavations, however, have confirmed the biblical chronology. (On this, see Joseph P. Free, **Archeology and Bible History,** Van Kampen Press, Wheaton, Ill., 1950, pp. 88ff., 98f.).

Despite his endorsement of the critical theory of the Pentateuch as an end-result of a series of forgeries, Marshall declares: "Although modern scholarship has demonstrated the gradual development of the Pentateuch, the church can still believe in the authority of the Bible as thoroughly as it did when it was thought that Moses wrote the whole Pentateuch" (TMA, p. 1108).

Marshall explains that he "finds the works of scholars important for establishing the intellectual respectability of believing in the authority of the Scriptures" (TG, p. 10).

It is hard to see any "intellectual respectability" in the view that even though the Bible is explained to be largely a collection of forgeries it still can have the same authority as it had when it was believed to have been written by the inspiration of God. God's Spirit is not a spirit of deception, and the forgery-theory necessarily implies the denial of the inspiration of the Bible. In reality, to speak of the authority of the Bible and at the same time to assert that it was largely born by way of forgeries, and that it contains great numbers of errors, is completely illogical and thoroughly dishonest double-talk. This shows what the liberals' much boasted-of "intellectual honesty" really is like.

A Christian does not seek the honor of "intellectual respectability" before men. He who does so is not a Christian and a servant of Christ (Jh. 5:44; Gal. 1:10).

2. Implications of Liberal Criticism

The Pentateuch states a number of times that the Lord spoke to Moses and told him what he had to speak to the children of Israel and what he had to do (e.g. at the beginning of chapters Lev. 1, 4, 6, 8, 11, 13-25, 27, Nu. 1, 2, 4-6, 8, 9, 13, 15, 17, 19). Ex. 24:4, Deut. 31:9 and 24-26 report that Moses wrote in a book all the words of the Lord.

The Book of the Law (TORAH) that Moses wrote was to be kept in the Most Holy of the Tabernacle at the side of the Ark of the Covenant. In Deut. 4:2 and 12:32 the Lord gives strict prohibitions against making any changes in it, adding anything to it or taking away anything from it. It was to be preserved and observed exactly as it was.

The Lord Himself impressed upon Joshua (1:7, 9) faithful observance of the written law of Moses. Joshua did the same to the Israelites toward the end of his life (23:6).

These passages show clearly that the Law of Moses, the TORAH, the Pentateuch, was "canonical" from the outset, beginning with the times of Moses and Joshua, since it was divinely given and inspired. It was the authoritative rule and norm of the religious, social, political and personal life of the Israelites.

When the liberals deny this, they assert that the Bible lies in these passages. They hold that the first canonical book was Deuteronomy, written (according to their theory) ab. 650-630 B.C., and made "canonical" in the reform of king Josiah in 621 B.C. The Bible teaches that it was God who made the Law of Moses (and the biblical books in general) canonical, to be the divine norm and rule of faith and life, by giving it and by inculcating obedience to it. The liberals hold that the "canonization" was done by men, by their official acceptance of them.

Deut. 11:29 reports that Moses gave the order to proclaim blessings and cursings at the mounts of Gerizim and Ebal, and in Deut. 27:11 - 28:68 the order was renewed, together with more detailed instructions and the words to be used. In Josh. 8:33f. we read how these orders of Moses were carried out at Gerizim and Ebal. The critics assert that these passages contain falsehoods: Dt., they say, did not exist until ab. 800 years later, and the book of Joshua, too, was composed several centuries later, so that the whole thing was a later story without historical reality.

In Josh. 22 we read how the tribes of Reuben, Gad and the half tribe of Manasseh, which had received their "inheritances" on the eastern side of the Jordan, built there an altar. When the tribes west of the Jordan heard that another altar, beside the one in the Tabernacle, had been erected, they were shocked because of this transgression of the law of Moses, according to which sacrifices were to be offered only on the altar that was in the Tabernacle. This law was in Deut. 12:5-28. The liberals say that the narrative in Josh. 22 is not historical, but a later fiction, and that the law in Deut. 12 was written by some priests in Jerusalem ab. 650-630 B.C., or ab. 800 years later, and did not exist in the time of Joshua.

2 Ki. 14:6f. and 2 Chr. 25:4 relate that when king Amaziah let the murderers of his father be executed he spared their children, "according to what is written in the book of Moses, as the Lord commanded, saying, The fathers shall not be put to death for the children, or the children be

put to death for the fathers; but every man shall die for his own sin." This precept is in Deut. 24:16. The critics hold that all these passages are false: Deut. did not exist in the time of Amaziah (ab. 840 B.C.), and consequently Amaziah could not do according to its precept.

1 Ki. 2:3 reports that David charged his son Solomon to walk in the statutes, commandments and ordinances of the Lord, as they were "written in the law of Moses." The critics hold that this passage is not historical and true, but just a later invented tale, since the written law of Moses did not exist at the time but was composed (forged) several centuries later.

Is. 1:10 has the exhortation of the prophet "to give ear to the law (TORAH) of our God." According to the critics, this passage cannot be from Isaiah, for the Law, TORAH, did not exist in his time (ab. 740 - 682 B.C.). Only the writings of "Jahvist" and "Elohist" existed, but they were mere individual literary works without canonical authority, and they did not contain much of the law.

Christ says in Mt. 5:18 that "one jot or one tittle shall in no wise pass away from the law," the Pentateuch. The liberals have left hardly any "jot or tittle" to remain in this law without declaring it to be forgery, and consequently not from God through Moses (or from God in general—forgeries cannot be from Him). What Christ categorically asserts the critics deny.

In Jh. 5:46f. Jesus says: "If ye believed Moses, ye would believe me; for he wrote of me. But if ye believe not his writings, how will ye believe my words?" The "writings" of Moses (plural!) obviously mean his Five Books. The critics deny that there are any writings from Moses (see e.g. the diagramatic table in Marshall's TMA: the time of oral tradition continues long after Moses).

According to the critics, such passages as Gen. 3:15 (seed of woman bruising the serpent's head) and Deut. 18:15-19 (great prophet) are not written by Moses: thus, Moses had not written of Him—Christ lied when He said so! The critics usually say that the Christian Church has applied these passages to Christ, but they deny the truth of Christ's words that Moses wrote of Him in them.

In Mt. 8:4 and Mk. 1:44 Jesus says that Moses had given the commandment that lepers had to go to show themselves to a priest and offer a gift, if they had been healed. This commandment is in Lev. 13:49 and 14:2ff. The critics aver that Lev. 13:1, 14:1 lie in saying that the "Lord said to Moses" this, and that Jesus likewise lied in saying that this commandment had been given by Moses. The book of Lev. was composed about a thousand years after Moses, and is a forgery, they say.

Mk. 7:9f. reports the words of Jesus: "Moses said, Honor thy father and mother; and he who curseth father or mother, let him surely die." The first of these words is in Ex. 20:12 and Deut. 5:16, and the second in Ex. 21:17 and Lev. 20:9. Some critics admit that the Decalog in Ex. 20 may be from Moses, but they deny that Ex. 21 and Lev. are from him. Both Ex. 21 and Lev. 20 state expressly that they contain words spoken by the Lord to Moses. The critics brand these statements, as well as the words of Christ, as lies.

According to Mt. 19:9, Moses gave the commandment concerning divorce in Deut. 24:1-4. The critics deny the truth of these words, explaining that Deut. is a forgery written ab. 800 years after Moses.

When tempted by the devil in the wilderness, Jesus used three passages of Deut. against the devil, saying, "It is written . . ." Could He have done so if Deut. was a forgery, as the critics assert?

Mk. 12:26 reports the words of Jesus, "Have ye not read in the book of Moses, in the passage about the bush, how God said to him, I am the God of Abraham..." The critics assume that the passage, Ex. 3:6, to which Jesus here refers is from "E", written about 750 B.C. or ab. 700 years after the time when God appeared to Moses in the burning bush, and was not written by Moses at all. Jesus did not know this (or, if He knew, did not speak the truth) —the critics claim to know better.

In his story of the rich man and Lazarus, Jesus relates as words of Abraham: "They have Moses and prophets... If they hear not Moses and the prophets, ..." (Lk. 16:29ff.). Jesus obviously refers here to the Five Books of Moses. The critics deny that they are from Moses.

Jesus says in Jh. 7:19: "Did not Moses give you the law, and yet none of you doeth the law?" The critics deny the truth of these words of Christ, that Moses had given the Israelites the law (the Pentateuch).

The **risen Christ** said, as Lk. 24:44 records, that "all things must needs be fulfilled, which are written in the law of Moses, and the Prophets, and the psalms..." The critics deny the truth of these words of the risen Lord, asserting that the "law of Moses" was not given by (through) Moses, and presuming that they know better.

In Mt. 12:39-41 Jesus speaks of Jonah as a real historical person and of the events of his life, recorded in the book of Jonah as actual happenings. "For as Jonah was three days and three nights in the whale's belly; so will the Son of man be three days and three nights in the heart of the earth. The men of Nineveh... repented at the preaching of Jonah..." Numerous liberals deny the truth of these words of Christ, holding that the story of Jonah is a "myth," an invented tale to illustrate certain truths.

* * * *

After His resurrection, Jesus opened the minds of His apostles to understand the Scriptures (Lk. 24:44f.), and on Pentecost the Holy Spirit came upon them and into their hearts to lead them to all truth (Jh. 16:13). After these events, Peter said in the fullness of the Spirit: "Moses indeed said, A prophet shall the Lord raise up . . .," quoting the words in Deut. 18:15 (Acts 3:22f.). Paul spoke in the Antioch of Pisidia (Acts 13:39) of the "law of Moses." In Rom. 10:5 and 19 he quotes the words of Lev. 18:5 and

Deut. 32:21, saying, "Moses writeth," "Moses saith." In 2 Cor. 3:15f. he speaks of the reading of [the books of] Moses. In the view of the liberals, all these passages are errors and lies as far as the Mosaic authorship of the quoted passages is concerned.

Note: Origin of some New Testament Books.

The LCA books THE MIGHTY ACTS OF GOD explains: "The pastoral epistles [1 and 2 Tim., Tit.] were written near the middle of the second century" (p. 217f.). The TALC book THE BIBLE: BOOK OF FAITH says: "The Pastoral Epistles, 1 and 2 Timothy and Titus, ... appear in their present form to be the work of someone other than Paul . . . after Paul's death" (p. 126). Of the First Epistle of Peter TMA (pp. 215f.) says that it was "produced toward the end of the first century," and that the letters "ascribed" to Peter "may have been written long after his death." The TALC book THE BIBLE: BOOK OF FAITH is more cautious and says: "It is wondered whether 2 Peter was written by Peter or someone living after Peter had died." This is the common way the liberals speak of these letters.

We read in 1 Tim. 1:1: "Paul, ... to Timothy ...," and in 2 Tim. 1: 1f: "Paul ... to Timothy." In both letters Paul speaks mostly in the first person ("I") personally to Timothy ("thou"), giving him instructions for his work. In Tit. 1:1-4 we read: "Paul ... to Titus." In this epistle, too, he mostly speaks in the first person. In all the three epistles Paul mentions by name contemporary persons, coworkers, and also enemies and perverters of the Gospel. In 2 Tim. and Tit. he sends greetings to some friends mentioned by name.

The critics deny that these epistles were written by Paul, asserting that the later writers lyingly ascribed them to him, and wrote them as though written by Paul.

However, the question arises: How would it have been possible that the congregations established by Paul would not have recognized them as forgeries, if they would have appeared several decades after the apostle's death?

The two epistles of Peter likewise begin with statements that it was Peter who wrote in them, and I Pet. 5:12 says that it was written through Silvanus (Silas), whom Peter used as his secretary. The critics hold that they were not written by Peter, but the later forgers composed them in a manner as though written by him in order that Christians would have better believed them. We have to ask again: How would it have been possible that Christians would not have recognized them as forgeries if they would have appeared several decades after Peter's death?

2 Tim. 3:16 and 2 Pet. 1:20f. speak of the scriptures as having been written by the inspiration of God, moved by the Spirit of God. Since the Spirit of God is the Spirit of truth, and all lie and deceit is of the devil, the liberal view implies the assertion that 1 and 2 Tim., Tit., and 1 and 2 Pet. were epistles written by the inspiration of the devil.

3. Critique of Liberal Arguments

The divine names

One of the basic arguments of the Graf-Wellhausen school for the multiple authorship of the Pentateuch is that proposed by J. Astruc: According to Gen. 4:26 ("J") the name YAHWEH was called on beginning from the time of Seth, whereas Ex. 3:13ff. ("E") and 6:3 ("P") relate that God revealed His name YAHWEH to Moses; to Abraham and the other patriarchs He has appeared by the name EL SHADDAI (God Almighty).

The critics explain that we have here two conflicting traditions set forth by three source documents, used in the compilation of Genesis and Exodus, namely, "Jahvist" (Jehovist, "J"), "Elohist" ("E") and "Priestly Code" ("P"). Of these, the last two agreed as to the use of the name YAHWEH.

In reality Ex. 3:13ff. and 6:3 say nothing of the **time** when the name YAHWEH first came into use. In Ex. 6:3 the Lord merely said that He had revealed Himself to the patriarchs by the name EL SHADDAI, and not by the name YAHWEH. The name YAHWEH had, to be sure, been known and used a long time before the patriarchs. But God had **appeared** to them by the name EL SHADDAI, and not by the name YAHWEH. This means that He had revealed to them that aspect of His being to which the name EL SHADDAI referred, and not that aspect which was implied in that of YAHWEH. This name was used of God as **covenant God,** and He revealed Himself by this name when He in the time of Moses began to make of Israel His covenant people.

God had in the time of Seth had a people of His own possession, the believing generation of Seth, in contrast to the ungody Cainites. He was the covenant God of the Sethites, who called on Him by the name YAHWEH. But after the Sethites had been (through intermarriages, Gen. 6:1-2) mixed with the Cainites, and general apostasy had set in (with the exception of Noah and his family), the covenant God name YAHWEH had lost its practical significance and fallen into disuse, although its existence continued to be known.

When God revealed Himself to Abraham, Isaac and Jacob, He still had no covenant nation but only (as had been the case in the time of Noah) a faithful family. It was therefore natural that He revealed Himself to them by the more general name EL SHADDAI, God Almighty. Only when He began to make of Israel a covenant nation to Himself did He again appear by the name YAHWEH. The critical assumption of two conflicting traditions concerning the time when the name YAHWEH **first** came into use is pure fancy.

In attempting to unravel the two assumed documents, "J" and "E," on the basis of the use of divine names, the critics have employed the **Masoretic** text, established by Jewish scholars, called Masoretes, ab. 600-900 A.D., and provided with vowel signs. When this text has been compared with the **Septuagint** Greek Version, which is nearly 1000 years older, and with the other old translations that likewise are several centuries older than the Masoretic text, the observation has been made that use of the names YAHWEH and ELOHIM is not identical in them. Out of the 148 cases in which the Masoretic text in Gen. 1:1 - Ex. 3:12 uses YAHWEH, the other texts use in 118 cases either ELOHIM or YAHWEH ELOHIM. This shows that the occurrence of the names YAHWEH and ELOHIM in the Masoretic text is wholly unreliable for the purpose of unraveling the (assumed) different source documents.

Studies of the use of the names YAHWEH and ELOHIM have given the result that ELOHIM is mostly used of

God as the Creator, Sustainer and Ruler of the world and the universe (about 2500 times), and the name YAHWEH mostly when God is spoken of (or when He speaks) as the God of Israel, the Lord of the covenant (about 7600 times). In numerous cases the names are used together: YAHWEH ELOHIM, the Lord God.

An example of this sort of usage is Gen. 39: The name YAHWEH is commonly employed in this chapter, since it speaks of God's care for Joseph. The name ELOHIM appears only in verse 9, since the wife of Potiphar did not know the YAHWEH of Israel.

Because of this fact even some liberal scholars have rejected the "JE-theory."

God's **name** and **knowing** God does not mean in the Bible a mere "historical" or intellectual awareness of the existence of God and His name. Rather, it means the experiential knowledge of God and of the **significance** of His name that a person has in faith-communion with Him. This is seen e.g. from the words in Jer. 9:24: "Let him who glorieth glory in this that he hath understanding and knoweth me, that I am the Lord, who exerciseth lovingkindness, justice. . ." It is also evident from the words of Jesus: "This is life eternal, that they know thee, the only true God, and him whom thou didst send, Jesus Christ" (Jh. 17:3; cp. Hos. 2:19; 4:1).

The fact that the mother of Moses had the name **Yochebed** (Ex. 6:20; Nu. 26:59), which a combination of **Yo** (abbreviation of YAHWEH) and **chebed** (Hb. chabod= glory), meaning, Yahweh is glory, whose glory is Yahweh, shows that the name YAHWEH was known and used before the revelation to Moses in the burning bush.* But its

---

* In reality Amram and Jochebed probably were ancestors of Moses and Aaron and not their immediate parents: Nu. 3:17-19, 27-28 tells that in the time of Moses Amram and his three brothers had in their family 8,600 males, all in all probably about 18,000 persons. There must have been an interval of 300-400 years between Amram and Moses. See on this below IX:1, chapter, "Age of the World and Mankind."

meaning became known again when God revealed it to Moses.**

Time of Deuteronomy

Another basic assertion of the Wellhausen hypothesis is that the book of Deuteronomy, the Fifth Book of Moses, was not known until it was found in the temple at the time of king Josiah, in 621 B.C., and that his reform was put into practice according to this book, not according to Ex., Lev., and Nu. The common assumption is that the priests of Jerusalem composed this book either in the time of Manasseh or in the early years of Josiah, and that its purpose was to accomplish centralization of sacrificial worship to the temple of Jerusalem. It was then "discovered" at an opportune time. According to this theory, the ordinance to offer sacrifices only on the altar that was in the Tabernacle did not exist prior to that time. The passage in Deut. 12:4-14 is as follows:

> "Ye shall not do [as the Canaanites] . . . But to the place which the Lord your God will choose out of all your tribes to put his name there, even to his habitation shall ye seek . . . And there shall ye bring your burnt offerings, and your sacrifices, and your tithes . . . when ye . . . dwell in the land . , .."

The decisive question is this: Is it true that Israel was before 621 B.C ignorant of an ordinance to offer sacrifices only in the Tabernacle? The matter is decided by what Josh. 22:9-29 records of an event in the time of Joshua: After the division of the land, the Reubenites, Gadites and the half of Manasseh, who had received their inheritance east of the Jordan, built there an altar. When the tribes

---

Wilhelm Möller, **Grundriss für alttestamentliche Einleitung (Berlin, 1958), gives examples (pp. 18f., 45f., 48) of the impossible and illogical results at which the critics have arrived in their attempts to unravel the "seams" of the different documents on the basis of the use of the divine names. E.g. in Gen. 17:1 and 21:1 the name YAHWEH is used in passages which, on the basis of other things, have been assigned to "P": according to the theory, this document represents the tradition that the name YAHWEH was not known until the revelation to Moses, recorded in Ex. 6:3ff. As the assumed "source documents" themselves thus are in conflict with the critical theory, this theory must be false.

west of the Jordan heard of it they were shocked because
of this glaring transgression of the ordinance that sacrifices
were to be offered only on one altar, the one that was in
the Tabernacle, which then was in Shiloh. They calmed down
only when the eastern tribes explained that the altar which
they had built was merely a memorial altar, and that they
had no intention to offer sacrifices on it. This event shows
that the ordinance to offer sacrifices only in the Tabernacle
was known in Israel from the times of Moses and Joshua on,
and was nothing new in 621 B.C.

The school of Wellhausen gets rid of Josh. 22 by explaining that it is a "late P-passage."* As H. Wouk points
out in the earlier quoted statement, Wellhausen used the
method of explaining as spurious (later interpolations, etc.)
all the passages that appeared to contradict his theory and
accepting as genuine only such passages which seemed to
be in harmony with it, or at least did not oppose it. By
means of this kind of method it is possible to "prove" almost
anything. But is this scientific and honest, is another
question. A pathetic fact is that so many theologians still
now follow Graf and Wellhausen in this sort of thoroughly
unscientific and dishonest treatment of the Bible.

The critical theory holds that Deut. ordained **Jerusalem**
as the only place for sacrificial worship. This assertion has,
however, no basis in the text of Deut. It does not say a
word on the **place** where the altar of sacrifices was to be
situated, but left this matter to the future guidance and
revelation of God. Its ordinance was in keeping with the
earlier one in Ex. 20:24: "An altar of earth thou shalt make
to me, and shall sacrifice on it thy burnt offerings, and thy
peace-offerings.... In every place where I put the remembrance of my name I will come to thee, and I will bless thee."

This passage does not say, as the critics falsely explain,
that sacrifices could be offered on more than one altar. The
word **altar** (MIZBEAH) is here in the singular, and in the

---

* Thus e.g. E. G. Gulin, Vanhan Testamentin synty ja kokoonpano/
Origin and composition of the OT/, Helsinki 1930, p. 58.

phrase "in every place" the word **place** is likewise in the singular (KOL HAMMAKOM). True, this phrase could mean several simultaneous places. The fact that the **altar** is in singular, however, shows that only one altar for sacrifices was permissible at each time.

This was also the actual situation in Israel from the times of Moses and Joshua on: There was at each time only one altar for the sacrifices offered by the Levitical priests. After settling down in Canaan, Israel had the Tabernacle and altar for several centuries at **Shiloh,** then in **Nob,** then in **Gibeon,** and finally in **Jerusalem** (Josh. 18:1, 8; 19:51; Judg. 18:31; 1 Sam. 1:3, 9; 2:14; 14:3; 21; 1 Chr. 16:39; 21:29; 2 Chr. 1:3; 1 Ki. 6-8, etc.). These were the different places in which, according to Ex. 20:24 and Deut. 12:4-14, the Lord chose to put the remembrance of His name.

In addition to the altar in the Tabernacle, there were **temporary altars** that were built at the special commands of God, and on which **other than** Levitical sacrifices were offered. Such were the altars built by Samuel (1 Sam. 6:9f.; 11:15; 16:5). Samuel was a prophet—not a priest who performed service in the Tabernacle (though he had been there in his childhood for training)—who offered sacrifices on special altars according to the directions that he received from the Lord. Elijah did the same on Carmel. These were not permanent altars beside the altar in the Tabernacle, but temporary ones, erected for sacrifices other than Levitical offerings.

The Israelites had, to be sure, "high places" (Hb. BAMOTH) and altars on them, but they were in conflict with the Mosaic law. Sacrifices were offered on them "by the people," not by Levitical priests, and they are repeatedly declared to have been wrong and in disobedience to the law of God (see e.g. Deut. 12:2; 1 Ki. 3:2; 13:1ff. 2 Ki. 14:4; Jr. 3:6).

Solomon worshipped and sacrificed on the high place of Gibeon because the Tabernacle was there at that time (1 Chr. 16:39; 21:29; 2 Chr. 1:3).

Time of the Levitical Law

The third basic assertion of the Wellhausen school is that the ceremonial laws of the "P" (Lev. plus about a half of the Pentateuch) were composed by Jewish priests either in Babylon during the exile or after it, or by Ezra, as though Moses had written it, and claiming again and again that the Lord spoke to Moses and gave the ordinances contained in it. The critics assert that the history of Israel, as it is set forth in Joshua, Judges, 1-2 Sam. and 1-2 Kings, knows nothing of these laws, and that only the Chronicles, written after the exile, are in harmony with them.

According to the Graf-Wellhausen theory, the Pentateuch got its final form after the exile, when its last component document, the "P," was written and combined by the final "redactor" (Ezra?) with the earlier ones, the "JE" and "D." The last "redactor" also revised the whole and made a number of additions of his own.

One of the arguments for the assertion that the laws of the "P" were unknown prior to the exile, is that Is. 1:11-15; Jer. 7:21ff.; Am. 5::21-25; and Mic. 6:6ff. speak against sacrifices.

We shall examine the real import of the critical arguments.

1. When was the Levitical law known? Deut. enumerates the various sacrifices which were to be offered in the Tabernacle, but it contains no instructions as to how they were to be performed. It clearly presupposes the laws of Lev. and Nu., which contain instructions for these sacrifices. Without them the Levitical priests would not have known how they had to proceed with regard to the sacrifices and other sacred acts.

The **book of Joshua** speaks of the law of Moses as an existing entity (1:7). Joshua charged the Israelites to observe the law given by Moses (22:5f.). In 24:2-10 he gave a short summary of the contents of the whole Pentateuch. This shows that it was in existence at that time.

HATH GOD SAID?

Josh. 22:23, 26f., 29 speaks of burnt, meal (cereal), and peace offerings. Only Lev. contains instructions on how they had to be performed, and it is thus plainly presupposed by this book.

Solomon organized the worship of the new temple, and 1 Kn. 8:62ff. reports that burnt, meal, peace, etc. offerings were sacrificed in connection with its dedication. Solomon's words at this occasion contained a number of references to Ex., Lev., Nu. and Deut., which shows that they must have existed then. According to the Welhausen theory, no part of the Pentateuch existed in Solomon's time, and even its first component document, the "J," was written after Solomon, who died in 931 B.C.

The critics of the Graf-Wellhausen school disregard the fact that 1-2 Chronicles are not the only historical books that speak of sacrifices ordained in "P." The books of Joshua, Samuel and Kings also speak of them (Josh. 22:23-29; 1 Sam. 2:13ff., 28; 7:9f.; 2 Sam. 6:17f.; 1 Ki. 8:62ff.). We repeat: There were no instructions on how the priests had to proceed with regard to these sacrifices except in Lev. or the "Priestly Code."

2. **Jer. 7:22ff.** is often quoted as a support for the theory that Levitical sacrifices ordained in the "P" were not offered before the exile. This passage states:

> "I spoke not to your fathers, nor commanded them in the day that I brought them out of the land of Egypt, concerning burnt-offerings and sacrifices; but this thing I commanded to them, saying, hearken to my voice."

This passage speaks nothing of the events of Sinai. The Lord says in it through the prophet that He had not spoken to the Israelites of sacrifices **in the day that He brought them out of Egypt.** Sacrifices were needed for expiation and forgiveness after Israel had transgressed God's commandments and broken His covenant at Sinai. It was after this that the sacrificial laws were given.

3. **Am. 5:25f.** is another passage that the critics use as

a support of their theory that the Levitical laws did not exist before the exile. We read in Am. 5:21-26:

> "I hate, I despise your feasts, and I will not take any delight in your solemn assemblies. Yea, though ye offer me burnt-offerings and your meal-offerings, I will not accept them; neither will I regard the peace-offerings of your fat beasts. Take away from me the noise of thy songs . . . But let justice roll down as waters, and righteousness as a mighty stream. Did ye bring me sacrifices and offerings in the wilderness forty years, O house of Israel? Yea, ye have borne the tabernacle of your Moloch and Chiun your images, the star of your god, which ye made to yourselves."

This passage is in harmony with Deut. 32:16-18:

> "They provoked him to jealousy with strange gods, with abominations provoked they him to anger. They sacrificed to demons, **not to God** . . . **Of the Rock who begat thee thou art unmindful, and** hast forgotten God who formed thee."

These passages do not intend to say that the sacrificial ordinances of the Mosaic law did not exist in the time of the wilderness journey, but only that the main part of Israel fell into idolatry. Stephen—who certainly had the entire Pentateuch—said (Acts 7:42-43): "Then God turned and gave them up to worship the host of heaven." After this Stephen quoted Am. 5:25ff.

4. Is. 1:11-16 has also been used by the critics to support the assertion that the Levitical laws did not exist before the exile. We read in it:

> "What to me is the multitude of your sacrifices? saith the Lord. I have had enough of the burnt-offerings of rams, and the fat of fed beasts; and I delight not in the blood of bullocks . . . or of he-goats. When ye come to appear before me, who hath required this at your hand, to trample my courts? Bring no more vain oblations; incense is an abomination to me; new moon and sabbath, the calling of assemblies, I cannot away with, it is iniquity, even the solemn meeting . . . when ye make many prayers, I will not hear; your hands are full of blood. Wash you, make you clean . . ."

This passage says nothing to the effect that the Levitical laws of sacrifices, incense, observation of sabbaths, new moons, etc., did not exist in Isaiah's time. On the contrary, the enumeration of these things, which were observed in the temple worship, shows that the laws concerning them did exist. The Lord only rebuked here the Israelites of shallow external ceremonialism that was connected with sinful life and impenitent hearts.

We conclude that not one of the passages that the critics have brought up really supports their theory that the Levitical laws did not exist until the exile. On the contrary, the history of Israel, as it is recorded in historical books of the OT, shows that these laws must have existed from the time of Moses and Joshua.

Passages used against the Mosaic authorship of the Penteteuch

The critics have frequently referred to the words in Nu. 12:3 as a proof that Moses could not have written the book that contains them: "The man Moses was very meek, above all men who were on the face of the earth." It has been asked: How could Moses in this way praise himself?

The Hebrew word that is here translated "meek" is 'ONI, and its basic meaning is **afflicted, distressed,** and only the secondary meaning is "meek." The people of Israel had just recently rebelled against Moses, and now his brother and sister criticized him and murmured against him. Who would not be afflicted and distressed in such a situation! In the German Bible this passage is translated correctly: Moses was **"ein sehr geplagter Mensch"**=Moses was a very afflicted man. Thus, when this passage is translated correctly it does not contain anything that Moses could not have written.

In Deut. 1:1, 5; 3:8; 4:41-49 the land east of the Jordan is called the land beyond the Jordan (in KJV these passages are translated "on this side Jordan," but the ASV renders them literally according to the Hebrew text, "beyond the Jordan"), although Moses was on the eastern side of the Jordan when he gave his last addresses. The liberals argue that passages like these show that Moses could not write

Deut., but that it must have been written later by men who lived west of the Jordan.

The term "beyond the Jordan" (Hb. BE'EBER HA'YARDEN) is used in Deut. **both** of the areas east of the Jordan and the ones west of it. It is used of the **western** area in Deut. 3:20, 25 (and also in Nu. 32:19). The expression "beyond the Jordan" means both the areas east and west of it in the same talk in Deut. 3:8, 20, and in Nu. 32:19 it means both of these in the same verse.

This strange variation is possibly due to the fact that beginning from the time of the patriarchs the Israelites had become accustomed to speak of the area east of the Jordan as the land "beyond the Jordan." When Moses spoke to the Israelites he sometimes used this customary expression despite the fact that he and his hearers then were themselves on the eastern side. This sort of variation is understandable from the point of view of the situation in which Moses gave the addresses recorded in Deut. If this book had been composed by priests who lived in Jerusalem, as the critical theory holds, the writers would have been consistent in using the term "beyond the Jordan." The inconsistent use of this term therefore speaks **for** the Mosaic authorship of Deut. rather than against it. —Another possibility is that Moses purposely used this kind of variation because a part of the tribes of Israel had already received their inheritances east of the Jordan, and he wanted to speak from the viewpoint of both groups of tribes, those east as well as those west of the Jordan.

The fact that Moses at times speaks in the first person ("I") and at times in the third person ("he") has sometimes been used as an argument against the Mosaic authorship of the Pentateuch. However, similar variation is found in the works of some ancient writers, e.g. of Julius Caesar, and this is not taken in their case as an indication that they were not authors of the books that go under their names.

We read in Gen. 12:6: "And the Canaanite was then in the land," and in Gen. 13:7, "And the Canaanite and Perizzite lived then in the land." These passages have been used against the Mosaic authorship of Genesis. The word "then," the critics explain, indicates that the land was in the possession of Israel at the time when this book was written, and that Moses cannot therefore be its author.

These passages should probably be understood as later explanatory insertions. Another possibility is that Moses wanted to notify in them that those parts of the land with which he dealt were inhabited by the Canaanites and Perizzites, while other parts were inhabited by other tribes. —The word "Canaanite" is used sometimes in a large sense, to denote the peoples of Palestine in general, and at other times in a narrow sense to denote only one of the many tribes of the land. In the referred passages the word is obviously used in the narrow sense. Whichever of the two possible explanations may be right, these passages do not give proof against the Mosaic authorship of Genesis.

Gen. 36:31 has the statement which also has been used against the Mosaic authorship of Genesis:

> "These are the kings who reigned in the land of Edom, before there reigned any king over the children of Israel."

The eight kings mentioned after this statement can well have all been before the time of Moses. At the time when the Israelites arrived at Kadesh there was a king in Edom (Nu. 20:14ff.). Esau had settled in this land more than 430 years earlier, and there is therefore no difficulty in assuming that there had been eight kings in Edom before Moses.

Moses knew from the promises given to Abraham, Isaac, Jacob and Judah (Gen. 17:6; 35:11; 49:10) and from the prophecies of Balaam (Nu. 24:7) that there would be kings in Israel, and he himself gave instructions concerning the election of a king (Deut. 17:14-20). The quoted statement contains the remark that there had been eight kings in Edom before the time of Moses, although the prophecies concerning a king in Israel had not yet been fulfilled.

Another possibility is that the second part of the statement ("before...") is a later explanatory addition, of which the Pentateuch seems to contain several. These insertions have been made in early times, and we may well believe that this has taken place under the guidance of the Spirit of God, so that they are just as true as the main text written by Moses. The most extensive of these later additions is the last chapter which records the death and burial of Moses, possibly written by Joshua or someone else under his guidance.

The so-called "doublets"

One of the arguments for the documentary theory is the existence of passages which have some similarity and which the critics explain to be "doublets" or two somewhat differing accounts of the same events.

The first of these "doublets" are the accounts of creation in Gen. 1 and 2. The critics hold that the story of creation in the second chapter is in conflict with the story in the first chapter.

Bible-believers have never found conflict between these two chapters. They have understood that part of the account (Gen. 2:4-24) which the critics call the second story of creation as being supplementary to the one in Gen. 1:1 - 2:3, giving additional information on certain points.

It is characteristic of the literary style of the OT (particularly its poetry) that the same things are told twice, so that the same matters are repeated in different words and by adding supplementary features (the second part may also give the contrast). In modern history books, too, the method is often used; a general account of certain events is followed by a more detailed description of certain events. This is also the case in the Genesis account of creation. Even such critics as Frankenberg and Gunkel have admitted that Gen. 2 contains no second account of creation.*

In the record of the great flood in Noah's time the critics also imagine to see two partly conflicting stories that

---

* Möller, **op. cit.**, pp. 16f. shows how the assumption of two accounts of creation leads to impossible and illogical conclusions.

have been weaved together. It is, however, quite obvious that the deluge account is one consistent whole. It suffers violence if it is divided into two different stories on the basis of the use of the two divine names YAHWEH and ELOHIM.**

Gen. 20 and 26 report that both Abraham and Isaac lied in Gerar, explaining their wives to be their sisters. The critics hold that these accounts are "doublets," that is, the event is actually one but has been applied to two persons, the father and the son. There is, however, no proof that this is the case; rather, it is impossible that these accounts could be doublets, for the details are quite different. They are obviously two different events. Why couldn't Isaac have made a somewhat similar mistake and sin as his father? Aren't children often doing about the same as their parents?

The critics have explained that the three explanations of the origin of Isaac's name in Gen. 17:19, 18:12 and 21:6 show that the story has been composed of three source documents. There is, however, no reason for such an assumption, for the account is one consistent whole. There is no difficulty in accepting the biblical account as it is, namely, that Isaac got his name (which means laughing) because both his mother and father laughed in connection with his birth, doing it for different reasons.

The merchants who bought Joseph and took him to Egypt are called, on the one hand, Ishmaelites, and, on the other, Midianites (Gen. 37:25-36; 39:1). The critics explain this to be an indication that the story has been combined of the accounts of two different documents ("J" and "E"), one of which called the merchants Ishmaelites and the other Midianites.

Judges 7:8 tells that Gideon fought against the Midianites, but 8:24 explains that these Midianites "had golden earrings, because they were Ishmaelites." This shows that

---

** Möller, op. cit., pp. 23ff. shows how all the conflicts that the critics claim to find in the account of the flood are fancied.

the same people were also later called both Ishmaelites and Midianites. The fact that both Gen. and Judg. use the two names shows the writers knew the reason for it, although it is not clear to us. A suggested plausible explanation is that Ishmaelites were largely merchants, and that other travelling merchants also were called "Ishmaelites."* The assumption of two sources is thus wholly uncalled-for.

4. Inner Testimony of the Pentateuch

The Pentateuch is both as to its language and contents one consistent whole, and the later books of the Bible from Joshua on clearly presuppose its existence. If it would have come into existence so that later "redactors" combined forged documents that were written 700-1000 years after Moses, making only minor adjustments, additions, etc., the result should have been different. Believing in the critical theory (or theories) implies from this point of view far greater difficulties than trusting in the testimony of the Bible that the Pentateuch is truly "the Five Books of Moses" (with the exception of certain later explanatory insertions and the last chapter).

As we have already pointed out, the Pentateuch itself contains a number of passages which state that God spoke to Moses, giving him revelations and instructions, and also some passages which tell that he wrote them in a book. That the liberals dare to call all these passages lies and pretensions shows how theirs is a shameless arrogance which has no understanding of what it means that God reveals Himself to man and speaks to him: No dishonesty and lying comes into question in such cases, for God is the God of truth and a "consuming fire" to all dishonesty.

In addition to the referred facts, and the statements in which Christ and the apostles speak of the Pentateuch as having been written by Moses, this book itself contains a

---

* On the alleged "doublets" in the books of Joshua and Samuel, see E. J. Young, **op. cit.**, pp. 178, 196f.

number of things that show that it must have been written by Moses.

The Tabernacle and its worship. The Pentateuch speaks of the Tabernacle as a movable tent. Had it been written after the time of Solomon, as the critics hold, the natural thing would have been to compose the ordinances concerning the sanctuary and its worship so as to fit them to the situation in Canaan and the temple. In reality they are as if written during the wilderness journey and applied to that situation, with the exception of a few directions that were given in view of the future settled life in the promised land. For instance, the ordinances concerning the celebration of the Passover, Lev. 23:5ff. and Nu. 28:16ff. (ascribed by the critics to "P," composed after the exile, about a millennium after Moses), were suited only to the period of the wilderness journey. There is no sense in the assumption that the priests of Jerusalem about a thousand years later would have composed for the direction of the temple worship of their own time a book whose ordinances did not at all fit to the situation of that time but only to the time of the wilderness journey.

When the Israelites arrived at the borders of Canaan, Moses gave them in Deut. 16:5f. a new ordinance for the celebration of the Passover, which made it suitable to the new situation. How is it possible to think—as the critics do—that the "P" (composed, according to the critical theory, about two centuries later) would have changed the ordinance of Deut. "backward" into a form that was wholly unfit to that time and suitable only to the time of the wilderness journey?

The regulations concerning the Tabernacle, the description of the consecration of Aaron and his sons, etc., in Ex. are very detailed and understandable only as having been written by Moses at the time of these events. Had they been written many centuries later, when Israel had a permanent temple, they would have been different. It is not at all probable that the priests of Jerusalem would have written such detailed descriptions of what happened during the wilderness journey—when their intention was to regulate the sacred acts of their own time. These descriptions must have been written by Moses.

Instrument music and singing. In the temple worship from David and Solomon on, the use of musical instruments and singing had a very important part in the temple worship. The Pentateuch, however, does not even mention music in connection with the Tabernacle worship. The critical assumption that the ordinances concerning the Tabernacle worship were composed at a time when music had long been an essential part of the temple worship is wholly improbable.

Jerusalem and its priesthood. The critics assert that large parts of the Pentateuch were composed with the purpose of establishing Jerusalem as the only place of worship and for the exaltation of its priesthood. If so, why is not Jerusalem and its priesthood mentioned at all in the Pentateuch? The only possible explanation is that it was written before Israel had contact with Jerusalem, that is, in the time of Moses.

One of the basic assumptions of the liberal theory is that the purpose of the reform of Josiah in 621 B.C. was to centralize worship in Jerusalem. This could not, however, have been its purpose, for the worship had been centralized to the temple of Jerusalem in the time of Solomon, about 350 years earlier. The purpose of the reform was to abolish idolatry, not to centralize the worship, and it was accomplished not only according to Deut. but primarily according to Ex.-Nu. There was nothing in the reform to show that Deut. was the sole guide in it.

Destruction of Canaanites and Amalekites. Deut. 7:1-4 contains the order given by Moses that when the Israelites would conquer the land of Canaan they should exterminate the Canaanites and make no alliance ("covenant") with them, in order that they would not lead them to idolatry. The Amalekites had to be destroyed because they had attacked Israel after it had left Egypt (Deut. 25:17ff.).

The liberals hold that these commands were written in Deut. a long time after these nations had been exterminated or amalgamated with Israel, so that they did not (for all practical purposes) exist any longer. There is no sense in this liberal assumption. Deut. must have been written by Moses.

The name "Lord of Hosts" was commonly used from the time of Samuel (c. 1050 B.C.) on, but in the Pentateuch it does not appear a single time. Had this book been written at times when this name was commonly used—as the liberals assume—it is wholly improbable that it would have never been used. The Pentateuch must have been written before Samuel.

Language of the Pentateuch. Language studies have come to the result that the Pentateuch has a clear Egyptian coloring, indeed, of the very period of the Egyptian history in which Moses lived. All that would point to later times, to Canaan or Babylonia, is missing. W. Möller (**op. cit.,** pp. 36f.) quotes A. Jeremias (**Das AT im Lichte des alten Orients,** pp. 241ff.):

> "The stories of Joseph and the exodus from Egypt show step by step genuine Egyptian coloring . . . The history of Joseph is throughout written in harmony with the conditions in ancient Egypt."

Möller also quotes Wiedman (**Geschichte von Alt-Agypten,** p. 69), who writes in the same tone:

> "All peripheral features of the biblical account, the description of the land and people, customs and methods is accurate and answers to what otherwise is known of them; the [royal] court is wholly Egyptian, free from all barbarisms."

The Egyptologist A. S. Yahuda* shows that the language of the Pentateuch evidences so much influence from the language of Egypt that it must have originated in the sphere of its cultural influence, particularly of the Middle

---

* **Die Sprache der Pentateuch in ihren Beziehungen zum Aegyptischen,** 1930, pp. 31ff., acc. to Möller, **ibid.,** pp. 37f.

Kingdom. Especially Genesis has a number of words which are not found in any Semitic language but which do exist in the language of Egypt. Such are e.g. ABRECH (Gen. 41:43), which, according to Yahuda, means, "Out of the way!" "Caution!" (in KJV: "Bow the knee"), and ZAPHNATH-PAANEAH (Gen. 41:45), which means, "The food of the land is this that lives."

The Tabernacle worship too had an Egyptian stamp on it (in external forms). If the instructions concerning its construction and worship had been composed in Babylonia or under its cultural influence (as the liberals assume), it should have a Babylonian stamp on it, and not Egyptian. The conclusion of Yahuda is that the Pentateuch evidences such an accurate knowledge of Egypt, and that of the very period of which it relates, that it must have its origin in those times. It is an impossible assumption that it could have been composed about a thousand years later in Palestine, which then was under the Babylon-Persian cultural influence, for the knowledge of Egypt contained in it would have been impossible so much later in a foreign country.

The Samaritan Pentateuch. As the Assyrian king Sargon III in 722 B.C. destroyed Samaria and the kingdom of Israel, he took a large part of its people to exile, and heathen people were brought to their place (2 Ki. 17:6, 24; Ezra 4:2). The remnant of the Israelites were probably still in majority, and the two elements gradually formed a mixed race, called Samaritans. When Cyrus in 537 B.C. permitted the exiled Jews to return to their own land and rebuild its temple, the Samaritans and other "people of the land" wanted to take part in this work. The leaders of the Jews, however (obviously remembering the injunctions of the Books of Moses against cooperation with the people of the land) answered to them: "Ye have nothing to do with us to build a house to our God; but we ourselves...will build" (Ezra 4). From that time on the relations between the Jews and Samaritans were unfriendly and hostile. Neh. 13:28 reports that Nehemiah dealt sternly with one of the grandsons of the high priest for marrying a foreigner. Josephus tells that this expelled priest was Manasseh, and that when Nehemiah drove him away he went to his father-in-law Sanballat, who then built a temple on Mount Gerizim and made his son-in-law the high priest. In this way the Samaritans built up a rival system of worship to that of Jerusalem (cp. Jh. 4:20). Manasseh made the five books of Moses, slightly amended, the basis of the life and work of the Samaritans, without accepting any other books of the Old Testament. Their Pentateuch was written in the old Hebrew characters that were in use before Ezra adopted the square script which has been employed since then. We do not know whether the copy of the Pentateuch that Manasseh had was one preserved in the area of the Northern Kingdom from earlier times or taken by him from Jerusalem at the time when he was driven away. It is, at any rate, quite like the Masoretic Pentateuch, having only certain minor differences, in many cases deliberately made by the Samaritans.

We ask: How is it possible to think that Manasseh and the Samaritans would have accepted for their sacred book a quite recent book composed in its final form at that very time, during the period of Ezra and Nehemiah? How is it possible to assume that Manasseh, a grandson of the high priest, belonging to the "inner circle" of the leading men, would have accepted the Pentateuch as an ancient book written by Moses, if it had been composed in his time by Ezra (though using older documents)? And how could the Samaritan Pentateuch be written in the older Hebrew script, if Ezra used the newer square script in composing it? The critical view does not make sense and fits the historical facts very poorly.

5. Tablets of Tell-el-Amarna and Testimony of Archeology

In 1887-88 a number of clay tablets were discovered at Tell-el-Amarna, in southern Egypt, all in cuneiform writing. They are letters from the time of Pharaoh Amenhotep III (ab. 1405-1352 B.C.), and in some of them Canaanite princes tell of the **Habirus** who were attacking some cities of southern Palestine. They refer obviously to the Hebrews who at that time were conquering the land under the leadership of Joshua.

Excavations conducted in the ruins of ancient Jericho have uncovered walls that have fallen flat to the ground, just as the Bible tells. John Garstang, the leader of the excavations has come to the conclusion that Jericho was destroyed about 1400 B.C. The necessary conclusion from this fact—as well as the Amarna tablets, which agree as to the time of the Israelite conquest with the results of the excavations of Jericho—is that Israel's oppression in Egypt must have been during the 18th dynasty (c. 1580-1335 B.C.) and not during the 19th dynasty (1335-1205 B.C.) as the liberals generally assume, holding that the chronology of the Bible at this point is wrong. The oppressor pharaoh must have been Thutmose III (1504-1450, or 1501-1447 B.C.) and the pharaoh of exodus Amenhotep III (1450-1424, or 1447-1420 B.C. (Free, **op. cit.**, pp. 88ff., 98f., 130, 136, Möller, **op cit.**, p. 44).

All this agrees well with the biblical chronology, according to which Moses was in Midian forty years (Ex. 2:23; Acts 7:23, 30), which means that it was at a time when there was a long-ruling pharaoh (Thutmose III ruled ab. 54 years). Since the exodus took place 480 years before the building of the temple of Solomon (1 Ki. 6:1), which started in 967 B.C., it must have taken place about 1447 B.C. Forty years after that, the Israelites conquered and destroyed Jericho. This agrees well with the information from the Amarna tablets and the excavations of Jericho (c. 1400 B.C.).*

Archeology has been able to throw light mainly on the background and environment of the Bible record. A remarkable fact is that in all the cases in which its findings have had contact with the biblical record they have confirmed it. Dr. Hugo Odeberg, professor (now emeritus) of exegetics at the University of Lund, Sweden, says:

---

* The view generally set forth in liberal works (and even in some conservative ones) is that the pharaoh of oppression was Ramses II (1292-1225 B.C.) and the pharaoh of exodus Merneptah (1225-1215). This view—which does not fit into the biblical chronology "has less support... in the light of the newer archeological evidence" (Free, op. cit., p. 90).

> "Truly genuine study, historical, archeological and linguistic, has in its newest discoveries and scientific conclusions more and more frequently proved that the Bible is true, refuting one critical theory on the Bible after another. But a truly notable fact is that up to this day and hour not a single new result of historical, archeological or linguistic research has confirmed a single assumption of destructive Bible criticism. It is not possible to show a single case in which a new discovery has given support or confirmation to a single afore-built assumption of Bible criticism. Instead, we could roll forth an immense amount of examples on how most of the archeological discoveries prove that the Bible is right, over against the assertions of Bible criticism" **(Karmel, Helsinki, No. 3, 1964, p. 58).**

5. Final Conclusions

The liberal criticism of the Pentateuch has come, as Möller **(op. cit., pp. 5f.)** says, to the point where hardly any critic believes what the other says. The result is a "complete field of ruins." The Pentateuch itself has not suffered from all its criticism, for, as Christ says, one jot or tittle will not pass from it till all is fulfilled (Mt. 5:18). But the critics and their students have suffered harm to their souls. Möller writes:

> "The first book of the Bible has a form that has on its front the stamp of internal and external unity, and it opposes division into sources [such as the liberal criticism has done], despite that its splitting up into sources still continues to have its assumed triumph" **(op. cit., pp. 14f.).**

Möller notes however: "We are not at all opposed to sources, we are only against those brought forth by the criticism, for they are nothing but fancy, and a poor one" **(ibid., p. 40).**

The book of Genesis itself contains statements which show what kind of sources Moses has used in writing it. It has ten "generations" or family records, which all have a somewhat similar heading:

1. Origin of heaven and earth: "These are the generations of the heavens and of the earth when they were created" (2:4).
2. Adam's family record: "This is the book of generations of Adam" (5:1).

3. Noah's family record: "These are the generations of Noah" (6:1).
4. Record of Noah's sons: "These are the generations of the sons of Noah, Shem, Ham, and Japheth" (10:1).
5. Shem's family record: "These are the generations of Shem" (11:10).
6. Terah's (Abraham's) family record: "These are the generations of Terah" (11:27).
7. Ishmael's family record: "These are the generations of Ishmael" (25:12).
8. Isaac's family record: "These are the generations of Isaac" (25:19).
9. Esau's family record: "These are the generations of Esau" (36:1).
10. Jacob's family record: "These are the generations of Jacob" 37:2).

It seems obvious that family records were prepared and carefully preserved from Noah on, possibly written on clay tablets, and Moses got his "historical" information from them, that is, from "first hand sources," and not from unreliable oral traditions, as the liberals hold (namely, that the "J," "E," etc., have got material from oral traditions current among people).

In writing in Gen. of creation, Moses either used an old written record that through Noah, etc., had come down from the antediluvian Sethites, or, then he got his information directly from God, or he got it partly from an old family record and partly directly from divine revelation as a "retrospective prophecy."

The use of different literary styles in the Pentateuch is no proof against its Mosaic origin. Many biblical authors have used varying literary styles as the subject matter has required. Even an ordinary historical study often contains narrative parts, lists, laws, poems, etc. The circumstance that legal ordinances are in the Pentateuch often in connection with or between historical accounts is in reality a proof for its Mosaic origin. The book(s) became naturally like this as Moses continued to write it while the events rolled onward and God gave him revelations and instructions. Had the books been written many centuries later in the settled circumstances of Canaan, it is entirely improbable that the result would have been the Pentateuch as we have it.

Liberal criticism has dimmed out and perverted normal thinking and reasoning to the extent that in the case of the Pentateuch it does not see and respect facts that otherwise should be plain and inescapable. If we didn't know that the Pentateuch is from Moses, the facts would force us to draw the conclusion that he must be the author. It contains so detailed and accurate accounts of him and his activity that it is completely unreasonable to assume that it could have arisen in the manner the liberal critics propose.

M. Segal, Jewish scholar, once professor at the Hebrew University of Jerusalem, writes of the "JEDP" theory:

> "Hebrew literature, or any other literature all the world over, cannot show another example of the production of a literary work by such a succession of recurring amalgamations and such a succession of compilers and redactors centuries apart, all working by one and the same method, as attributed by the Theory to the formation of the Pentateuch. But beside this striking artificiality, the Theory also puts forward highly improbable assumptions without offering any evidence for their veracity . . . we must reject the Documentary Theory as an explanation of the composition of the Pentateuch. The theory is complicated, artificial, and anomalous. It is based on unproved assumptions. It uses unreliable criteria for the separation of the text into component documents. A careful reading of the contents of the book [of Genesis] shows clearly that the book is the work of an author with a definite and preconceived purpose, and not a compilation of disconnected fragments put together by late redactors . . . The hypothetical pseudonymous legislators and critics, working in exilic and post-exilic times, who ascribed their legal composition to Moses, would have written their laws as written and complete compositions, and not as oral and incomplete addresses" (**Scripta Hierosolymitana** VIII, Studies in the Bible, edited by Chaim Rabin, pp. 95, 98, 108; quoted from Otten's **op. cit.**, pp. 178f.).

Samuel R. Külling* shows that all the arguments of the critics for the late date of those parts of the Pentateuch that

---

* **Zur Datierung der "Genesis-P-Stücke," namentlich des Kapitels Genesis XVII,** J. H. Kok N. V. Kampen, The Netherlands, 1964, pp. 166-208.

are ascribed to "P" are invalid. The theory of the post-exilic date of the "P" "has no historical value." The late dating of the "P" material turns the history of Israel upside down, on its head (p. 282).

Moses would have been extremely inconsiderate if he had not recorded in writing the great events and divine revelation acts in which he was a mediator and which had a profound significance for Israel and mankind, but had left the matter to the uncertainties of oral tradition. All that he had accomplished, and even the divine revelation through him would have in that case soon become distorted, ruined and forgotten.

Additional facts.

We add a few more facts which point in the direction of the authenticity of the Pentateuch.

Josh. 24 has a record of the building of an altar on Mt. Ebal, and this was done in compliance to the orders given through Moses in Ex. 20:24 and Deut. 27:2. How could this have been done if Ex. and Deut. did not exist at that time?

Josh. 14:6-15 and Judg. 1:20 refer to the promises in Nu. 14:24 and Deut. 1:36 concerning Hebron as Caleb's inheritance. How could this be understood if Nu. and Deut. did not exist at that time, as the critics assert?

The first part of Deborah's song in Judg. 5 leans clearly on the blessing of Moses in Deut. 33, and v. 17 on the words Gen. 49:13f. How should this be understood if Deut. and Gen. did not exist at that time?

According to 2 Ki. 18:4, Hezekiah broke in pieces the brazen serpent that Moses had made because the Israelites used it as an idol and burned incense to it. This presupposes the narrative of the brazen serpent in Nu. 21. How should this be understood if Nu. was written later?

The words of Micaiah in 1 Ki. 22:17 are a verbal quotation from Nu. 27:17, and his words in vv. 27f. are based on Deut 18:21f. This shows that Nu. and Deut. must have existed at that time (c. 850 B.C.), and that the critical theory of their later origin is false.

According to Ezra 9:1-12, Ezra was grieved because the Jews who had returned from the exile had, in conflict with the commandment of the Lord, practiced intermarriages with the heathen. This ordinance is in Lev. 18:24f. and Deut. 7:2f. How should this be understood if Lev., according to the critical theory, belonged to "P" and was "published" later than this, after the arrival of Nehemiah?

The critical theory holds that the reforms of Ezra and Nehemiah were accomplished according to the "P." However (according to the critical division of the source document), this code does not contain any law that prohibits intermarriages with other nations. but it is in Deut. 7:3f., and this was one of the most notable parts of the reforms. This fact too is fatal to the critical theory of the origin and time of the assumed "P."

Deut. 27 is almost full of references to the middle books of the Pentateuch. How should this be understood if these books had been composed centuries later, as the critics hold?

Note: Opposing liberal theories.

The Graf-Wellhausen Documentary theory (in various modifications) continues to be the dominant trend, and it is this theory that is set forth in the recent Sunday School books of different denominaions. There are, however, liberal critics who reject this theory as having no basis in historical facts.

Several Scandinavian scholars have attacked the "bookish" approach of the Documentary Theory and declared that it is just a product of the fancy of the scholars, and is in principle wholly wrong. These scholars have replaced the assumed "J," "E," etc., with the living community of Israel and especially its leaders. The literature of Israel consists of various traditions, and some individuals may have played an important part in shaping them, but this does not mean that they wrote such documents and "J," "E," etc. The documents called "JEDP" have never existed, these scholars hold. They propose that the materials that we have in the Pentateuch were first written down by the Israelite community in the Babylonian exile.

Most liberal scholars feel that this new hypothesis cannot be proved or even showed to be probable (H. W. Harrelson, **Interpreting the Old Testament, 1964, pp. 33f.**). In reality it is no better than the Documentary Theory.

The fact that the different trends of liberal criticism offer theories so far apart, regarding one another's theories as just so much fantasy shows that they all are moving in the wide field of subjective imagination.

The Pentateuch, as we have it in the Bible, is a simple, clear and consistent book, a real masterpiece, even from a literary point of view. It can be the work of Moses only, who wrote it under the inspiration and guidance of the Spirit of God, being the greatest of the OT prophets. The critics have torn loose practically all the "building blocks" of this magnificent edifice and formed from them heaps according to their misdirected fancy. And after doing so they have asserted that this is genuine historical and scientific Bible study! (cp. Möller, **op. cit.,** pp. 131f.).

And now the majority of American Protestantism has started to teach this sort of "scientific" view of the Bible from the Sunday School children on! What a devilish travesty!

VI. INTERPRETATION OF BIBLICAL PROPHECIES

Alongside the Pentateuch criticism the question of the nature and interpretation of biblical prophecies has been the most important area of conflict between Bible-believers and liberals.

1. Liberal Criticism of Prophetical Books

The liberal criticism of the prophetical books of the Bible is as motley a field of conflicting theories as is the Pentateuch criticism. They have in both areas only one thing in common, and it is their assertion that, just as the Pentateuch, so also the prophetical books are products of series of forgeries and their conglomerations. Robert J. Marshall sets forth a rather general liberal view when he writes:

> "The prophets themselves did more speaking than writing. Even when prophecies were written, pupils continued to memorize and recite the teachings of their master. When all the bits of written and memorized material were finally brought together, the compiler arranged them according to a scheme of his own, which could be helpful or confusing" (TMA, pp. 99f.).

E. G. Gulin, formerly professor of Biblical Exegetics and then (till 1966) a Lutheran bishop in Finland, describes the liberal view of the origin of prophetical books as follows:

> "The prophets did not produce their books in the form which they now have in the Bible... Isaiah mentions in 8:16ff. the circle of disciples among whom he wanted to seal his teaching, and Jeremiah also has his friend Baruch who writes down the words of the prophet. Thus, connected with the prophets there were circles of disciples and friends, and their heritage was fostered among them and possibly also developed further. Several books may have been sometimes formed from the proclamation of the same prophet. When they were later combined, the result was that there was con-

fusion in the final book, which was not the fault of the prophet himself...

"As books in ancient times in general had no heading, the books that were written in the same scroll and which originally were independent could later be regarded as one... Thus, e.g. the book of Isaiah probably contains three different books* which originate from different periods in the history of Israel... Further, the additional material that later accumulated to this literature is particularly noteworthy. We should keep in mind that in the difficult situation of the exile and even after it the Jewish congregation devoted itself to a special study of prophetical literature. The small fragments were gathered together into collections, and books were composed out of these collections. At the same time there was a desire to have the literary records, which often proclaimed severe judgments, in such a form that the reader and the congregation in hard circumstances got encouragement and consolation from them. The compilers liked to arrange the remnants of prophetical proclamation in such a manner that the declarations of judgments were placed at the beginning and the predictions that contained brighter hopes were put to the end. If the records... did not have this kind of more comforting material, it was taken from elsewhere, or it was created according to models. Spurious pictures of bright future were produced in this manner particularly at the end of the collection, or as a conclusion of shorter series."

Where the liberals have got this sort of information on the process by which prophetical literature was produced, they do not say. Historical sources offer no such information—and so it must be from their own fancies.

In America, this theory of the origin of OT prophetical books is set forth e.g. in the previously mentioned works of R. H. Pfeiffer and W. Harrelson. This theory has been the critics' guide in their destructive criticism of this section of the Scriptures.

After this kind of work, the German critics W. Nowack and B. Duhm left of the book of Micah only c. $\frac{1}{4}$, of Jeremiah a little more than 1/5, of Ezekiel c. 1/7 and of

---

* The LCA book **The Mighty Acts of God** has a diagrammatic table in which the book of Isaiah is divided into **four** books written at different times and by different authors.

Hosea c. ¼ that they ascribed to these prophets themselves. Ernst Sellin defended in his commentary on the Twelve Minor prophets (1929-30) the authenticity of the bulk of their books, tearing down according to the old model only Joel and Obadiah. R. E. Wolfe spoke in 1925 of a 13-fold tampering of the text of the Minor Prophets. Out of 1050 verses he left intact only 547. In their criticism of Isaiah, even the most conservative critics, such as A. Dillmann, F. Koenig, O. Procksch and E. Sellin, have acknowledged as genuine only c. 1/3 of the book.

We ask: What are the historical and factual arguments by which the critics support their theory and criticism? Do we have any historical records of this sort of "redactorial" and collecting work? Or do the prophetical books themselves contain indications and evidences of their formation in that manner? Is it true that in ancient times books were commonly without headings, so that fragments or books by different authors because of this could be combined?

The answer to all these questions is totally negative. As we have already said, the critics have gotten all these ideas from their own imagination.

We can ourselves easily find the answer to the question concerning the headings of prophetical books by looking at the first verses of the biblical books of the prophets: Every one of them has a heading which mentions the author of the book and usually also gives information on the time of his ministry. There is not a single exception to this rule. In view of this fact it is wholly inconceivable where the critics have gotten their idea that the prophets in general did not provide their books with headings.

The fact that the critics are at variance concerning their conclusions on the authors and composition of the prophetical books is an indication of the subjectivistic arbitrariness of their "theology." Judges 21:25 describes the anarchic conditions of that time: "In those days... every man did that which was right in his own eyes." The same is true in liberal theology: Each theologian of this trend proceeds in his criticism of the prophetical and other biblical books as it seems right in his eyes, without respect for what the Bible itself says, naturally being influenced by the particular "school" in which he has gotten his training.

Bible-believing theologians who in scientific competence are at least on a par with the liberals have arrived in their study of the prophets at entirely different conclusions. Möller (**op. cit., p. 133**) writes:

> "If it can be proved that all the prophetical books without exception are structures that have been built in a masterly way, comparable to cathedrals, their breaking down into their individual building blocks is something that is in direct conflict with the intentions of these men of God, for that which is before our eyes speaks against it."

Möller shows in the case of every prophetical book of the OT how it is a consistent whole and obviously written in its final form by the very prophet whose name is in the heading. The liberal breaking down of these books into sections that are assumed to be from different times and different authors is void of any historical or factual foundation.

Concerning the liberal assumption that the prophetical books are end-results of repeated "editing" Möller writes:

> "We should be... mindful of the fact that good care was taken of the preservation of the Word of God. The newer theology imagines that the text of the sacred writings was in free use in the sense that its margin was, so to speak, open to anyone's whims for any kinds of remarks and notes to the extent that, in fact, we should in many cases think of the marginal notes and additions as more extensive than the text—which hardly would have any space left if all that would be included which is assumed to be later additions. Thus it would be e.g. in Hosea in which hardly anything (according to some critical extremists) authentic would be left; such an assumption is unhistorical and in conflict with all parallel cases in the history of religions. Even if we wholly disregard the preservation of the sacred texts in other religions, the OT has sufficient number of passages which show how their preservation, keeping and making known was taken care of: The Decalog was written by the

Lord's own hand on two tables and placed in the ark of the covenant, Deut. 10:1ff. The book of the law that is mentioned in Deut. 31:26, and that can be only the entire Pentateuch up to Deut. 31:23, was, according to vv. 24ff., at the side of the ark of the covenant. In the feast of the Tabernacles of the Year of Release [every seventh year] it was to be taken out and read, 31:9ff. The future kings had to have a copy of it made for themselves in order that they would compare their reign with the law of God. The law was to be written on Mt. Ebal on stones... In Josh. 24:25 we read: '... And Joshua wrote these words in the book of the law of God; and he took a great stone and set it up under the oak that was by the sanctuary of the Lord.' ... we read in 1 Sam. 10:25, 'Then Samuel told the people the manner of the kingdom and wrote it in a book and laid it up before the Lord,' doing it, as it appears, ... with solemn ceremonies in the presence and sight of all the people. 2 Ki. 22:8ff. and Neh. 8-10 report a sort of a new acknowledgement of the canonical material and of obligating the people to obey it. The former passage shows how the sacred books were kept in the holy place... According to Deut. 4:2 and 13:1, nothing should be added to them nor diminished from them, which ordinance is... repeated in Prov. 30:5f. and Rev. 22:18... The whole tribe of Levi, according to Deut. 33:9, had the special task... not only to keep themselves the precepts of the law and to preserve it, but to teach Israel the statutes and ordinances" (op. cit., pp. 382f.).

The liberal assumption of a full freedom to tamper with the sacred texts is not only refuted by the passages referred to by Möller but also by the fact that from ancient times on the Israelites were so strict in their preservation without alteration that they did not even dare to correct the copyist's mistakes that had crept into the text at early times but only put notes on them in the margin. When scholars have compared the text of Isaiah found in a cave near the Dead Sea in 1947—which is from the second century B. C. —with the Masoretic text that is almost a thousand years younger, they have found them practically identical.

The liberal assumption on a "free" attitude toward the sacred texts and on an arbitrary liberty to tamper with them in Israel is wholly unhistorical, a product of their own fancy.

2. Liberal and Biblical Views of Prophecy

Attitude toward the Supernatural

One of the basic tenets of the liberal view of prophecies is that what is in them in the form of predictions of future events has in reality been written after the "foretold" events, and that they are actually only "pious frauds."

The fundamental reason for the liberals' suspicious or negative attitude toward predictive prophecy is their attempt to apply the Kantian theory of knowledge, followed in secular sciences, to the interpretation of biblical prophecies. According to this axiom, no supernatural factors can be considered and admitted, but all the phenomena are to be explained from natural causes.

Miracles and fulfilled predictions were formerly regarded by Christians as irrefutable evidences for the truth of Christianity and the reliability of the Scriptures. In our time the liberals, although they call themselves Christians, regard miracles and predictions of future events as a great hindrance to the acceptance of Christianity on the part of scientifically trained modern men.

The fact, however, is that if the supernatural element is removed from Christianity, it ceases to be Christianity. It becomes mere human religious, churchly and social activity which has hardly anything in common with the Christianity of the Bible, at least not in essentials.

"Situation" in Prophecies.

One of the guiding principles of liberal interpretation of prophecies is that the prophets have spoken to the people of their own time on the issues of the day, and not to future generations. A. B. Davidson, a late professor at Edinburgh, Scotland, who in his times was one of the most influential advocates of the critical view, described the function of the Hebrew prophet as follows:

> "The Prophet is always a man of his own time and it is always to the people of his own time that he speaks, not to a generation long after, nor to us. And the things of which he speaks will always

be things of importance to the people of his own day, whether they be things belonging to their internal life and conduct, or things affecting their external fortunes as a people among other peoples" (Hasting's **Dictionary of the Bible** IV, 118b; quoted from Oswald T. Allis, **The Unity of Isaiah**, 1951, p. 2; abbr. AUI).

If applied consistently, this definition of the function of prophets leads to a denial of predictive prophecy. Foretelling of future events is not essential in Hebrew prophecy, this view holds. More than a century ago J. A. Alexander described the critical attitude toward this kind of prophecy, and the words are still true:

> "The successive writers of this modern school, however they may differ as to minor points among themselves, prove their identity of principle by holding that there cannot be distinct prophetic foresight of the distant future" (**The Earlier Prophecies of Isaiah**, p. xxxviii, acc. to AUI, p. 3).

In order to bring biblical prophecies into harmony with the described theory of the nature of prophecy, the liberals have changed the "situation" or "seat in life" (**Sitz im Leben**) of these prophecies. This means: Whenever Scripture has predictions of future events which it sets forth as having been fulfilled at a later time, or when they refer to far distant events, the critics have explained that they cannot have been uttered by the prophets to whom they are ascribed, but they must have been uttered shortly before, at the time of, or after the events to which they refer; for a prophecy cannot deal with a "non-existent situation," such as did not exist at the time of its utterance. Or, then, it is explained that the prophecy which speaks of an event in the distant future was originally a general, vague and indefinite utterance that dealt primarily with current or near future events. The editor ("redactor") or editors have later, in the time of or after the "fulfilment" revised and molded it so as to apply to the event in question. According to the liberals, "the history of Hebrew literature ... is a history of revisions" (J. M. Powis Smith, "The Study of O. T. and of the Religion of Israel," in **A Guide to the Study of the Christian Religion**, 1916, p. 152; acc. to AUI, p. 4).

This means that the earlier writings (or "documents") of the OT have been brought into harmony with the facts of history by means of an almost continuing series of forgeries and falsifications.

Examples of the Liberal Procedure

Gen. 15:13 tells of the divine revelation to Abraham, that his descendants would sojourn in a foreign land and be oppressed there, 400 years. In order to remove a foretelling of future events from this passage, the critics have explained that the two source documents, "J" and "E," of which this passage is assumed to have been composed, were combined about 650 B.C., and that the youngest of its sources, "P," was still later. The final "editing" of the Pentateuch took place about 450 B.C. When these "documents" were revised in the course of centuries, the prediction to Abraham was "colored" by the actual events. The final "redactor" added to it the words, "and they will afflict them, four hundred years." He did this on the basis of the story found in the last document, the "P," which told of the "fulfillment" of this "prediction." In this manner the critics have changed this passage into a "prediction" **post eventum,**" after the event, in other words, into a deception.

1 Ki. 13:1ff. tells of a man of God who came from Judah to Bethel in Israel (the Northern Kingdom) at the time when Jeroboam I (931-910 B.C.) was standing by the altar that he had erected to burn incense.

> "And he cried against the altar by the word of the Lord and said, O altar, altar, thus saith the Lord: Behold a son will be born to the house of David, Josiah by name; and on thee will he sacrifice the priests of the high places who burn incense on thee, and men's bones will they burn on thee."

According to the critics, this kind of prediction of a future event in which even the name of the person was mentioned was impossible. The **Westminster Study Edition** (pp. 468f.) explains, "Since Josiah carried out this destruction, his name became attached to this prediction (2 Ki. 23:17)." C. H. Cornill explains that this prophecy is "a quite late production" (**Introduction to the OT,** 1892, Engl. transl. 1907, p. 213; acc. to AUI, p. 9). In this case too the predictive prophecy is denied and the passage is asserted to have been written after the event, being a "pious swindle."

2 Ki. 10:28-31 records that the Lord gave Jehu, who destroyed Baal worship in Israel, the promise that his sons "of the fourth generation" would sit on the throne of Israel. In order to get rid of real prediction in this passage, the critics have explained that the "Deuteronomic redactor" (who is assumed to have played an important role in the composition of the Books of the Kings) "revised" this passage by inserting into it the words "of the fourth generation." This was done after the dynasty of Jehu had ruled in four generations and then been overthrown, that is, when the events referred to had become facts of history. This is a simple way to turn the prophecies of Scripture into fraudulent tricks.

According to Ps. 110:1, this psalm was written by David. Jesus appealed to it in His argument with the scribes and Pharisees as a proof that Messiah, who was David's son (descendant), also was David's Lord and therefore greater than David. He asked: "If David then calleth him Lord, how is he his son?" (Mt. 22:41-45).

The critics have explained that relatively few of the psalms which are ascribed to David were actually composed by him (This assertion, however, has no factual basis.*). Even those psalms, the critics say, which originally were composed by David were in the course of time more or less "revised" and changed. They speak of Ps. 110 as "popularly supposed to be written by David," and that the Jews held that David wrote Ps. 110:1, regarding it as Messianic. By this they suggest that "David may not have written Ps. 110"

---

* Professor R. D. Wilson made a thorough study of "The Headings of the Psalms" and published his results in an article with the quoted heading in the **Princeton Theological Review,** 1926, pp. 1-37, 353-395. His conclusion was: "As far as the Objective evidence goes the headings of the psalms are presumptively correct." (p. 395; acc. to AUI, p. 11).

(Westminster Study Edition, NT, pp. 60f., 100f., 154; acc. to AUI, p. 11). This means: the Davidic "situation" and authorship of this psalm may be denied, but the conclusion may still be upheld that David's Son must be greater than His father David. In reality this liberal interpretation implies that Jesus lied, or at least erred, when He stated that David spoke the words in Ps. 110:1.

Is. 7:8 contains a prophecy concerning Israel (often called Ephraim, according to its leading tribe): "Within threescore and five [65] years will Ephraim be broken, that it is not a people."

Bible-believing scholars have long recognized that this prediction was fulfilled by three steps: (1) Tiglath-pileser, king of Assyria, weakened the kingdom of Israel c. 733-732 B.C. by crushing its army and deporting many of its people to Assyria (2 Ki. 15:27-31; 16:7-9); (2) Sargon III captured Samaria in 722 B.C. and made an end of the kingdom of Israel (2 Ki. 17:6); (3) Esarhaddon, king of Assyria (c. 680-669 B.C.), repopulated cities of Israel with people brought from other parts of the empire (Ezra 4:2; 2 Ki. 17:24). The prophecy of Isaiah was given a short time before the first phase (c. 734 B.C.), and from it to the last phase was c. 65 years. It was through these three blows that Israel was broken and ceased to be a nation.

Many critics, however, explain that the fulfillment of the prophecy in Is. 7:8 was the destruction of Samaria in 722 B.C., and that a later "redactor" added to it the words, "threescore and five years," after Esarhaddon had repopulated the cities of Israel with foreigners. Other critics explain that Isaiah overestimated the time needed for the overthrow of the Northern Kingdom: Instead of 65 years it took only about 12 years. The purpose of these critics is to show that in his "guess" Isaiah made a mistake of more than half a century, and that Is. 7:8 contains no prediction that has actually come true.

In Is. 9:5 we have the familiar "Christmas text":

> "Unto us a child is born, unto us a son is given; and the government will be upon his shoulder; and his name will be called

Wonderful, Counsellor, Mighty God, Everlasting Father, Prince of Peace."

This is an obvious Messianic prophecy. Liberals have wanted to translate it: "A wonderful Counsellor is the mighty God, the Father of eternity, the Prince of Peace," with the explanation: "The Messiah's name describes the nature of God for whom he is to rule" **(Westminster Study Edition, p. 939; acc. t. AUI, p. 14)**. But if understood in this manner, these names of the Messiah do not essentially differ from many other names of the same type in the OT, such as ELIMELECH (My God is king), JEHORAM (Yahweh is exalted), GEDALIAH (Yahweh is great), ELIJAH (My God is Yahweh), etc. This liberal translation and interpretation of Is. 9:5 empties it of all real Messianic meaning, transferring the names to refer to God the Father, while they actually are here applied to God the Son.

Is. 13 contains "the burden of Babylon," in which the overthrow of that city is predicted to take place by the Medes. The Medes and Persians, led by Cyrus, conquered Babylon in 539 B.C. This event was the beginning of its downfall, which was completed later. Liberals explain that this prophecy was not uttered by Isaiah but was inserted here at the time when Babylon's fall was in sight **(Westminster Study Edition, p. 945, 955; acc. t. AUI, p. 15)**. The only reason for this explanation is the liberal assumption that real predictive prophecy is impossible; the utterance of this prophecy must therefore be transferred to the time of the historical event spoken of in it.

Jer. 50-51 contains a long detailed prophecy of the same event, the conquest of Babylon by the Medes and Persians, "great nations from the north." In the critics' view, Jeremiah could not write this prediction many decades beforehand; it must have been written about 540 B.C., at the time when the Medo-Persian armies were approaching Babylon. G. A. Smith sxplains: "The compiler, or the editor of the Book, has (51:60) erred in attributing this long prophecy to Jeremiah" (AUI, p. 17). The only "warrant" for this liberal assertion is unbelief, the denial of the possibility of God to reveal future events through His prophets.

Mic. 5:2 contains the prophecy of the Messiah's birth in Bethlehem:

> "Thou Bethlehem Ephratah, which art little among the thousands (clans) of Judah, out of thee shall come forth to me one who is to be ruler in Israel; whose goings forth are from of old, from everlasting."

Mt. 2:1-12 records how the chief priests and scribes of Jerusalem explained to Herod and the Magi that this passage was a prediction of the Messiah's birth in Bethlehem. The critics explain that this passage is "parabolic" (**Westminster Study Ed. NT,** p. 26), or that it is a "Christian Midrash rather than authentic history" (Gore, Goudge and Guillaume, **A New Commentary,** Mt. 2, acc. to AUI, p. 16). The only reason for this interpretation is the liberal refusal to admit the possibility of real predictive prophecy, and that Mic. 5:2 was fulfilled in Christ's birth in Bethlehem.

These examples (for additional ones, see AUI, pp. 10-19) show what sort of methods the liberals use for "explaining out" predictive prophecies from the Bible: **First,** they change the "situation" given in the biblical text either near the foretold event or after it, so that the "prediction" becomes a story written on the eve or after the historical event; **second,** they tamper with the prophecies by cutting from them their essential features or by denying them, so that they become hazy and indefinite; **third,** they explain the predictions to be mere literary tricks whereby the "editors" who lived at the time of the "predicted" events spoke by the authority of renowned men of God in the past; **fourth,** they explain that later "editors" or "redactors" have changed and molded prophecies that have come down from older times so as to bring them into harmony with historical events, adding to them the passages that plainly refer to them.

The use of such methods leave us in a complete uncertainty as to what the prophets have actually said and written, and what the later "redactors" have put in their "mouth." In this manner they cease to be prophecies **according to Scripture** and become prophecies **according to the critics,** in other words, pious swindles.

Liberal critics assert that their theory of the nature of biblical prophecies is based on careful objective studies of them. In reality it is built on subjective and arbitrary assumptions which lay aside or reject the Bible's own testimonies. If the Scriptures are taken as they are, the result is entirely different.

Much emphasis is put by the liberals on the necessity of finding out what the prophetical utterances meant to the people of their time, to whom they spoke. This original meaning is to be distinguished from what they have meant to later generations, and from the one which they have received in the light of their "fulfillment." According to the liberal view, the prophecies can have significance for later generations only through the application of the principles that the prophets once taught in the situations of their own times.

Biblical prophecies, to be sure, contain revelations of the principles of divine world government and His dealings with men. These principles apply to every generation, and are fulfilled again and again. Such principles are e.g. those shown in Jer. 18:6-10, Ez. 3:17-21 and 33:1-19: God's saving grace and punishing justice deal with men according to their attitude toward Him and His word, namely, whether they humble themselves to repentance and obey Him or not. Such passages, however, make up only a small fraction of all prophecies. Liberal critics interpret the prophets almost as philosophers whose messages contained principles that apply to different situations, but who were not able to give real predictions of future events (AUI, pp. 4-21).

Biblical Teaching of Prophecy and the Liberals' Attitude to It.

Scripture teaches a great number of times that God has spoken to and through the prophets. "God, who at sundry times and in diverse manners spoke in time past to the fathers by the prophets, hath at the end of these days spoken to us in Son . . ." (Heb. 1:1f.). We read e.g.: "And the Lord said to Moses..." (Lev. 24:13;25:1). "And the Lord said to Joshua..." (Josh. 3:7). "Then the Lord said to Samuel..." (1 Sam. 3:11). "The word of the Lord came to Nathan..." (2 Sam. 7:4). "I heard the voice of the Lord saying..." (Is. 6:8). "The word which came to Jeremiah from the Lord..." (Jer. 18:1). "The word of the Lord came unto me..." (Ez. 6:1). "Then said the Lord to me..." (Hos. 3:1). "The word of the Lord that came to Joel..." (Joel 1:1).

Ez. 21:21 tells us how the Assyrian king used three forms of divination to find out what he should do when he set out on his campaigns. One of the most common ones was "looking into the liver," of which a large number of cuneiform texts speak. All these pagan methods (some of them are mentioned in Deut. 18:10f.) were abominations before God, and their use was forbidden in Israel at the pain of death.

In most cases, as in the cited ones, the prophets simply say that the Lord said to them, or that His word came to them, without explaining how this took place. To Moses God spoke "mouth to mouth" (Ex. 33:11), or through His angel Gal. 3:19). He also spoke in dreams, visions, etc. (Nu. 12: 6-8; Acts 12:7; 27:23f.).

Information concerning the time, sometimes even the month and day when received, the situation, etc., is frequently connected with the biblical prophecies (e.g. Is. 1:1; 20:1; Jer. 25:1; Ez. 40:1). In numerous cases the prophecies, however, did not deal with things of the time and contemporary people but with matters of a more or less distant future. The prophecies uttered by Jacob on his deathbed referred to relatively distant future events (Gen. 49). The same was true of the predictions of Balaam (Nu. 23-24), Moses' prophecies on the Plains of Moab (Deut. 28-29), the prediction of the man of God against altar of Jeroboam I (2 Ki. 13), Isaiah's prophecy on the overthrow of Babylon (Is. 13), Micah's prophecy of the destruction of Jerusalem (3:12), Ezekiel's prediction of the overthrow of Tyre (26-27), Elijah's prediction of the destruction of the family of Ahab (1 Ki. 21, though its fulfillment was not very far). In all these cases the predictions dealt with quite definite "situations," but they were not those at the times when they were uttered but ones in more or less distant future.

Anonymity is, according to the critics, a characteristic feature of many or most of the OT prophetical utterances: they do not contain the names of men who gave them. The liberals aver that this is the result of careful studies of these prophecies; however, they have arrived at this "result" by disregarding the headings of the OT prophetical books themselves and by splitting up these books into small fragments, which they then have declared to be independent utterances.

This arbitrary critical method reduces the book of Isaiah to a small library of mostly anonymous prophetical utterances. The critics disregard the statement in the first verse of the book and several other passages which state that they were prophecies given through Isaiah. To each of the several hundred fragments into which certain critics have divided this book they have tried to invent its own "situation" which is independent from the general situation mentioned at the beginning of it.

Scripture itself regards the authorship of each prophecy as essential, and the same is true of the time and situation in which it was given. This is seen from the fact that the author's name is in the beginning. The critics arbitrarily disregard these statements of Scripture itself and set forth their own subjective guesses, claiming "scientific" value to them. They are not able to support their assertions at this point by any historical facts. The only reason for their procedure is their axiom of unbelief: God has not been able to give any real predictions of future events.

Fulfilled Predictions and the So-Called Prophetical Perfect

Scripture has a number of predictions that give the length of the time after which they were to be fulfilled, such as: 65 years (Is. 7:8), 70 years (Is. 23:15; Jer. 25:11; 29:10), four generations (2 Ki. 10:30), 400 years (Gen. 15:13), 70 year-weeks or 490 years, middle of the last year-week or after 486.5 years (Dan. 9:24-27), three years (Is. 16:14; cp. 20:3), within a year (Is. 21:16), tomorrow (2 Ki. 13: 1ff.). In numerous instances the OT prophecies on Christ and the new covenant have been fulfilled (e.g. Is. 7:14— Mt. 1:22f.; Mic. 5:2—Mt. 2:5f.; Ps. 110:1—Mt. 22:41-46; 24:1-44; cp. AUI, pp. 25-28).

Biblical prophecies have been fulfilled with amazing accuracy, and many of them are in the process of fulfillment in our time (e.g. Dan. 7:8, 20f. 24f,; Is. 11:11ff.; Rev. 13 and 17). This is a plain proof of their divine origin—and at the same time an evidence that the liberals have gone miserably astray in their unbelief.

The liberal theory of the "situation" of every prophecy at the time of its utterance is also in conflict with the so-called "prophetical perfect." This means that the prophets often spoke of future things in the past tense, as though the predicted events had already taken place. In Is. 5:13 the prophet says: "Therefore my people have gone into captivity ...," although the exile of Judah at the time of Isaiah was c. 150 years in the future. In Is. 9:1ff. we read: "The people who walked in darkness have seen a great light ... For unto us a child is born ..." At the time of the utterance of this prophecy its fulfillment in Christ was c. 700 years hence. Is. 10:28-32 contains a detailed and picturesque description of the advancement of the Assyrian army in the perfect tense, although it dealt with a future event, as even the critics in this case generally admit.

Jer. 50-51 speaks of the conquest of Babylon in the perfect tense: "Say, Babylon is taken, Bel is put to shame ...," although this prediction was about 50 years ahead of the event. The prophecies about the end time in the Book of Revelation are in the past tense, although their fulfillment at the time of the apostle John was almost two millenniums ahead, and for the most part they still are in the future.

Although it is rather usual that biblical prophecies of future events are in the past tense, there are others which are in the future tense, and at times the past and future tenses alternate.

Thus, with regard to a large part of biblical prophecies, the liberal assertion does not hold true that the situation of each prophecy is the actual situation of the time of its utterance. If we take the prophecies of Scripture as they are and do not, as the critics do, arbitrarily explain them to have been written at the time or after the events dealt with in them, we observe that the prophets speak quite often from the viewpoint of future situations as though present or past.

Original Intention, Later Understanding and "Adjustments"

As already pointed out, the critics emphasize the principle that a clear distinction should be made between the original intention of the prophet and the manner in which his utterance has been understood later, at the time of its fulfillment.* Scripture itself, however, does not make this kind of distinction: The intention and meaning of a prophecy is the one seen in its fulfillment, for God's progressive revelation is one consistent whole. Just as the real nature of a grain of wheat is seen in the full-grown wheat, so the real meaning and purpose of each prophecy is seen when it has come true. God Himself has shown or shows in the fulfillment what He has meant by the prophecies that His Spirit has given in times past.

The critics deny this kind of supernatural activity of God and connection between the original prophecy and its fulfillment. They may say that the OT prophecies were **applied** in the Christian Church to Christ, although they did not originally mean that. This is, however, a denial of the interpretation that God Himself has given through the fulfillment, and it implies that Scripture cannot be relied on as its own interpreter.

True, the prophets who received predictions did not

---

* The consistent critics deny real foretelling of future events, and in their view there is, therefore, no true "fulfillment."

always understand their meaning, or did so only in part. This is implied in the words of 1 Pet. 1:10f. that "the prophets have inquired and searched about this salvation," promised in the coming Messiah. They "searched what person or time was indicated by the Spirit of Christ within them when he predicted the sufferings of Christ and the glory that would follow."

It is probable that Jacob did not fully perceive the meaning of the prophecies that God gave through him in Gen. 49. Their implications became clear in the course of the history of Israel, as they were realized. The critics have, according to their method of unbelief, explained that these prophecies were later adjusted so that they came to be in harmony with the actual course of events.

The OT contains prophecies that pertain to the last times. Some of them are now in the process of fulfillment, others will be fulfilled in the future. The prophets through whom they were given probably understood little of their real meaning, for they were given for later generations and not for their own time. Such are e.g. the prophecies in Is. 2:1-5; 11:1-15; 65:17-25; Ez. 35-39; Zech. 12 and 14; in the NT Mt. 24 (Mk. 13; Lk. 21); 2 Thess. 2:1-12; Rev. 13-22, etc.

Since numerous Scripture prophecies deal with things in distant future, some of them thousands of years after their utterance, it is obvious that they were not spoken to the contemporaries but for future generations. Their "situation" or "seat in life" could not be the time when they were uttered, but later times. In speaking of the prophets who searched about the person, time and salvation that the Spirit in them indicated, Peter writes: "...not to themselves, but to you they ministered the things, which are now reported to you..." (1 Pet. 1:12). These words of Peter refute the liberal theory that the prophets ministered only to their own time: Peter states the very opposite to the liberal theory, namely, that when the prophets predicted things pertaining to Christ and the new covenant salvation they did not serve their contemporaries or speak to them, but to the people of the new covenant time. The liberal theory is thus in direct conflict with what the Bible itself clearly says.

In the question of the nature and interpretation of biblical prophecies we are face to face with this alternative: Either we accept the biblical prophecies as they are, and the teaching of Scripture concerning the nature and fulfillment of the prophecies as we find them in the Holy Writ, or reject what the Bible says and adopt the preconceived theory of the critics, which makes of practically all biblical predictions forgeries and swindles.

The liberal critics claim that they study and interpret biblical prophecies in a scientific, objective and historical manner. In reality their way to deal with them is extremely unscientific, subjective and unhistorical. Its main purpose seems to be to throw down the Scripture-based faith that God truly "has of old spoken to the fathers in the prophets" (Heb. 1:1), and that He has done nothing, and is doing nothing important unless He has revealed His secret to His servants the prophets (Am. 3:7).

VII. UNITY OF ISAIAH

Until the latter part of the 18th century, the Book of Isaiah was believed to have been written by Isaiah, son of Amoz, about 700 years B.C. Professor A. B. Davidson wrote: "For about twenty-five centuries no one dreamt of doubting that Isaiah the son of Amoz was the author of every part of the book that goes under his name" (**Old Testament Prophecy,** p. 244, acc. to AUI, p. 41). But since J. C. Doederlein in 1775 published his commentary on Isaiah (**Esaias**), liberal scholars have generally held that the book of Isaiah comprises at least two distinct works, namely, the actual book of Isaiah, chapters 1-39, and the other part, chapters 40-66, usually called "Second Isaiah" (Deutero-Isaiah), an anonymous work assumed to have been written about 545-537 B.C. The usual explanation is that by some accident it has been attached to the book of Isaiah.

However, the criticism has not stopped here. It has also split the first part of the book of Isaiah into a number of units which it claims to be from different times and by various authors. Many critics even break the second part of this book into two or more fractions.

1. Liberal Splitting of Isaiah

R. H. Pfeiffer is one of the leading Protestant liberal critics in America, and we use him here as a representative of that trend.

Pfeiffer ascribes a number of passages in the first part of Isaiah, such as 7:15, 18-25; 8:9f., 19-22; 9:1-7, to much later times, denying that they were written by Isaiah. The same he does to the vision of judgment and God's kingdom in chs. 24-27, and also chs. 32-35 (**op. cit.,** pp. 417-420, 435-442; Harrelson, **op. cit.,** pp. 226f., sets forth about the same liberal view).

Pfeiffer explains that the first part of Isaiah was

originally "a collection of separate little books. They circulated as separate small collections of oracles which were repeatedly "edited" or revised, before they were all copied on a single roll of papyrus. About 200 B.C. the final editor copied the material in chs. 40-66 after the material in chs. 1-39, and so the book of Isaiah was born, as we have it (**op. cit.**, pp. 447f.).

According to A. B. Davidson, this kind of splitting up of the book of Isaiah is based on the general "canon of interpretation" that the "prophetic writer always makes the basis of his prophecies the historical position in which he himself is placed," and that "the purpose of prophecy as exercised in Israel was mainly ethical, bearing on the life and manners of the people among whom the prophet lived" (acc. t. AUI, p. 44).

We have seen how this "canon of interpretation" is a fanciful preconceived idea of the critics, having no biblical and historical basis. True, it applies to a part of biblical prophecies, namely, to the ones that deal with the prophets' contemporary situations and people; but it does not apply to prophetical predictions.

The only reason why the critics deny the Isaianic origin of such passages as 7:18-25, chs. 13-19, etc. is the fact that they contain predictions of future events.

The book of Isaiah—like many other prophetical books—contains a number of predictive prophecies of events so far in future that it is impossible even for the critics to explain that they were written at the time or after their coming true. We ask: Does it really help, from the point of view of the said liberal "canon," to ascribe these prophecies to times a few centuries later, as they even in that case contain prophecies whose fulfillment was centuries and even millenniums in the future? Does it really make much difference if the fulfillment of a prophetical prediction is, let us say, 300 or 700 years later? If the divine Spirit who revealed future events through the prophets could span the period of 300 years, why could He not as well span 700 years? Does God have some limit in His foreknowledge, so that He is still able to see 300 years into the future, but not more?

If God who has planned everything and guides the course of events according to His counsel, knowing everything from the beginning to the end, has really spoken to and through the prophets, we have no reason or right to limit the scope of prophetic foretelling and no reason to ascribe to later times those portions of the book of Isaiah that deal with future events.

The liberals pay some lip-service to God, but in reality they deny the existence of the living God of the Bible. The "god" of the liberals, who does not see much farther into the future than men see, who has not been able to reveal to the prophets future things, and to accomplish much more than ordinary men can, is no true God but an idol, a creation of these critics "after their own image," as ignorant and powerless as they are.

The historical section in Is. 39-49 is usually explained by the critics to be an "extract from the Kings." In reality the corresponding section of the Kings (2 Ki. 18-20) must be from Isaiah, and not **vice versa**: 2 Chr. 32:32 report that Isaiah wrote a history of king Hezekiah. Since 2 Ki. was written ab. 150 years after Isaiah, its writer must have used this history book by Isaiah. How could an earlier writer use a book that was written so much later?

One of the central themes of the first part of Is. is the deliverance of Jerusalem and Judah from the Assyrian army of Sennacherib. This event is spoken of several times in this part of the book, at first in its predictions, and then in the historical record of their fulfillment. Is. 29:5-8 has one of these predictions, the clearest one:

> "The multitude of thy foes shall be like small dust, and the multitude of the terrible ones as chaff that passeth away; yea, it will be in an instant, suddenly. She [the Assyrian army] will be visited by the Lord of hosts with thunder, and with an earthquake, and great noise, with whirlwind and tempest, and the flame of devouring fire."

HATH GOD SAID?

This was the manner in which an "angel of the Lord went forth and smote in the camp of the Assyrians 185,000 men," as we read in Is. 37:36, and not by "epidemic in the camp," as Robert J. Marshall explains (TMA, p. 97), following the usual liberal interpretation that does not care for what the Bible says.

Pfeiffer (**op. cit.**, pp. 435f.) explains that God did not really save Jerusalem in 701 B.C., as the Bible reports. The story of this event, Pfeiffer says, arose a century later: People believed then that Hezekiah had turned to the Lord in prayer, and that the Lord had repented of the evil that He had pronounced against Judah and Jerusalem. From this there was only one step to say that Sennacherib's army had been destroyed in the night by an angel of the Lord.

Thus, according to Pfeiffer, all this was later invention and forgery. He, and other critics who follow a similar line, have no other basis for their imaginary explanation than their unbelief that does not permit them to admit supernatural divine miracles.

2. Cyrus and the "Servant of the Lord"

The second part of the book of Isaiah contains two main groups of prophecies and two great themes: The first of them deals with the deliverance of the Jewish exiles from Babylon through Cyrus and the second with the greater spiritual deliverance of sinners through Christ.

With regard to the second part of the book of Isaiah, chs. 40-66, the critics agree only on one thing, that it was not written by Isaiah son of Amoz. They are sharply divided in their opinions on practically everything else in these chapters. Pfeiffer (**op. cit.**, pp. 453-459) classifies their views on the structure and authorship of Is. 40-66 as follows:

1. These chapters are a unity. This is the opinion of C. C. Torrey **(The Second Isaiah)**, E. Koenig **(Das Buch Jesaja)**, L. Glahn **(Die Einheit von Kap. 40-66 des Buch**

Jesaja), W. F. Albright (**The Archeology of Palestine and the Bible**) etc.

2. Chs. 40-55 and 56-66 have been written by two different men. A. Kuenen (**De godsdienst van Israel** II, 1889) held that chapters 50-51, 54-56 were written for the most part in Palestine by the "school" of Second Isaiah. According to B. Duhm and K. Marti, the Second Isaiah wrote chapters 40-55 shortly before 538, and the Third Isaiah wrote chs. 56-66 after 538 in Palestine. This theory of Duhm and Marti is widely accepted among the critics (Harrelson, **op. cit.**, pp. 247-252, belongs to this group).

3. Many critics divide chapters 40-66 into several separate units, written by different men.

The variety of the critical opinions on the second part of the book of Isaiah shows that they follow here, too, their subjective methods, each of them bringing forth what seems good in his own eyes.

Acts 8:21ff. tells how the Ethiopian eunuch asked Philip, of whom did the prophet speak in Is. 53, of himself or some other. Despite the clear answer given by the NT that the prophet spoke here of Christ and His sufferings on Calvary, the critics, disregarding this testimony of Scripture, continue to ask this question and set forth their own subjective opinions, which they claim to be "scientific theology."

The critical theories fall into two types: Those that regard the "servant of the Lord" as a personification of the people of Israel, and those that hold that he is an individual.

Pfeiffer (**op. cit.**, 459-462) lists the following theories:

1. The servant is the people of Israel.

2. He is a historical character of past or contemporary history: Moses, Hezekiah, Jeremiah, Jehoiachin, Zerubbabel, the Second Isaiah himself (as described by his followers).

3. An unnamed contemporary of the author: A teacher of Torah afflicted with leprosy, or a pious sufferer.

HATH GOD SAID?

4. The dying and resurrected god of vegetation of pagan mythology: Tammuz—Adonis or Eshmun.

5. The Messiah, either future Messiah in general, or Jesus Christ.

6. The Servant is both Israel and an individual. Franz Delitzsch (**Bibl. Kommentar ueber den Propheten Jesaja**, 4th ed. 1889, p. 432) conceives the Servant under the figure of a pyramid in which the basis is Israel as a whole, the middle level being Israel according to the spirit, and the apex Messiah, the Redeemer.

* * *

The conservative view, which takes the Bible's own interpretation as authoritative, holds that the "situation" of the utterances of the prophecies in Is. 40ff. is given in the final verses of ch. 39:

When envoys came to Hezekiah from Merodach-Baladan, king of Babylon, he showed to them all his treasures and other resources. Ostensibly the envoys had come to congratulate Hezekiah for his recovery from his illness, but in reality they wanted to secure his support in the Babylonian king's struggle against Assyria.

Isaiah obviously saw in the act of Hezekiah human boastfulness that deserved rebuke. He predicted to him that Judah would be taken captive to Babylon, and that the things that Hezekiah had shown to the envoys also would be taken there.

When Isaiah, through divine revelation, saw all the calamities that would befall Jerusalem and Judah, and its exile in Babylonia, he received from the Lord additional revelations which were intended to help and guide the exiles at the time when their deliverance from the exile was at the doors. This was the **situation** of Is. 40ff.

The Lord did not, however, limit His revelations to the deliverance from the exile through Cyrus. He also gave the prophet additional revelations concerning the future Messiah and salvation through Him. The Messianic prophecies of the first part of Is. (9:1-7; 11:1-5; 25:6-8, etc.) were supplemented by these new ones, which described the coming salvation in more detail.

* * *

Is. 40-48 speak 7 or 8 times of Cyrus and deliverance from the Babylonian exile. The most important of them is the elaborate song of praise in 44:24-28, where the name of Cyrus is mentioned the first time and which speaks of the deliverance in the "prophetical perfect," as though already accomplished—although it was in the future. The heathen idols are "vanity," and the Lord shows His pre-eminence over them as the sovereign Ruler who reveals beforehand what will take place in the future.

Some interpreters have thought that such titles as "my shepherd" and "his anointed" applied to Cyrus are indications that the prophet hailed him at first as the Messiah; only after Cyrus had attributed his victories to Marduk, chief god of Babylon, instead of the Lord of Israel, did he realize his mistake and projected his hope of salvation to the future "Servant."

However, this view has no basis in the text. The prophecy states quite clearly that Cyrus was not a worshiper of the Lord of Israel: "Thou hast not known me" (45:4f.).

Cyrus was not the only foreign ruler whom God used to accomplish His ends and to whom titles of this type were applied. Jeremiah called Nebuchadnezzar a "servant" of the Lord (25:9; 27:6; 43:10). Hazael, king of Syria, was anointed by Elijah at the command of the Lord (1 Ki. 19:15). That Cyrus is called a "shepherd" and "anointed" of the Lord did not imply that any Messianic expectations were attached to him (cp. AUI, pp. 48-55).

Josephus (**Antiquities** XI, 1:50f.), who lived in the first century A.D., speaks of Isaiah as the author of the book under his name. He also refers expressly to the prophecy on Cyrus. He relates that "Cyrus read this [prophecy in the book of Isaiah] and admired the divine power," and that "an earnest desire and ambition seized upon him to fulfill what was so written" (AUI, pp. 56f.).

The critics lay aside this statement of Josephus as though void of historical value. Pfeiffer writes: "Josephus glibly states that Cyrus read the prediction about himself in the book which Isaiah had left behind" **(op. cit.,** p. 415). The liberals have, however, for this view of theirs no other basis than that, according to their theory, the second part of Isaiah could not have been written by Isaiah son of Amoz, since it was impossible for him to predict events that were nearly 200 years ahead.

The event related by Josephus shows that the whole book of Isaiah was in existence in 539-537 B.C. and was then believed to have been written by Isaiah.

* * *

The second and far more important theme in Is. 40-66 is salvation through the "servant of the Lord."

This term does not mean the same thing every time. It is used several times of the people of Israel (e.g. 41:8f.; 44:1f.; 45:4; 49:3). When used in this sense in chs. 54-66 it is always in the plural.

We are, however, here concerned with the special "four songs of the Servant" in 42:1-4; 49:1-6; 50:4-9 and 52:13-53:12, in which this term is used of the future Messiah. The most important of these Servant Songs is ch. 53, which is the summit of OT prophecy. From the Apostolic Age on Christians have seen it as a prophetic description of the events of Calvary. Is. 61:1-3 should be included in these Servant Songs: Christ applied it to Himself in His speech in the synagogue of Nazareth (Lk. 4:18f.). The word "servant" is, however, not used in this passage.

The NT quotes Is. 53 several times, always speaking of it as a prophecy of Christ. The quotations are as follows:

Mt. 8:17 quotes Is. 53:4 as fulfilled in Jesus' ministry of healing.

Lk. 22:37 quotes in part Is. 53:12 as fulfilled in Jesus' burial.

Jh. 12:38 and Rom. 10:16 quote Is. 53:1 as fulfilled in the refusal of the Jews to accept Jesus as the Messiah and to believe the Gospel proclaimed by His messengers.

In Acts 8:32ff. the evangelist Philip explains Is. 53:7f. as having been fulfilled in Christ.

1 Pet. 2:22 refers to Is. 53:9 as predicting the sinlessness of Jesus.

1 Pet. 2:24f. uses phrases taken from Is. 53:5f. as having been fulfilled in the substitutionary suffering of Christ and healing through His wounds.

Refusing to accept this NT interpretation as normative, the critics have offered almost every other conceivable possibility, as we have seen. Their basic reason is the same as the one given for the rejection of the Isaianic authorship of other passages that contain predictions of future events. Thus they deny the truth of the quoted statement in 1 Pet. 1:12 that in speaking of Christ and His suffering the prophets ministered to the people of the new covenant time.

It is impossible to interpret the Suffering Servant of Is. 53 as Israel or some historical Israelite personality, for His sufferings were **substitutionary**; he carried the sins of others for their salvation, being Himself sinless. It was "our sins" that He bore.

The Israelites' sufferings in the exile were not substitutionary, for the Bible teaches clearly that they suffered the punishment of their own sins. Ez. 14:14, 20, written in the exile, says that even if such righteous (though not sinless) men as Noah, Daniel and Job were in the sinful city of Jerusalem they could save only "their own selves by their righteousness," not even their son or daughter. These passages clearly reject the idea of a substitutionary and saving suffering of the "pious remnant" of Israel. The critical idea that Is. 53 speaks of Israel or its pious remnant or some historical person (past or contemporary) suffering for the salvation of others is therefore in plain conflict with the teachings of the OT.

The One who, according to Is. 53, "bore the sins of many" cannot be anybody else than Jesus Christ. It is of Him that this chapter speaks, according to the NT.

The critics admit that the NT parallel is obvious: the sufferings of Jesus on Calvary resemble greatly the sufferings of the Servant in Is. 53; but they do not want to admit that they were the **fulfillment** of this prophecy, as the NT teaches. The critics speak of how the NT **applies** Is. 53 to Christ, but they deny that it is a predictive prophecy of His vicarious suffering and death on Golgotha for the salvation of sinners. Their basic reason is their denial of real foretelling prophecy, and their theory that the prophets always spoke to their contemporaries, not to future generations.

If one would consistently apply the critical theory of the nature of prophecy both to the passages on Cyrus and Is. 53, he should conclude:

Since the Cyrus prophecies speak vividly of the victories of this conquerer, as if he were on the point of striking at Babylon, they must be dated shortly before the fall of that city, or about 540 B.C. Likewise, since Is. 53 describes the sufferings of Christ just as vividly, as though the writer had been present at Calvary, this chapter must have been written by an eyewitness after these events, not earlier than 30 A.D., for this is the exact "situation" of this chapter.

This is, however, impossible, for Is. 53 existed before Christ: It was in the Septuagint, translated ab. 300-200 B.C., and it is also in the Dead Sea Isaiah scroll that was copied in the second century B.C.

Some critics are inconsistent: Although they follow the critical theory that Isaiah was not able to write the Cyrus prophecies, they still believe in Is. 53 as a prediction of Christ's sufferings on Calvary. They do not see that such an intermediate position is inconsistent and untenable. The very arguments that deny the Isaianic authorship of the Cyrus prophecies, if logically followed, also destroy the Messianic character of Is. 53.

Consistent critics deny all Messianic prophecy in the OT. E. W. Heaton states the position of such critics as follows: : "There is nothing in the Old Testament which can properly be interpreted as a prediction of the Messiah of the New Testament" (**His Servants the Prophets,** p. 112; acc. to AUI, p. 100).

An infidel interpretation of the Bible like this destroys the foundation of the Christian faith.

It is plain inconsistency to deny the possibility that Isaiah son of Amoz has written the Cyrus prophecies and at the same time admit that Deutero-Isaiah is the author of the Servant of the Lord poems, which undeniably are messianic.

It is in general inconsistent to break up the book of Isaiah into fractions that are from different times on the basis of the theory that the prophets spoke only from the point of view of their contemporary situation and of things that were important to the people of their time—and at the same time admit that many of these (supposedly anonymous) prophecies contain predictions that to their authors were in a more or less distant future.

Modern Sunday School Material

R. J. Marshall sets forth in the LCA book THE MIGHTY ACTS OF GOD and its TEACHER'S GUIDE the common liberal view that Is. 40-66 was not written by Isaiah but by an anonymous person writing about one and a half centuries later. He denies that Is. 53 is a prediction of the suffering and death of Christ (thus rejecting the NT interpretation) and explains: "The prophet did not connect the suffering of the servant with the Messiah, because the Messiah was still thought of in the narrow sense as an earthly king. In 45:1 it is Cyrus who is called the anointed, in other words, the Messiah. Thus Second Isaiah used the title to refer to a person chosen for the time to fulfill God's purpose" (TG, p. 101). The book explains that the "servant of the Lord" in Isaiah 40-66 is Israel, which is personified in these poems. Marshall says that the Second Isaiah "also likes to think of the Jews as personified in an individual" (TMA, p. 125).

Marshall admits that Jesus "applied" the prophecies of the suffering servant to Himself; but he asserts that they were not originally so intended. "By assuming the title 'servant of the Lord,' Jesus showed that he was taking the place of Israel as the agent of God's salvation" (TG. p. 101). "Jesus accepted the servant passages as the best explanations of his work" (TG, p. 127). The "early church relied on it heavily to explain Jesus' death" (TG. p. 191).

Thus, in the typical liberal manner these LCA books deny the prophetic quality of the Servant passages, namely, that they are predictions of Christ, as the NT interprets them. According to this liberal interpretation set forth by Marshall e.g., the following passages originally meant the people of Israel: "He was wounded for our transgressions, he was bruised for our iniquities; the chastisement of or peace was on him; and with his stripes we are healed. . . . the Lord laid on him the iniquity of us all . . . He had done no violence, neither was any deceit in his mouth . . . Thou wilt make his soul an offering for sin . . . By his knowledge will my righteous servant justify many; for he will bear our iniquities."

It would hardly be possible to give any more unbiblical, impossible and senseless interpretation of these passages than to assert that they originally spoke of the people of Israel!

In fact, Marshall—and with him the liberals in general—claim that they know and understand the real meaning of the passages better than Christ and His apostles.

True, Marshall speaks of the fulfillment of the OT Messianic prophecies in Christ (TG, p. 132); but this is, in the main, empty lip-service, since he denies the true predictive nature of most of them.

A considerable part of the OT Messianic prophecies is in the Psalms, and the NT refers freqently to them as predictions fulfilled in Christ. Marshall writes of them: "Though very little in the Psalms should be considered prophecy, the New Testament writers often looked to them for Messianic predictions" (TG, p. 144).

Marshall represents here the common liberal view that Christ and the NT writers erred at this point, and that they, the liberal critics, know the thing better.

Marshall explains Is. 9:6 ("For to us a child is born, . . . and his name will be called Wonderful, Counsellor, Mighty God, Everlasting

Father, Prince of Peace") as follows: The term 'Mighty God' comes from a Hebrew phrase that can mean 'mighty hero.' 'Father' was used because the king was head over all the families of the realm" (TG, p. 85). "Since the king was called 'Messiah,' a title arising from the anointing ceremony at his coronation, Isaiah's hope came to be called Messianic' " (TMA, p. 99).

By means of this kind of interpretation Marshall robs the clearest predictions of the OT concerning the coming Christ of all real prophetic meaning, following the general liberal denial of true predictive prophecy, or trying to limit it as much as possible.

The ALC book THE BIBLE: BOOK OF FAITH, moves in the interpretation of Isaiah along similar lines of liberal unbelief. It says of Is. 40-66: "The 'Edict of Cyrus' (538 B.C.) freed the Jews. This forms the background for the writings in Isaiah 40-66, chapters later attached for uncertain reasons to the sermons of Isaiah of Jerusalem from the eighth century. In glorious poetry the unknown author of Isaiah proclaims that the faithful Israelites constitute a 'Suffering Servant.' Through the sufferings of the Israelites the redemption of the world was coming nearer (words which Christians see fulfilled in the sufferings of Jesus Christ, who is 'Israel reduced to one')" (pp. 43f.).

Thus, this TALC book also denies that Is. 53, etc., was a real prediction of Christ. According to the OT, the Israelites were a sinful nation (Is. 1:4: "Ah sinful nation, a people laden with iniquity..."), but according to Is. 53:9 the Suffering Servant was sinless: "He had done no violence, neither was any deceit in his mouth." Being Himself sinless, He bore the sins of mankind, for "the Lord laid on him the iniquity of us all."

If the "faithful Israelites" constituted the Suffering Servant, who was sinless and our sinbearer, why was Christ needed at all?

There is no consistent and tenable intermediate position between the liberal and Bible-believing positions. We must choose one of them, **either** the critical stand of unbelief, which denies the possibility and reality of predictive prophecy, and practically everything supernatural, **or** the biblical position which believes in the reality of divine revelation. In the prophecies of Scripture this revelation is directed partly to the past, partly to the present, and partly to the future.

By rejecting the Christ-given apostolic interpretation

of OT prophecies the critics have taken a stand against Christ Himself, denying Him as true God in whom all the treasures of wisdom and knowledge are hidden, and in whose mouth there was no falsehood. Scripture says of those who deny Christ:

> "Every spirit that confesseth not Jesus is not of God; and this is that spirit of the antichrist, whereof ye have heard that he cometh; and even now already it is in the world" (1 Jh. 4:3).

The words of Christ still stand:

> "Heaven and earth will pass away; but my words will not pass away" (Mk. 13:31).

> "He who rejecteth me and receiveth not my words, hath one that judgeth him: the word that I have spoken will judge him on the last day" (Jh. 12:48).

3. Historical Facts that Support the Unity of Isaiah

There is not a single historical fact that would support the liberal splitting of the book of Isaiah into two or more parts that are by different authors and from different times. On the contrary, all the known historical facts support its unity and authenticity. We list the most important of them:

1. Every OT prophetical book without exception has a heading which gives the name of its author. This universal rule renders inconceivable the critical assumption that large parts of several prophetical books are combinations of anonymous prophetical oracles, possibly by unknown disciples of known prophets.

2. The most ancient manuscripts of Isaiah give no support to the theory that it is a conglomeration of writings of different men who lived at different times, most of them unknown. The whole book is in the Isaiah scroll found in a cave near the Dead Sea in 1947, dating from about the middle of the second century B.C., and the whole book is in the Septuagint version that is about a century older.

3. The OT and ancient Jewish history knows nothing

of the existence of a great prophet in the late exilic and early post-exilic times. This is a serious objection to the theory of the existence of such a prophet. It is hard to believe that one of the greatest prophets would have lived in that time, but that no mention would be found of him in any OT book or in any Jewish source.

4. Is. 40:9 and 62:6 show that the city of Jerusalem existed at the time of the writing of this part of the book of Isaiah:

> "O Zion, that bringest good tidings . . . ; O Jerusalem, that bringest good tidings, lift up thy voice with strength; lift it up, be not afraid; say to the cities of Judah, Behold your God."

> "I have set watchmen on thy walls, O Jerusalem, who shall never hold their peace."

How could an unknown prophet speak in this way of Jerusalem and the cities of Judah at a time when they were in ruins, and when no watchmen were on the walls of Jerusalem—as the liberal theory holds?

5. Outside the OT, the earliest evidence of the existence of the whole book of Isaiah is in the apocryphal Ecclesiasticus, written c. 180 B.C. We read in this book (48:24ff.) a statement on Isaiah, how he saw "what would come to pass at the last, and he comforted those who mourned in Zion." The words obviously refer to the words in Is. 40:1: "Comfort ye, comfort ye . . ." and thus presuppose the existence of the second part of Is.

It is wholly impossible that—as some critics assume—some of the prophecies of Is. could date from the century of the writer of Ecclesiasticus (Jesus, son of Sirach), and that this book could have been given its final form in his lifetime, for the whole book of Isaiah was believed at that time to be an ancient book written by Isaiah son of Amoz about five centuries earlier.

6. The NT mentions Isaiah about 21 times (E. J. Young, **op. cit.**, pp. 219f., gives a list of these passages),

that is, more often than all the other writing prophets altogether. The citations are almost equally from each of the main parts of the book. Thus, the NT clearly supports Isaianic authorship and the unity of the book of Isaiah. For every believing Christian this is decisive—and all other known facts are in harmony with this NT testimony.

Note:

Differences in Style and Theories of Multiple Authorship

One of the arguments that the critics have given for their multiple-authorship theories of the Pentateuch, Isaiah and some other biblical books (Zech., 1-2 Tim., Tit., etc.) are the the differences in style found in these books (in the case of Paul's epistles, between the Pastoral epistles and the rest).

Pastor A. Q. Morton of Scotland published in the Nov. 1963 issue of THE OBSERVER his article: "A Computer Challenges the Church," in which he told of his computer studies of the epistles of Paul. According to his report, these studies gave the result that five of Paul's letters were by a single writer, and that the rest of them had been written by five different authors. Morton based his study on the theory that the use of certain common words, such as in, but, and, etc. was the key to the writer's style. The freqency and pattern of the use of these words was assumed to remain remarkably constant in each writer's production, being as individually distinctive to a man's writing as the pattern of his fingerprints to his hands.

Dr. John W. Ellison, an Episcopal minister in Winchester, Mass., applied Morton's method to his own articles in THE OBSERVER. He divided Morton's first article into three parts and studied by means of a computer the frequency with which seven common words appeared in the different parts. Then he compared these results with the frequency of the same words in Morton's second article in THE OBSERVER (Nov. 10). His result was that the pattern fluctuated from part to part moderately to wildly. The pattern of the first article did not match the pattern of the second one (which was Morton's reply to his critics). According to Dr. Ellison, the computer studies could not prove that Morton's articles were written by the same man, and yet this was beyond doubt the case, for they were signed by him. The frequency of the words varied from one portion of his article to another from the mean use by anywhere from 5 to 88 per cent.

Ellison asserted that he "could prove [by computer studies] that five authors wrote James Joyce's Ulysses," and that none of them wrote the

"Portrait of the artist as a Young Man." At least six authors could thus be assigned to the two novels, Ellison suggested. "This demonstrates," Ellison said, "that in one writer, a wide pattern of variation can exist" (McCandlish Phillips, "Computer in Search of Authors. Can Find them in Bible or Joice," Jan. 22, 1965, The New York Times; acc. to Christian Beacon, Feb. 18, 1965, p. 3).

Certain critics have used essentially similar methods in their studies of the Pentateuch, Isaiah, the epistles of Paul, etc., concluding that the differences in the use of certain words show differences in authorship. Dr. Ellison's results show that this method is wholly unreliable, and that the theories of the multiple authorship based on them are sheer fancy.

VIII. AUTHORSHIP AND RELIABILITY OF THE BOOK OF DANIEL

The book of Daniel is of fundamental significance for the NT revelation. According to Mt. 24:15, Jesus based His prediction of the destruction of Jerusalem on what was "spoken of by Daniel the prophet." These words of Jesus show that the prophet whose name was Daniel really existed, and that his prophecy was true (He referred to Dan. 9:27; not to Dan. 11:31, for this passage speaks of a different abomination and desolation, namely, that produced by Antiochus IV).

It was from the book of Daniel that Jesus took the term "Son of Man" which He used of Himself, indicating thereby that He was the one "like the Son of man," who was to "come with the clouds of heaven" and receive "dominion, glory, and kingdom, that all peoples, nations, and languages should serve him" (Dan. 7:13f.). Jesus used almost the same words as He spoke of His second coming:

> "They will see the Son of man coming in the clouds of heaven with power and great glory" (Mt. 24:30).

Jesus obviously referred to the passage of Dan. also when He said to Caiaphas:

> "Hereafter ye will see the Son of man sitting at the right hand of Power, and coming on the clouds of heaven" (Mt. 26:64).

The prophecies of the book of Revelation concerning the last beast-power that blasphemes God and makes war with His saints, and which will be destroyed at the second coming of Christ, are built on the prophecies of Dan. 7 concerning the last horn or beast, which is described in Dan. and Rev. in about the same manner.*

---

*On this, see U. Saarnivaara, **Harmageddon—before and after** (Minneapolis, Minn., 1966), chapter 11.

The NT teaching of the resurrection of the dead, both of the righteous and the wicked, is likewise closely connected with Daniel (12:2f.). The prophecy of seventy year-weeks in Dan. 9:24-27 contains an accurate prophecy of how the Messiah was to "make reconciliation for iniquity, and to bring in everlasting righteousness, ... and ... confirm the [new] covenant," and also of the destruction of Jerusalem in 70 A.D. The teachings of the NT on these things are closely tied up with this prophecy of Daniel.

The early Christians appealed to these and some other prophecies of Daniel as proofs of the supernatural character of the Bible and the reality of the divine inspiration of the prophets.

1. Criticism of Porphyry

Pagan writers had made many assaults on Christianity, but they had not been able to shake it. Christian authors had refuted them with undeniable facts and effectively. The pagan neo-platonic philosopher Porphyry used a new method in his book AGAINST THE CHRISTIANS (c. 270 A.D.). As the Christians often appealed to the book of Daniel and showed how its prophecies had come true, Porphyry aimed his attack against this book and tried to show that it was not written by Daniel but was a literary forgery composed in the time of the Syrian king Antiochus IV Epiphanes and the Maccabeans in the second century B.C. He could not deny the historical reality of the first four kingdoms in Dan. 2 and 7, but he attempted to undermine trust in this book (and the Bible in general) by showing that instead of containing real predictions of future events its "predictions" were in reality forgeries written after the events. He asserted that the writer wrote correctly of the events up to his time, but could not see into the future. "Daniel did not so much foretell coming events as he told of things that had taken place. What he told up to Antiochus was true history; if he guessed something after that point of time, it was error, for he did not know the future" (acc. to Jerome, J. P. Migne, **Patrologia latina XXV:491**).

HATH GOD SAID? 139

The most important of Daniel's prophecies on the world-empires are the image-prophecy in Dan. 2 and the beast and horn prophecies in Dan. 7-8. They are as follows:

1. The golden head of the image=the first lion-like beast=Babylonia.

2. The silver breast of the image=the second bear-like beast=the ram with two horns=Medo-Persia.

3. The brazen belly and thighs of the image=the third leopard-like beast with 4 wings and 4 heads=the he-goat with a great horn that broke, and 4 horns came up in its place=Alexander the Great's empire and the 4 kingdoms into which it was divided after his death. The "little horn" that came up from one of the 4 horns was Antiochus IV Epiphanes.

4. The iron legs of the image=the fourth beast with iron teeth=Rome.

5. The 10 horns of the fourth beast=the 10 kingdoms that were formed in the area of Rome when it broke down.

6. The two feet of iron and clay of the image and their 10 toes=the little horn of Dan. 7:8, 20ff. that came up from among the 10 horns of the fourth beast (Rome) and that later looked larger than the others, and which blasphemed God and made war with His saints, till one like the Son of Man comes with the clouds of heaven, and this horn-beast will be destroyed=the last beast of Rev. 13, 17, 19 with its ten horns, which blasphemes God and makes war with His saints, and which will be seized at the second coming of Christ and cast into the lake of fire.

In the image-prophecy the stone that smites the image at its feet and toes, crushing them and the whole image and becoming a great mountain that fills the whole earth describes the same event as Dan. 7:13f., namely, the coming of the one like the Son of Man on the clouds to take dominion and kingdom over all the nations of the earth, in connection with which the last blaspheming beast that makes war with the saints of God will be destroyed.

In order to refute these prophecies of Daniel, Porphyry limited the brazen belly and thighs of the image and the corresponding third leopard-like beast to Alexander's empire, transferring the four kingdoms into which it was divided into the fourth beast (=the legs of iron in the image). He explained that this beast's ten horns meant ten

Syrian kings, counting Antiochus IV as the eleventh. He identified the "little horns" of Dan. 7 and 8.

Porphyry calculated: By showing that the book of Daniel was a late literary forgery that contained no real fulfilled predictions he would shake the entire building of Christianity.

Porphyry's philosophical presuppositions were about the same as those of modern liberal critics, namely that real divine revelation and predictive prophecy are impossible. He explained that the writer of the book of Daniel was a deceiver who used Daniel's name as disguise, but did it with the purpose to encourage the Jews in the difficult times of the Syrian oppression.*

2. Modern Liberal Criticism

Christian teachers refuted the assertions of Porphyry, and his thoughts remained for a long time in the museum of historical peculiarities. The eighteenth century Rationalism, however, dug them up from this museum. Modern liberal criticism, its successor, has adopted Porphyry's main thoughts as irrefutable facts, and it holds about the same view of the book of Daniel as did Porphyry. Many of these critics go so far as to question the very existence of Daniel.**

The ALC book THE BIBLE: BOOK OF FAITH explains (pp. 45f.) that the book of Daniel was written in the time of Antiochus IV Epiphanes and the Maccabeans, and

---

* On Porphyry, see E. J. Young, op. cit., pp. 382f., LeRoy Edwin Froom, **The Prophetic Faith of our Fathers** I (Washington, D.C., 1950), pp. 326-33.

Harrelson, op. cit., p. 458, writes: "We cannot determine whether this Daniel of the stories (Daniel 1-6) ever lived." A. Lauha, formerly professor of OT in the theological department of the University of Helsinki and since 1964 bishop of Helsinki, writes: "In my view ... it is wholly improbable that there existed and acted in the exile a certain famous Daniel, who later became the hero of the book that has the same name" (Israelin profeettain historiankäsitys**/The Israelite Prophets' View of History/, Helsinki 1938, p. 67).

the LCA book THE MIGHTY ACTS OF GOD does the same (table p. 7 and p. 146).

The arguments of the critics are commonly the following:

1. The text in Dan. 2:4b-7:28 is late western Aramaic which was used in Palestine after the exile, but was not used in Babylonia, where eastern Aramaic was the language of the people. The Hebrew in Dan. 1 and 8-12 is late Hebrew and contains several words of Greek origin.

2. In telling of the events of older history the author of this book makes many mistakes. He says e.g. that the Jews were taken into the exile in the third year of king Jehoiakim (1:1), that Babylon was conquered by Darius, that he was a Mede, and that the Chaldean Belshazzar was Nebuchadnezzar's son (he was son of Nabonidus). The statement that Darius was son of Xerxes (Ahasuerus, 9:1) is also a mistake, and so is the statement that he was succeeded by Cyrus (6:28; 10:1). As the OT accidentally mentions only four Persian kings, the book of Daniel assumes (11:2) that the entire Persian rule comprised only these four kings. These mistakes show that the author of the book of Daniel had a deficient knowledge of the times when Daniel was supposed to have lived, although he had accurate knowledge of the events of the later Greek period which were significant to the Jews. In about the same way as Porphyry, the liberals commonly explain that the "little horn" of Dan. 7:8, 20ff. and the "little horn" of Dan. 8:9ff. are the same, namely, **Antiochus IV** Epiphanes. The sections of Dan. that deal with this king and the Maccabeans is, according to the liberals, history already lived, but in this book it has been put in a prophetic-apocalyptic garb. Some liberals (such as Gulin) assert that the author of Dan. was ignorant of the death of Antiochus in Persia in 164 B.C., and therefore they conclude that this book must have been written before this event, in 165-164 B.C.* Gulin

---

* We have followed here Gulin, op. cit., pp. 302ff. He represents a common liberal view; there are differences in minor details, but these are the rather general liberal arguments against the authenticity of Dan. Harrelson, op. cit., p. 464, identifies the "little horns" in Dan. 7 and 8.

explains that the writer of Dan. expected (12:11) the Messianic time to break in 1290 days after the desecration of the temple, or in the summer of 164 B.C.—which, however, failed to be realized. The 70 year-weeks of Dan. 9:24-27 are interpreted to end at the time when Antiochus caused the daily sacrifice to be discontinued in the temple and when it was desecrated.

3. What is the Truth?

In order to find out whether the book of Daniel is a true prophetical book or a forgery, we must examine the critical assertions point by point.

Languages of the Book of Daniel

The Hebrew and Aramaic languages are used both in Daniel and Ezra. This was natural at a time when the Jews were in the process of transition into the use of Aramaic as their every-day language, but when the Hebrew also was still employed. This transition took place in the period of the exile and after it. In the Maccabean period the transition was already behind, and Aramaic alone was used as every-day language. As early as in the time of Ezra and Nehemiah, less than a century after the exile (although a part of the Jews returned to Palestine with Ezra), most Jews were unable to understand the law in Hebrew, but it had to be interpreted for them in the Aramaic, as we read in Neh. 8:8 (this is the probable meaning of this passage).

The use of the two languages, Hebrew and Aramaic, was natural in the time of Daniel, the period of transition, while it would have been unnatural in the Maccabean age, when the transitional period was in the past.

The languages of Daniel and Ezra are closely related both in their Hebrew and Aramaic parts, whereas the Targums or Aramaic translations of the OT that were prepared by the Jews before Christ differ considerably from the Aramaic of Daniel and Ezra. In the Elephantine papyri which were written by the Jews who lived in Egypt about 500-400 B.C., or the time soon after Daniel, the Aramaic is quite like the Aramaic of Daniel. These linguistic facts support the conclusion that the book of Daniel must have been written in the period of the exile and soon after it (Dan. 9-12 belong to the time after the exile) and not in the Maccabean age.

Both Daniel and Ezra lived much of their life in Babylonia. The fact that both of them use the same type of western Aramaic shows that this was the language of the Jews both in the exile and after it. Since both of them wrote primarily for the Jews, they naturally employed the western Aramaic that was their everyday language, and not the eastern Aramaic that was used by the Babylonians.

The Hebrew language ceased to be the everyday language among the Jews but it never became extinct among the learned Jews who studied the OT in Hebrew and also used it to some extent as their literary language down to our time, when it has again become the living language of the Jews in Israel. With regard to the book of Daniel, the decisive thing is that its Aramaic is the Aramaic of the time of the exile and after it, and not the Aramaic of the Maccabean period.

The existence of some Greek words in the book of Daniel is natural, for the influence of Greek culture has been observed in Mesopotamia about five centuries before Daniel. The Greek words in Dan. are names of musical instruments (3:5, 15). Cultural products like these have been from ancient times international in nature, and they have been easily exported and imported from land to land (Möller, **op. cit.,** pp. 313-7.).

One of the critical arguments of the liberals against the authenticity of Dan. is that the term "Chaldeans" is used in 2:2, 4; 4:4, etc. of a certain group of "wise men" in Babylonia. Gulin (**op. cit.,** p. 301) writes: "It is impossible to think that in the period of the Chaldean rule the term Chaldeans could have been used in the sense of 'diviners,' 'interpreters of signs.'"

The "Chaldeans" who were the ruling nation in the empire of Babylonia did not inhabit an area within the actual province of Babylon but some distance south of it (see map). The use of this name of a certain group of wise men or diviners is probably due to the fact that they were from the Chaldean district. Herodot, a Greek historian who lived about a century after Daniel, in the period of Ezra and Nehemiah, speaks of a group of Babylonian priests who were called "Chaldeans," and his language implies that this group had existed in Babylonia a long time (Young, **op. cit.**, pp. 386f.).

In the Gospel of John (9:22 etc.) the term "Jews" is used of the leaders of the people, even though the nation as a whole was also called "Jews." As it would be wrong to assert that the Gospel of John could not have been written in the period of the apostles since the leaders of the Jews are called "Jews," so is the liberal assertion concerning the use of the term "Chaldeans" in the book of Daniel without factual foundation (cp. **The Pulpit Commentary,** Dan. 2:2).

Historical Facts

Dan. 1:1-4 reports that Nebuchadnezzar beseiged Jerusalem in the third year of the reign of Jehoiakim (608-597 B.C.). The Lord gave the city into his hands, and he took to Babylon not only a part of the vessels of the temple but also young men of the king's seed and of the princes, among them Daniel and his three friends. But in Jer. 25:1 we read that the first year of Nebuchadnezzar was the fourth year of Jehoiakim. The critics say that there is a mistake of one year in Dan. at this point.

The Babylonian historian Berosos writes that while his father Napobolassar still lived, Nebuchadnezzar went with an army to Syria and Palestine. While there, he defeated the army of pharaoh Necho at Charchemish, conquered Syria, Palestine, etc. He apparently besieged Jerusalem a short time, but after king Jehoiakim had fallen in his hands, the city surrendered. Jehoiakim probably apologized of his rebellion and was allowed to continue as king of Judah as vassal of Babylonia. Soon after this, Nebuchadnezzar received word about the death of his father, and he hurried to Babylonia, to take government in his own hands. The last two clay tablets of Napobolassar's reign are (according to our calendar) from the May and September of 505 B.C., and the first tablets of Nebuchadnezzar from the August and September of the same year. Thus, Nebuchadnezzar was obviously in Palestine in the summer of 505 B.C.

The discrepancy between Dan. 1:1-4 and Jer. 25:1 is not real: The first year of Nebuchadnezzar was partly Jehoiakim's third and partly his fourth year, and probably the events mentioned in Dan. 1:1-4 belonged partly to both of them. It is also possible that Dan. 1:1-4 speaks of Nebuchadnezzar as king at the time when he still was the crown prince—which is a common manner of speech among men.*

For the first group of Jews, the exile began in 605 B.C. (other groups were taken to Babylonia in 597 and 586 B.C.). The 70 years of the exile, mentioned in Dan. 9:2, Jer. 25:11f., 29:10 and 2 Chr. 36:21, which the Jews had to "serve the king of Babylon," started from this point of time. The period from 605 to 536 B.C., when the first group of Jews returned to their own land, was 70 years (Free, **op. cit.,** pp. 224f., 237; Jamieson-Fausset-Brown Commentary, 2 Chr. 36:6; Jer. 25:1; Dan. 1:1).

In older times, liberal critics asserted that such a king as Belshazzar had never existed. They have had to give up this position after some cuneiform scripts have been found which tell of how Nabonidus, the last king of Babylonia, "entrusted royal power" to his son Belshazzar, giving him the rule of the province of Babylon, and possibly of the whole empire. Nabonidus himself withdrew to Teman in

---

* Harrelson, **op. cit.,** p. 458, writes: "The story [of Daniel] begins with the exile of Daniel and other Jews in the third year of Jehoiakim (606-605 B.C.). This incorrect dating of the Babylonian Exile is only one of the historical inaccuracies found in this book." — In reality, this statement of Harrelson is one of the many historical inaccuracies in **his** book. The book of Daniel is historically accurate.

Arabia. When the Medes and Persians conquered Babylonia, they did not put him to death but gave him a pension. The words in Dan. 5:16, 29, that Belshazzar made Daniel the "third ruler in the kingdom" probably refer to this situation: Nabonidus was the first, Belshazzar was the second, and Daniel was (for a few hours) the third ruler.

That Nebuchadnezzar is called in Dan. 5:11, 18 the father of Belshazzar, although he was son of Nabonidus, contains no real historical error as the critics (e.g. Harrelson, **op. cit.,** p. 458) hold: Certain facts point in the direction that Nebuchadnezzar was Belshazzar's mother's father, that is, his grandfather, and the Bible often uses the term "father" to mean descendence in general, whether immediate or more distant. Another fact is that the Hebrews, Arameans and Babylonians used to call the successor of a king his "son," and the predecessor "father," whether a blood-relationship existed between them or not (Möller, **op. cit.,** pp. 328f.; Free, **op. cit.,** pp. 232-235).

One of the problems of the book of Daniel is, who was the "Darius the Median" (Dan. 5:31) who "took the kingdom, being about 62 years old," after Belshazzar had been slain in the night when the handwriting had appeared on the wall with the words, MENE, MENE ,TEKEL, UPHARSIN. Harrelson (**op. cit.,** p. 458) expresses the common liberal view in writing: "No Darius the Mede (5:30) succeeded Nabonidus or his son Belshazzar in Babylon."

The ancient historians Herodot and Xenophon report that the city of Babylon fell into the hands of Medes and Persians in connection with a great feast, just as we also read in Dan. 5. Xenophon relates that Cyrus did not conquer Babylon for himself but acted as a representative of his uncle and father-in-law Cyaxares II. It is obvious that this Cyaxares II was the "Darius the Mede" of Dan. 5:31 and 6:1ff. The word "Darajawus" was in Persian a title that meant "ruler," and the word "Uwakshatra" (Cyaxares) likewise was a title, meaning "sovereign." This explains why the same ruler was known by both names.

According to Xenophon, Cyaxares gave, after the conquest of Babylon, his daughter to Cyrus for wife and Media for dowry. He notes that Cyaxares had no (male) heir. This information confirms the statement of Dan. 5:31 that Darius was a Mede, and that Cyrus is mentioned as king after him (10:1). The fact that the Bible speaks, on the one hand, of Cyrus as the conquerer of Babylon, and on the other hand, of Darius as the conqueror, has its explanation in what has been said: Darius was the actual king, but being old, he let Cyrus take care of leadership in the conquest. The Bible thus contains no discrepancy or historical error on these things.

This holds true also concerning the statement in Dan. 9:1 that Darius (=Cyaxares II) was son of Ahasuerus. We have mentioned how e.g. Gulin identifies this Ahasuerus with Xerxes and declares that Dan. 9:1 contains a historical error.

The solution for this problem is found from the fact that many oriental rulers are known by several names. Before becoming king, Cyrus used the name Agradates. Smerdis, the successor of his son Cambyses, is called Ahasuerus in Ezra 4:6. As already pointed out, "Darius" was a title of Persian rulers, and several kings were therefore called by this name. Likewise, in the case of the name "Ahasuerus" we should find out who is the person meant, since besides referring to Cambyses, the OT uses this title also of another Persian ruler.

The Ahasuerus of Dan. 9:1 was **Astyages**, father of Cyaxares II=the Darius of Dan. 5:31, not Xerxes, as many critics explain. Cyrus was the son-in-law and successor of his son Darius or Cyaxares II, as already pointed out. The "Ahasuerus" of the book of Esther was a different man, the king who is known as Xerxes in secular history. The Artaxerxes of Ezra 6:7, 11, 17, 23 was Smerdis (not Cambyses, as Scofield explains), while the Artaxerxes of Ezra 7:1 was Artaxerxes Longimanus. The Darius of Ezra 5:5 was Darius Hystaspes.

The assertion that Dan. 11:2 has an error in stating that the Persian empire had but four kings disregards the fact that the Bible has many somewhat similar "gaps," but in no such case are we justified to speak of errors. In Mt. 1:8 we read that "Joram begat Ozias (Uzziah)," although there were three generations between them. Ezra 7:3 speaks of Azariah as son of Meraioth, although six generations were between the two. As already pointed out, in biblical language such terms as "father," "son," "begat," etc., mean that one is descendent of another, whether immediate or more distant.

Four Persian kings are referred to in Dan. 11:2 [three of them are mentioned in Ezra 4:6f., 23; 5:5: 1. Ahasuerus= Cambyses; 2. Artaxerxes=(Pseudo) Smerdis (Xenophon's Tanaoxares); 3. Darius (Hystaspes)]. The fourth king who came after them was the Ahasuerus or Xerxes of the book of Esther, known for his wars with the Greeks and the defeats that he suffered (the most important of them was the defeat at Salamis). After these defeats, the Persian power was, from the point of view of world politics and the biblical record, practically speaking dead, although it continued to exist. Because of this, Dan. 11 skips over the kings after Ahasuerus-Xerxes and takes up the thread of the story at Alexander the Great, in whom the third empire came to its summit and became important for Israel (see Jamieson-Fausset-Brown's Commentary, Dan. 11:2-3).

Daniel's Place in the OT Canon

The Hebrew OT usually has the book of Daniel in the third section, or the Writings (Kethubim). The critics explain that the reason for this is that "the canon of the prophets was regarded as being completed about the middle of the third century." Daniel's book was not accepted into it because it was written later. They add to this another argument, namely, that the apocryphal Ecclesiasticus, which was written about 180 B.C., does not mention Daniel in its list of Israel's famous men (Gulin, **op. cit.**, p. 301; cp. Harrelson, **op. cit.**, p. 547).

It is not true that the "canon of prophets" was finished and closed in the middle of the third century (Gulin: before 200 B.C., **op. cit.,** p. 347). This was done already c. 430 B.C., which is the latest possible time of Malachi, the last prophetical book of the OT. But at that time the Writings also existed and were regarded as sacred books, authoritative like the rest. The grandson of Jesus son of Sirach, author of the Ecclesiasticus, wrote about 130 B.C. that at the time of his grandfather the Writings belonged to the canon of the sacred books, alongside the Law and the Prophets. The fact that Jesus son of Sirach failed in his desire to have his book (Ecclesiasticus) accepted into the OT collection of sacred books shows that its limits were closed at that time. Josephus, who lived in the time of the apostles, wrote (on the basis of the OT Scriptures) in his history of the Jews **(Antiquities,** XI, 8:5) that the sacred books of the OT were written between Moses and the Persian king Artaxerxes I (464-424 B.C.), in whose time Ezra, Nehemiah and Malachi lived. The critics have rejected this statement of Josephus, but have given no valid reason.

In his list of OT books Josephus enumerates the Five Books of the Law, thirteen prophetical books, and four books in the Writings, which must be Job, the Psalms, the Proverbs, and Ecclesiastes. Daniel was in his list among the Prophets. This shows that the Jewish division of the OT was not yet definitely fixed at that time, but took place later. The often repeated liberal argument concerning the place of Daniel in the Hebrew OT has therefore no validity.

That the Jewish scribes placed the book of Daniel in the third division gives no indication of its age. The Writings (Kethubim) contain a number of psalms by David and his contemporaries Asaph and Jeduthun (c. 1020-975 B.C.), and the book of Job also must be from a time long before the exile since Ezekiel, who lived in the exile, speaks of him as a renowned godly man (14:14, 20). The critics date Job as post-exilic, but without valid reasons. The book of Daniel was placed among the Writings probably because he was, as to his official status, not a prophet but a statesman. He never stood up among his own peaple to proclaim to it the word that he had received from God, calling it to repentance. He lived in pagan royal courts as a high official. He had the gift of prophecy, but not the status of a prophet (Möller, **op. cit.,** pp. 339f; Young, **op.. cit.,** p. 38).

That Daniel is not mentioned in the poem that the grandson of Jesus son of Sirach wrote on the great men of Israel does not prove that it was written in the Maccabean period, about 165-4 B.C. This poem is not complete, and it does not contain such men as Ezra and Mordecai. Another possible explanation for the omission of Daniel's name is that he did not live and work among his own people and thus, in a sense, did not belong to the great men of Israel, although he was of Jewish extraction.

The assertion of some critics that the book of Daniel must have been written before the death of Antiochus IV since it does not speak of his death is based on error, for this book speaks of it twice:

"He [Antiochus] shall be broken without hand" (Dan. 8:25).

"He shall come to his end, and none will help him" (Dan. 11:45).

Antiochus died of severe illness, and no one was able to help him when the terrible disease made an end of him. Harrelson's **(op. cit.,** p. 457) assertion that Daniel's description of Antiochus' coming end "hardly corresponds with the actual end of this monarch," is strange indeed, for what Daniel says of the matter is in complete harmony with the manner in which Antiochus came to his end.

Among the manuscripts that have been found in the cave near the northwest end of the Dead Sea are some sections of the book of Daniel. The manuscripts are from the middle of the second century B.C. It is impossible that the Qumran community would have had Daniel among its sacred books alongside Isaiah, etc., if it had been composed in the lifetime of these people.

The first book of Maccabees which tells of the events of the period of Antiochus IV Epiphanes refers to Daniel as an accredited sacred book, and even refers to the Septuagint version of it, which must have been prepared in the previous century, as was the LXX in general. 1 Macc. 2:59f. speaks of the three friends of Daniel who were saved from fire because of their faith, and of Daniel who was saved from the mouths of lions because of his innocence. This shows that the writer of 1 Macc. knew the book of Daniel and used it. That he used in 1:54 the same expression, "abomination of desolation" (**bdelygma eremoseos**), as the Septuagint did indicates that the LXX version of Daniel existed at that time. The translation of Daniel in LXX is very poor. The translator(s) obviously was a stranger to the ideas and vocabulary of Daniel and in many cases did not understand the meaning of the text (because of this, Theodotion's version was substituted for it in the early Church). This would be inconceivable if this book would have been written in the same period as it was translated (Möller, **op. cit.,** pp. 338f.).

Reliability of Daniel's prophecies.

The liberals follow Porphyry in asserting that what the book of Daniel sets forth as predictions of future events are historically correct up to 165-4 B.C., but faulty after that point of time. Many critics* hold that even the prophecy of the 70 year-weeks in Dan. 9:24-27 ends at the Maccabean period in the 2nd century B.C.

Daniel was primarily a prophet of world empires. The most important of his world-empire prophecies are the following:

Chapter 2: Vision of the great image.

        7: The four beasts; ten horns; the last horn or beast that blasphemes God and persecutes His people; the coming of one like the Son of Man, destruction of the beast-horn and setting up of His universal kingdom.

---

* Puukko, **op. cit.,** pp. 310, 331; Gulin, **op. cit.,** p. 303; Harrelson, **op. cit.,** p. 465.

8: Medo-Persia, typified by a goat with two horns; Alexander the Great's Greco-Macedonian empire, typified by a ram with a great horn; the four kingdoms into which it was divided; Antiochus IV Epiphanes, symbolized by a horn that broke forth out of one of the four horns.

11: Wars between various kings, beginning with Alexander the Great, and then between kings of Syria and Egypt; the "vile person" and king described in vv. 21-45 was Antiochus IV Epiphanes (not the Antichrist of end time, as some think).

A rather common interpretation among the liberals is the one set forth already by Porphyry that the second bear-like beast of Dan. 7 was Media, the third leopard-like one Persia, the fourth terrible beast Alexander the Great, and the "little horn" that came forth from among the ten horns, (identical with the "little horn" of Dan. 8:9ff.), Antiochus IV Epiphanes.**

This interpretation is in conflict with the plain words of the book of Daniel and also with the interpretation that was prevalent in the Christian Church before the onrush of liberal criticism.***

The book of Daniel does not deal with **Media and Persia** as two separate kingdoms but as one double kingdom. In Dan. 8:3ff. the **goat** that symbolizes Medo-Persia is **one animal** with two horns, which refer to its two main parts, Media and Persia. They cannot be interpreted—as the liberals do—as two separate kingdoms without changing the

---

** So e.g. Harrelson, **op. cit.**, p. 464, Puukko, **op. cit.**, pp. 316, 325; Nikolainen, **op. cit.**, pp. 41f., 45f.

*** On this, see Le Roy Edwin Froom, **The Prophetic Faith of our Fathers I-III**, Review and Herald, Washington, D.C., 1946-50, Index, words Beasts, four, Four empires, Bear, Leopard.

biblical text and the historical facts into something different from what they are.*

The "little horn" of **Dan.** 7 comes up from among and after the **ten** horns of the **fourth** beast or the ten kingdoms that were formed in the area of Rome when it disintegrated, whereas the "little horn" of **Dan.** 8 comes out of one of the **four** horns into which the **third** (Alexander's) empire was divided, having its historical fulfillment in Antiochus IV Epiphanes of Syria (so e.g. Scofield's Reference Bible and Jamieson-Fausset-Brown, Dan. 8:9).

The liberal critics disregard the biblical text and historical facts, when they confuse and identify the "little horns" of Dan. 7 and 8 merely because a somewhat similar name is used (the original text has in Dan. 7:8, qeren zeirah, and in Dan. 8:9 qeren mits'irah). The "little horn" of **Dan.** 7 belongs to the **sixth** empire-phase, whereas the "little horn" of **Dan.** 8 belonged to the **third** empire-phase.

By disregarding the clear text of the Bible, the critics try to get around admitting that the book of Daniel contains here real predictive prophecy which does not end in the Maccabean period but extends to a time about 2500 years later, just before the second coming of Christ and even after it, to Christ's universal kingdom which includes all the nations "under the whole heaven." In order to make the prophecies of Daniel cease with the Maccabean period, the critics have had to distort its text to **mean** something entirely different from what it **says**.

By explaining that the **seventy year-week prophecy of Dan. 9:24-27** ends with the events in 165-4 B.C., the liberals want to deprive it of all predictive content. Their interpretations, however, differ from one another in certain details. Puukko (**op. cit.,** p. 331) sets the starting point of the 70 year-weeks (7 × 70 years = 490 years) at the **destruction** of

---

* In contrast, e.g. Scofield's Reference Bible interprets Dan. 2:32; 7:4; 8:20 correctly as meaning the double kingdom of Medo-Persia, and so does Jamieson-Fausset-Brown's commentary.

Jerusalem in 586 B.C.—although the text states that they start at the time when the word went forth "to restore and rebuild Jerusalem" (v. 25). Harrelson (**op. cit.**, p. 465) thinks that the starting point was 537 B.C., when Cyrus gave his edict whereby he allowed the Jews to return to their own land and to rebuild the temple of Jerusalem. Harrelson assumes that the "anointed prince" (v. 25) was Zerubbabel, and that the "prince who is to come" (v. 26) and "destroy the city and sanctuary" was Antiochus IV Epiphanes. The "strong covenant" that this prince was to make "with many for one week" means, Harrelson says, that Antiochus received "strong support" "from the Judeans who had become enamored of the new culture."

This liberal interpretation is point by point in conflict with the plain statements of Scripture.

The "anointed one, the prince" of 9:25 could not be Zerubbabel, whom Cyrus appointed governor over the Jews who returned to their own land, for he was never "cut off" (put to death), but died peacefully after a relatively successful service. The prediction of 9:24 was obviously not fulfilled in the time and through Zerubbabel, namely, "... to finish transgression, to make an end of sins, and to make reconciliation for (to purge away) iniquity, and to bring in everlasting righteousness, and to seal up vision and prophecy, and to anoint the most holy place." These words speak clearly of the work of Christ: He was the "anointed one" (MASHIAH, Messiah), who made reconciliation for (purged away) the sins of the world and brought in everlasting righteousness (to be accepted by penitent sinners from the promise of the Gospel). Only in and through Him were the OT visions and prophecies "sealed" or fulfilled. It was after His finished work that the "most holy place," the Kingdom and Church of God (His "temple"), was "anointed" by the pouring out of the Holy Spirit upon it on Pentecost. He, the Anointed Prince, was "cut off" on Calvary, and it was thereby that He took away the sins of the world and accomplished reconciliation of the world. There is no possibility to apply these words to Zerubbabel.

Since the 70 year-week prophecy deals with the death

of Christ and the reconciliation that He accomplished, the starting point of the 7 x 70 or 490 years cannot be 537 B. C. The "commandment to restore and build Jerusalem," from which the 490 years started, must be the one given to Ezra in 457 B.C. (Ezra 7:7-14) by the Persian king Artaxerxes I (464-424 B.C.). This "commandment" authorized Ezra to "restore and build Jerusalem" spiritually, morally and socially, and its outward reconstruction took place by the authorization of the same king a little later in cooperation between Ezra and Nehemiah. 490 years from 457 B.C. is the year 33 A.D. The prophecy divided the time of 70 year-weeks into three main sections:

1. The first "seven weeks" or 49 years were the period of Ezra and Nehemiah, when the religious, social and external reconstruction took place, laying the foundation for the Jewish life for the millenniums that followed.

2. The second section of 62 year-weeks or 434 years was the "intertestamental period" from thea time of Ezra and Nehemiah to the beginning of the public ministry of Christ in 27 A.D.

3. The last section or the 70th year-week was the time of Christ's public ministry and of the founding of the Christian Church, the seven years 27-33 A.D.

The Revised Standard Version translates 9:27: "And he shall make a strong covenant with many for one week; and for half of the week he shall cause sacrifice and offering to cease; and upon the wing of abomination shall come one who makes desolate, until the decreed end is poured out on the desolator." It seems that the translators of the RSV have been here influenced by the liberal theory that Antiochus IV Epiphanes was the prince spoken of in this passage, and that the abomination and desolation of which it speaks was the one accomplished by him.

One of the basic principles of sound Bible interpretation is that it must be allowed to interpret itself. Especially when Christ Himself interprets an OT passage, that is decisive. So it is in this case: According to His words in Mt.

24:15-20, Mk. 13:14-18 and Lk. 21:20-23, the "abomination" and "desolation" spoken of by Daniel in this passage took place when the people (at least many of them) who heard His words saw Jerusalem compassed by the armies of the Romans in 70 A.D., and when these armies destroyed it. The word "abomination" pointed to the Roman ensigns and idolatrous symbols that were taken into the temple. The "desolation" was the thorough destruction of Jerusalem and its temple by the Roman army. The "prince" who accomplished this was Titus, who later became emperor of Rome. The decreed end that was to be poured upon the desolator (not "desolate," as KJV erroneously translates) was the destruction of the Roman empire several centuries later (not the miserable end of Antiochus IV, as the liberals explain).*

Dan. 9:27 is translated partly wrong both in KJV and ASV, and the rendering of RSV is the worst of all. The literal translation is: "And he will confirm (or make strong) covenant with many one week; and half of the week he will cause sacrifice and offering to cease." The words "one week" (Heb. SHABUA' EHAD) and "half of the week" (HATSI HASHABUA') have no prefix or preposition. The starting point for the right understanding of this verse is Christ's statement in the referred passages. According to His explanation, the abomination and desolation was to take place during the life time of many of His hearers ("When ye see Jerusalem compassed with armies...") through enemy armies. Consequently, the other events spoken of in the same verse, before the words concerning the abomination and desolation, must belong to the same period, to take

---

* The Darbyan dispensationalists interpret the abomination, the desolation, and the prince as referring to the end time, when the Antichrist will perpetrate these things in the Christian Church. This interpretation, however, disregards Christ's statement in the referred passages and is consequently false. — The erroneousness of the liberal interpretation is also seen from the fact that v. 26 speaks of the destruction of the city. Antiichus IV did **not** destroy the city of Jerusalem. It was done by the Romans in 70 A.D.

place before the destruction of Jerusalem and its temple by the Romans.

The only "confirmation of covenant" that took place at that time was the confirmation of the new covenant by Christ through His death and resurrection and the pouring out of the Holy Spirit. This took place in 30 A.D., or in the middle of the last year-week, which was in 27-33 A.D.

Dan. 9:27 speaks of the events of the 70th year week, just as does v. 26 and the first part of v. 17, being supplementary to them. Because of this, the context requires that it should be translated:

> "And he will confirm a covenant with many in one week; and in the midst of the week he will cause the sacrifice and offering (or oblation) to cease."

The OT sacrifices and offerings were "shadows" or "types" which pointed toward the future sacrifice of Christ. When He was "cut off" and died on Calvary, His all-sufficient sacrifice caused all the old covenant sacrifices to cease to be in force before God. Their time was over, and sinners had to seek reconciliation, forgiveness and justification in Christ's sacrifice alone. The ceasing of the OT sacrifices before God took place in the midst of the last year-week or in 30 A.D. The new covenant was confirmed in (during) this year-week (not **"for** one week," as KJV, ASV, and RSV all falsely translate). The "times of the Gentiles" started after it, as is seen from Christ's words in Mt. 21:33-45: The kingdom was to be taken from Israel after they had cast "out of the vineyard" the Son of its Owner and killed Him, and it was given to the Gentiles, till the times of the Gentiles are fulfilled (Lk. 21:24). This is obviously implied in the words at the beginning of the 70 year-week prophecy: "Seventy weeks are determined upon thy people..." After these 70 year-weeks, or in 33 A.D., the times of the Gentiles were to begin, since Israel as a nation rejected the new covenant and the reconciliation and free justification prepared by the Messiah in the middle of the last year-week.

The 70 year-week prophecy of Dan. 9:24-27 dealt with

things that at Daniel's time were many centuries ahead, but for us it is completely fulfilled prophecy.*

The book of Daniel has three passages which speak of abomination and desolation, namely 9:27, 11:31, and 12:11. Christ can mean in the referred passages only Dan. 9:27, for it alone is in a context which speaks of the destruction of the city of Jerusalem. Dan. 11:31 and 12:11 speak clearly of the time of Antiochus IV Epiphanes, when the "abomination" of Greek pagan religion was put into the temple of Jerusalem, and when this temple became "desolate" for over three and a half years. The numbers of days in Dan.

---

* Scofield's Reference Bible represents the Darbyan Dispensationalistic view that separates the last year-week from the previous ones, explaining that the Church Age is like a "parenthesis" or "gap" between them. According to this interpretation, the 70th year-week is still ahead. The prince who will confirm a covenant will be the Antichrist, and he will do it for one year-week or seven years with the Jews, but will break it in the middle of the week, or after three and a half years, and cause to cease the sacrifices that have been started again in the rebuilt temple of Jerusalem. The Antichrist will take his seat in the rebuilt temple of Jerusalem, which will be the abomination of desolation.

This interpretation is in conflict with Christ's words in Mt. 24, Mk. 13 and Lk. 21, and consequently false, since, according to Him, the abomination and desolation was the one accomplished by the Roman armies in 70 A.D. All the 70 year-weeks were successive, and there is no biblical justification for separating the last week from the rest. Most early Christian interpreters explained the 70 year-weeks as successive and the abomination and desolation to have been the destruction of Jerusalem and its temple in 70 A.D., and having no reference to the future Antichrist (see Froom, op. cit., p. 277f.). The **Lutheran Confessions** give the correct older interpretation in explaining that the Antichrist will take his seat in the "temple" of the Christian Church. The Roman Church will be a part of the realm of the Antichrist. This statement indicates that the Antichrist will be the supreme head of the united World Church of end time, and he will be the Pope (**Smalcald Articles IV:9-10; Treatise on the Power and Primacy of the Pope, 39; Apology XV:18**). The OT temple of Jerusalem will never be rebuilt, for when Israel, after the war of Gog, will get the temple area, it will be converted to Christianity, and as a Christian nation it will have no need and desire to rebuild the OT temple and to start again its sacrifices (see Ez. 38-39; Joel 3; Zech. 12).

12:11-12 (1290 and 1335) refer to the various phases in the history of the Maccabean period.

Many liberal critics identify the three and a half years (time, two times and half a time) in Dan. 7:25 and 12:7, because they assume that the "little horn" of Dan. 7:25 is Antiochus IV Epiphanes.

As we have seen, the "little horn" of Dan. 7:25 belongs to the **sixth** empire-phase at the end of the present age, while the "little horn" of Dan. 8 belonged to the **third** empire-phase, being Antiochus IV. The "little horn" of Dan. 7, which later is larger than any other world power prior to it (v. 20), is obviously the same as the first beast of Rev. 13 and the scarlet colored or red beast of Rev. 17, for both Dan. 7 and Rev. 13 and 17 describe it as blaspheming God and making war against His people, and both Dan. 7 and Rev. describe it as the last world power, to be destroyed at the second coming of Christ. In it the enmity of the ungodly world against God and His people reaches its climax. The 3.5 years of Dan. 7:25 are therefore probably the same as the 3.5 years in Rev. 11:3; 12:6, 14; and 13:5, possibly the time of cooperation between the scarlet-red world power and the great harlot Babylon-Church. It will be the time of great tribulation for the true Church, for both the red world power and the apostate World Church will persecute those who remain faithful to Christ and the Word of God (Rev. 13:7; 11ff.; 17:3-6, 14f.). After this, the red world power and its ten satellite states will destroy the great harlot church (Rev. 17:16).

The ten toes of the two feet of the great image in Dan. 2 have been interpreted (so e.g. Scofield's Reference Bible) as symbolizing the same thing as the ten horns of the fourth beast in Dan. 7, that is, the ten kingdoms that rose in the area of the Roman empire. This interpretation is, however, impossible. The stone that smites the image at its feet and toes typifies Christ in His second coming and the destruction of the ungodly world power of that time, and His becoming the ruler of the whole earth, that is, the same thing as the coming of one like the Son of Man in the clouds to take

dominion under the whole heaven (Dan. 7:13f., 27). This
did not take place in the period of the ten kingdoms, which
came to its end in 1917 A.D., when the "little horn" or "scarlet colored beast" (Rev. 13: 1ff.; 17:3ff.) arose from the sea
of nations. Since the two feet and ten toes symbolize the
last world power that Christ will destroy at his second coming, it must be the same as the "little horn" of Dan. 7 and
the scarlet colored or red world power of end time, pro-
phesied in Rev. 13, 17, and 19. The final battle in which its
destruction will take place will be the battle of Harmageddon (Armageddon), at the time of which Christ will come.
(Rev. 16:13-16; 19:19-21; Dan. 7:12ff.).

While the liberals limit the prophecies of Daniel to the
time prior to 164 B.C., the Dispensationalists have gone to
the other extreme and applied passages that clearly speak
of Antiochus IV to the Antichrist of end time. The ungodly
king of Dan. 11:21-45 has been frequently interpreted as
the Antichrist. In reality this passage speaks of Antiochus
IV Epiphanes. Scofield interprets 11:21-35 as speaking of
Antiochus IV, but identifies the king spoken of in vv. 36ff.
with the "little horn" of Dan. 7:8, 24-26, and the time described here as the time of the Antichrist. Jamieson-Fausset-Brown gives the correct interpretation, for the whole
section 11:21-45 speaks obviously of the historical events of
the time of Antiochus IV, and the last verse speaks of his
death. It is wholly wrong to connect Dan. 11:36ff. with
Dan. 9:26f. as Scofield does, for, as we have seen, Dan. 9:
26f. speaks of the time of Christ and the destruction of
Jerusalem in 70 A.D., while Dan. 11:36ff. continues to speak
of Antiochus IV Epiphanes.

Antiochus was a type of the Antichrist only in the sense
that as he set up a false god (an image of the Greek Zeus)
in the temple of Jerusalem, leading numerous Jews, the
people of God, astray to this false religion, so the Antichrist
of end time will take his seat in the temple of Christendom
(united World Church) and set up there a falsified Christianity, leading numerous church people astray. Antiochus
was a political ruler, and **as such** he was **not** a type of the
Antichrist who will be the supreme leader of the united

HATH GOD SAID?

World Church of end time and not a political world dictator, as many assume. According to 1 Jh. 2:18f., all the antichrists will go out of the Christian Church, and they are all, as 2 Jh. 7 shows, "deceivers" in the Church, and not political rulers. We have already pointed out how the Lutheran Confessions rightly remark that the Antichrist will sit in the temple of God, in the united World Church, and not on the throne of a political state or empire (Apology XV:18).

4. Proofs of the Authenticity of Daniel

Ezekiel refers to Daniel twice: "... even if these three men, Noah, Daniel and Job, were in it [Jerusalem], they would deliver but their own souls by their righteousness" (14:13f.; the same thought in v. 20), and : "... say to the prince of Tyrus ... thou art wiser than Daniel; there is no secret that they can hide from thee" (28:2f.).

According to the critics (e.g. Puukko, **op. cit.,** pp. 307f.; Gulin, **op. cit.,** p. 302; Harrelson, **op. cit.,** p. 458), these passages show that Daniel was a renowned man of a distant past, not a contemporary of Ezekiel. Puukko and Harrelson suggest that the Daniel spoken of in Ezekiel may be the Daniel mentioned in the Canaanite texts that have been found in Ras-esh-Shamra in 1929, in which he seems to be a ruler-judge.

This assumption, however, is impossible: How could the Lord (who speaks in the first person in the referred passages of Ez.) speak of a **pagan idolater,** such as the Danil of Ras-esh-Shamra, as a righteous and wise man? Ezekiel (or, rather, the Lord through him) speaks obviously of the **Israelite Daniel** who was known as a righteous and wise man and revealer of secrets. The Daniel who was Ezekiel's contemporary was the **only** Daniel who is mentioned in the Bible who has had any significance (the Daniels mentioned in 1 Chr. 3:1 and Ezra 8:2 have had no significance in the history of Israel, except that their names are mentioned). He was taken into exile in 605 B. C., or about eight years before Ezekiel experienced the same fate. At the time when Ezekiel began his prophetical ministry (592 B.C.) Daniel was already renowned of his righteousness and wisdom, for he had then been for more than a decade the head of the wise men of Babylon (Dan. 1-2), and for many more years at the time when Ezekiel wrote the cited words.

Were the book of Daniel a forgery, written about four centuries after the exile, the writer could have done nothing more foolish than to put it in the name of a man of whom the Jews knew he had not lived in the exile but a long time before it. The suggestion of critics that Daniel may have been the ancient Danil mentioned in the Ras-esh-Shamra texts is inconsiderate, to say the least.

It is obvious that time has in this case no significance: As Noah and Job belonged to periods that were separated by a long distance of time, why could not Daniel be a famous righteous and wise man of Ezekiel's time? This is the only possibility, since the history of Israel does not know of any other renowned righteous and wise Daniel (Möller, **op. cit.**, pp. 336f.).

Josephus (Antiq. XI, 8:4) reports how Alexander the Great, after having conquered Gaza, proceeded toward Jerusalem. While approaching it, he met a procession of priests and people and showed peculiar respect for Jaddua, the high priest, and the Jews in general. When one of his men asked him reason for this, he told him that while still in Macedonia he had seen in a dream a high priest, and that he had recognized Jaddua as the man whom he had thus seen. Josephus tells further that the book of Daniel was shown to Alexander, and that he read in it the prediction (ch. 8) that a king of Greece (Javan) was to make an end of the Persian empire, and that he understood it to refer to himself.

The liberals have tried to discredit the story of Josephus, but the only thing that they have against its historicity is that, according to their theory, the book of Daniel did not exist in the time of Alexander the Great (ab. 330 B.C.).

We have already mentioned how the 1 Macc. refers to Daniel, and probably its writer has used the LXX translation of it, prepared sometime 300-200 B.C. The so-called predictions of Sibylla from ab. 140 B.C. speak of the beast that has ten horns and of a horn that comes forth from between them. This presupposes plainly the knowledge of Dan. 7:8, 20-24. We have already mentioned that the book of Daniel is among the Dead Sea (Qumran) scrolls, and that the Essenes regarded it as a part of the OT. If it had been written during the second century B.C., or the time when the Essene community already existed, they certainly would not have regarded it as a part of the OT canon.

Our study of the book of Daniel has led us to the conclusion that everything in and about it points in the direction that it must have been written by the Daniel who lived in exile from 605 B.C. to about 530 B.C., and that the book is reliable in every respect.

IX. "DIFFICULT PASSAGES" OF THE BIBLE

The liberals have said again and again that the Bible contains so many obvious errors and conflicts that intellectual honesty prohibits them from believing in its inerrancy.

We have already dealt with a number of such passages and shown that they do not contain any errors or discrepancies, when other Scripture passages are used for their interpretation, or when they are taken in the light of historical facts. The liberals have merely misrepresented them.

There are, however, many other passages to which the liberals appeal as proof for their assertion that the Bible is not reliable. But before setting out to examine such passages we have to pay attention to the reasons and nature of difficulties in the Bible and the right attitude toward them.

First, we should realize that the Bible is the record of God's revelation to men. He is infinitely great, holy, wise and powerful, and we men are small, finite and weak, and our minds are in many ways dimmed and confused by sin and the various false ideas current in the world. It is therefore no wonder that Scripture contains many things that seem to us hard to understand. Even the wisest and best of us are just beginners in comprehending the things of God and His world. "We know in part... For now we see in a mirror, in an enigma (KJV: through a glass, darkly)" (1 Cor. 13:9, 12).

Second, the fact that we cannot now solve a difficulty in the Bible does not mean that it cannot be solved. The fact that we at the present time are unable to answer an objection does not prove that it cannot be answered. Christian modesty and humility requires us to say: Though I at this time see no possible solution to this difficulty, someone who is wiser than I may find it. And even if there should be a

HATH GOD SAID?

difficulty that no one in this age is able to solve, when we enter into the kingdom of glory all things will be solved there and we will see things as they are (1 Cor. 13:10, 12).

Third, the difficult passages are quite insignificant in comparison to the great bulk of the Bible which is plain and clear, when a Spirit-enlightened Christian reads it. To the carnal mind, even the essentials of the Scriptures remain dark and impossible to understand. Someone has admitted: The most difficult passages of the Bible are not those that I do not understand, but those that I understand.

In dealing with the relationship between the glories of Scripture and its difficulties, to which the critics pay so much attention, R. A. Torrey **(Difficulties in the Bible,** Moody Press, p. 15) writes to the point: What should we think of a man who is studying a masterpiece of art and concentrates his whole attention on what looks like a fly-speck in the corner? A large part of the much vaunted "critical study of the Bible" is a laborious investigation of supposed fly-specks. A person who does not want to spend his time for such a study of fly-specks but devotes his labors to what is essential in Scripture is counted in some quarters as not being "scholarly and up to date."

Fourth, the difficulties seem to be of immense importance to superficial readers, but they (at least most of them) disappear rapidly on careful and prayerful study. A humble and careful student of the Bible who prays God for guidance and enlightenment experiences year after year how these difficulties disappear one after another.

As we have already pointed out, some of the difficulties in the Bible (e.g. in King James' Version) have been caused by errors made by copyists. Many of them have been removed by the study of the most ancient manuscripts. Some of them have been caused by inaccurate translations. We shall deal with several difficulties of these types, in addition to the ones already discussed. Certain difficulties have arisen from false interpretations of the biblical texts and disappear when they are interpreted correctly. We shall also discuss some difficulties of this kind.

Whenever we find a difficulty in the Bible it is best to acknowledge it frankly and to try to find an honest solution. There must be solution somewhere if we are patient and search for it with a prayerful heart and mind.

1. The Genesis Account of Creation
The "Firmament" and Waters Under and Above It

Ancient people thought that heaven or sky is like a huge dome or cupola in which stars are fixed, or, then, that the stars are really holes in this solid dome, through which light shines from the world of God. Is it true that the Genesis account of creation gives this view in speaking of a "firmament" that separates waters under it from waters above it? (Gen. 1:6ff.)?

The Hebrew word for "firmament" is RAKI'A which means something that is spread out or expanded. Gen. 1:20 speaks of birds flying "in the open firmament of heaven." The birds do not fly in a solid dome but in the air. The RAKI'A, therefore, obviously means "expanse," and like our word "sky" it includes both the atmosphere and outer space, for according to Gen. 1:14ff. the sun, moon, and stars also are in the RAKI'A.

In creating the earth, God established such an order that water evaporates from the earth, namely, from the seas, lakes, and moist ground, etc., so that there are large amounts of it above the "expanse," in the atmosphere, and from there it comes down as rain. This circulation of water is one of the most important conditions of life on earth. It is at the same time a symbol of how the prayers of Christians go up from the earth to God, and "showers of blessing" (Ez. 34:26) come down from heaven in answer to them.

It is also possible, and even probable, that the waters above the RAKI'A were great amounts of water that formed an invisible vapor "canopy" around the earth and worked as a regulator of its atmosphere, causing a much more uniform warm temperate climate than it has now, having something like a "greenhouse" effect.*

The Two Parts of the Creation Account

Gen. 1:11f. states that on the third day God ordered the earth to bring forth vegetation, but Gen. 2:4ff. tells us (we use here the RSV, which in this case expresses better the meaning of the text): "In the day that the Lord God made the earth and the heavens, when no plant of the field was yet in the earth and no herb of the field had yet sprung up—for the Lord had not caused it to rain upon the earth, and there was no man to till the ground; but a mist went up from the earth and watered the whole face of the ground—then the Lord God formed man of dust from the ground, and breathed into his nostrils the breath of life." Thus, according to Gen. 1:26f., man was created on the sixth day, but according to Gen. 2:4ff. it seems as he had been created much earlier. How should we understand this? The liberals say that these are two partly conflicting stories of creation.

The statement that there were no plants on the earth, for the Lord had not caused it to rain upon the earth, obviously speaks of the situation between Gen. 1:10 and 11: God had separated the land areas from the seas but had not yet created vegetation, which took place on the next day, neither had He created the natural law that determines the circulation of water, spoken of above. Gen. 2:6f. skips over the creation of the various forms of life (plants and animals) and gives then a more detailed description of the creation of man and of the garden of Eden, supplementing here the account of ch. 1. There is no conflict between chs. 1 and 2. They are not two different stories of creation, but they supplement each other.

Creation of Light, Sun and Moon

Gen. 1:3-5 relates that God created light and ordained the alternation of day and night on the first day (or rather, the first day came when God created light), but vv. 14-19

---

* On this, see Henry M. Morris and John C. Whitcomb, Jr., **The Genesis Flood**, 5th printing, 1964, pp. 240f., 253-258.

tell of the creation of the sun, moon and stars on the **fourth day** to divide day from night. How should we understand this?

Science does not know how our solar system and the stellar systems of the universe have come into existence. Various theories have been set forth, but none of them is satisfactory. Only God, the Creator, knows how the various parts of the universe have come about, and we must accept as truth what He says of it in the biblical account of creation. It is our only real source of information in this respect.

The sun of our solar system is not the only source of light, but there are many other sources of it. The rotation of the earth around its axis must have begun on the first day (unless it had started from the beginning), and the alternation of day and night from the first day on must have been caused by this rotation. What was the source of light toward which the earth turned its various sides before the creation of the sun we do not know.

Many evangelicals hold the theory (set forth e.g. in Scofield's Reference Bible, Gen. 1:3) that Gen. 1:14-18 merely means that the sun, moon and stars were made to appear, became visible, on the fourth day. The light came from the sun from the first day on, but thick layers of water vapor diffused its light till the fourth day, when the sun appeared in an unclouded sky the first time. This explanation is not possible, for the Hebrew word YA'AS (from 'ASAH) means **made**, not "caused to appear." The same word is used in 1:7 of making the firmament, in 1:25 of the creation of land animals, and in 1:26 of the creation of man. In none of these passages does it mean "to cause to appear," "to make visible," but clearly refers to God's creative activity.

Structure of the Universe

Is it true, as the liberals frequently assert, that the Bible teaches an antiquated view of the structure of the universe and therefore is not true in this respect?

At the time when the books of the Bible were written, the earth was commonly thought of as the center of the solar system, and that the sun and stars circled around it. Many people even thought that the earth was flat and floating on waters, and that the sky was like a solid dome above it. There were, however, among the ancients men who knew that the earth was globular, like a ball, and that it was circling around the sun.

Is. 40:22 speaks of the "circle" (Hebrew HUG, roundness) of the earth, and Job 26:7 says that God "hangeth the earth upon nothing." These passages show that according to Scripture the earth is round or globular in form and in "empty space." All this is in good harmony with the modern scientific view. The Spirit of God led the holy writers to give the correct view at these points, and to avoid the wrong popular conception of those times.

That the Bible speaks of the rising and setting of the sun does not mean that it teaches the sun to be circling around the earth. We "moderns" use the same expressions although we know that the earth revolves around the sun; even scientific astronomers use this common manner of speech.

Those who hold that the Bible teaches the ancient popular view appeal to such passages as Ps. 24:2, "He hath founded it upon the seas, and established it upon the rivers," and Ps. 136:6, "...who spread out the earth upon the waters."

These passages seem to give support to the assertion that the Bible teaches the ancient conception of the earth as floating on waters when translated as they are in KJV, ASV and RSV. All of them, however, have a wrong translation of the Hebrew text. True, the Hebrew 'al that is used in both of these passages may mean "upon," but it also has the meaning "above," and this is obviously its meaning in these passages. The Bible translators have transgressed here the basic rule that when a word has more than one meaning the context determines how it should be translated. We too say that a certain land area is so and so many feet (or meters) **above** the sea level. Thus, when Ps. 24:2 and 136:6 are translated correctly, they do not contain any antiquated view but simply state that God has established dry land areas to be **above** the waters and seas.

Origin of the Universe and the Laws of Thermodynamics and Morpholysis

Many modern people hold that according to the scientific view the universe, the earth included, has come about by way of gradual evolution and not by divine creation as the Bible teaches. How should we understand this issue?

The two most basic universal laws of nature, recognized by all scientists, are the so-called first and second laws of thermodynamic (Greek **thermos**=heat, **dynamis**=power, energy). The **first law of thermodynamics** is also called the **law of conservation of energy.** It means that energy can be transformed in various ways, but it can neither be created nor destroyed. The universe is an immense and complicated system of various forms and sources of energy. How could it have come about without creation and Creator, for (at the present) energy cannot be created or destroyed but only transformed? It must have been once created.

Atoms are like very tiny solar systems. In each of them electrons (negatively charged particles) revolve around the nucleus (composed of various kinds of particles) at immense speeds. The simplest is the hydrogen atom which has one electron. Nuclear fission (breaking up of atoms) has revealed that atoms contain enormous amounts of energy. The universe is an immense system of various kinds of energy and solar systems from the tiny atoms to huge galaxies. All the processes of the universe—physical, biological, geological, etc.—involve transformations of the various forms of energy, the total amount of which cannot be increased or decreased, but which has once come to be. This must have taken place through creation by God. Only a fool can imagine that it has just jumped out of nonexistence into existence without any designer or creator.

The **second law of thermodynamics** means in a certain sense that in all energy transformations there is a tendency for some of the energy to turn into non-reversible heat energy, which means that the availability of the energy of a system or process for the performance of work is reduced. It "wears out" or "runs down." The measure of the amount of energy thus depleted from a system is called **entropy.** The second law of thermodynamics states that entropy in a closed system always tends to increase; it never decreases. This means that its available energy always decreases.

The so-called **law of morpholysis** (Greek **morphe**=form, **lysis**=loosing, breakdown) is an application of the second law of thermodynamics. It means the generally known fact that all things, both the ones made by man and plants, animals, etc., lose their form and order, break down, when left without care. Wherever there is order, an ordering agent must have been at work. The formation of crystals is no exception to this law, for the order of the atoms and molecules in the crystal is determined prior to its formation. Neither is the multiplication of plants and animals an exception to it, for they produce offspring similar to themselves, and this sheds no light on their first appearance on the earth. When molten metal or a piece of metal is put into a machine which produces parts for another machine or implements for human use, there is an ordering agent, the machine, or rather the man (men) who has (have) designed and made that machine. But if these metals or machines are left on their own, they soon lose their form, break down into the raw materials in the form of which they are usually found in nature. The statement of God, "Dust thou art, and unto dust shalt thou return" (Gen. 3:19), is a universal law, the law of morpholysis. In other words, left to chance objects tend to move from complex to simpler substances.

The evolutionary assumption that atoms and molecules have come about by themselves and then formed at first simple and then more complicated organisms is in obvious conflict with the second law of thermodynamics and the law of morpholysis. In order that organisms would be formed, solar energy and other factors are necessary, but by themselves they are not able to bring them about. On the contrary, morpholysis, decay, disintegration, "turning into dust" necessarily takes place, when natural forces are active without an ordering agent, that is, without a living organism. Organic compounds are formed with considerable difficulty in the laboratory, but no chemist has been able to put life into them. Could biological processes have started and proceeded in nature in conflict and against the universal laws of thermodynamics and morpholysis, without the Creator as the ordering agent? Impossible!

The universal cosmic process determined by the second law of thermodynamics and the law of morpholysis produces disorder, breakdown, "running down." Those who hold the macroevolutionary theory that the different forms of life which have lived or are living on earth have gradually evolved from some simple one-celled form of life* assume that somehow this process has functioned despite and against the otherwise universal laws of thermodynamics and morpholysis. This is, however, impossible. "The fool saith in his heart, 'There is no God'" (Ps. 14:1).

Origin of Species

There are many theologians and others who hold the theory of "theistic evolution," according to which evolution has been God's method of creation. After the evolutionary process had led to the stage of man, God took one pair of these man-like animals into fellowship with Himself, making of them true men. What should we think of this theory? Can the Genesis account of creation mean something like this?

It cannot mean anything like that, unless it is taken as

---

*Microevolution or variation within existing groups is a different thing, a fact that no one denies. We are speaking here of the macroevolutionary theory that holds that new forms of life have emerged on the earth by way of evolution, without a Creator.

a "myth" or "parable" and interpreted to mean something else than it says. Neither can the facts of nature be brought into harmony with the macroevolutionary theory, unless they are interpreted to mean something else than they are.

There are particularly two groups of facts which show that the different forms of life that have lived or are living on earth cannot have come about by way of evolution, but must have been created by God.

The first of them is that the laws that govern **heredity** in plants and animals (which hold true in man as well) permit **only variation within existing groups,** that is, differentiation into races, strains, varieties, and in some cases into forms that may be classified as parallel closely related species. These laws do not allow the emergence of new forms of life. (On this, see e.g. Dr. Walter E. Lammerts, "Mutations and Evolution," in **The Challenge of Creation,** Bible-Science Association, 1965, pp. 1-11; Lammerts is a professional geneticist).

The second group of facts that is against the macroevolutionary theory belongs to the field of **paleontology** or that branch of historical geology which deals with the past forms of life that are known from their fossil remains. Paleontologists have observed that the **various groups** of plants and animals that have existed or live now on earth **have been separated from one another by bridgeless gaps from their first appearance on.** They have appeared upon the earth group after group without intermediate forms.* This indicates that they cannot have evolved from common ancestors.

Another fact, inexplainable from the viewpoint of the evolutionary theory, is that the earth has in our time all the **groups** of plants and animals that have ever existed from the "simplest" to the "highest" forms. Why should some have evolved and others remained practically unchanged?

---

* This is admitted by evolutionists themselves. See e.g. G. G. Simpson, **Tempo and Mode of Evolution** (New York, 1944), p. 107.

The usual evolutionary explanation is that when the environment remains unchanged, the forms become fixed. This is, however, a far-from-satisfactory explanation, for the environmental changes have not been great, and they cannot account for the appearance of new forms of life.

The **biblical account of creation** shows that God created first plant life, then animals living in water and winged creatures, after that land animals, and finally man. The various forms of life thus appeared upon the earth group after group. **Nature** testifies to the same thing: Plants and animals have always been grouped (from the time they have come into existence) in the same manner as they are now. Even when classified according to the theory of evolution, the fossil-bearing rocks show that the various forms of life have appeared upon the earth group after group (in reality the fossil-bearing rocks show the sequence of sedimentation in the great Noachian flood, not their evolutionary sequence of emergence). They have been from the beginning separated from one another by bridgeless gaps, which shows incontestably that they must have been created, and cannot have come about by way of evolution.

The necessary conclusion from the testimonies of both Scripture and nature is, first, that both plants and animals have been **created group after group, "after their kinds,"** and second, that they also **produce off-spring and multiply "after their kinds."** The theory of "theistic evolution" is an attempt to combine the truth of creation with the false macroevolutionary theory, and it is therefore necessarily wrong. God did not create the various forms of life by way of evolution but separately, group after group, as both Scripture and science show.

Origin of Man

The Bible tells in Gen. 1:27 and 2:7 that God formed man of the dust of the ground, breathing into him the breath of life and making him in His own image. But evolutionistic scientists say that, according to the testimony of the skeletal remains of ancient men, apes and men have gradually developed from common ancestors. What is the truth in this matter?

Evolutionists have for some time explained that the first phase in man's evolution was the one when the lines that led to apes and men began to differentiate. To this phase belong the early **Dryopithecines**, the ape-like "**Proconsul**," etc. The **second** phase is represented by such early forms of the line that led to man as the African **Kenyapithecus, Ramapithecus** and the early **Australopithecines**. The third phase is represented by such early stages of man with low sloping foreheads as the **Pithecanthropus** of (Trinil) Java, the **Sinanthropus pekinensis** (Chinaman of Peking), etc. The **fourth** phase includes all modern men from the late Pleistocene (Ice Age) to the present time, including the Neanderthal man (who had a low and sloping forehead and prominent browridges) as an extreme variation.

Dr. Louis B. Leaky, a British anthropologist, has recently wanted to make a rather thorough revision of this theory (which is quite generally set forth in text-books). He holds that the **Pithecanthropus** and **Sinanthropus** did not belong to the line that lead to the modern man but were side-branches without modern descendents. Leaky thinks that the skeletal remains that he has found in the Olduvai Gorge of Tanganyika, East Africa (which otherwise resemble those of modern man but are small in size) have belonged to the first real man, since they are from very ancient times. According to him, the **Australopithecines** of South Africa do not belong to a line that has led to man. Thus, Leaky holds, the four-phase theory has fallen, for its second and third phases have turned out to be mere side branches that are not parts of the line that has led to the modern man. The **Homo habilis** (as the Olduvai man is called) has taken their place.

We may, however, note: Even now there are many pygmy tribes in Africa, small or dwarfed in size. The "Homo habilis" is obviously an early representative of these pygmies and not an evolutionary stage of man.

In addition to the Olduvai finds, two older discoveries

have been fatal to the evolutionary theory of the origin of man, namely, those made at **Swanscomb**, England, in 1936, and at **Fontechevade**, France, in 1947. Both of them represent men who have lived long before the Neanderthal age, not far from the time of the **Pithecanthropus** of Java and **Sinanthropus** of Peking, and both of them have belonged to men of the modern type with high and smooth foreheads. The necessary conclusion has been that from the oldest known times on there have been men of different types, some with high and smooth foreheads and others with low sloping forheads. Both of them have been contemporary variant forms and not evolutionary stages. The Swanscomb and Fontechevade discoveries already led to the drop of the "third stage." J. O. Buswell III, an American anthropologist, wrote in 1956 in an article that was checked by about ten other anthropologists: "Those who hold to the theory of evolution no longer believe that the older the fossil remains are the more ape-like they become... The famous missing link is now an antiquated concept." Buswell quoted the words of the renowned British anthropologist F. M. Ashley Montagu: It is an erroneous assumption to equate "primitiveness with morphologically brutal traits. The facts, as we know them, do not lend support to the notion of a beast-like early man" (from Montagu's book **Introduction to Physical Anthropology, 1952**). According to Buswell, modern anthropology has come to the conclusion that "all men can be regarded as the same species, Homo sapiens, but they have been divided into races, both living and extinct, whose properties cannot be proven to be of different quality" ("The Creation of Man," **Christian Life,** May, 1956, p. 17).

Ales Hrlicka, an American anthropologist, made in the 1930's careful measurements among American academicians (university men) and common people and arrived at the surprising result that academic people have in the average a little lower and more sloping foreheads than common people. This showed, Hrlicka concluded, that the form of the forehead has nothing to do with the evolution or intelligence of man. This does not depend on the form of the bones of his skull but on the quality of his brain. (Hrlicka, **Observations and Measurements on the Members of the National Academy of Sciences,** Washington, D. C., 1937, pp. 8f). Thus, the theory of evolution has "fallen" even among the scientists (although most of them still hold to it, despite the facts). Those Christians who still believe in the theory of evolution and try to combine it with the biblical doctrine of creation (in the form of the "theistic evolution" theory) are "behind the times" from the scientific point of view. Historical anthropology (human paleontology) has come to the conclusion that man has appeared upon the earth suddenly, without any earlier forms that would point in the direction of evolution. Scripture is thus in good harmony with science when it teaches the special creation of man.

Age of the World

When the age of the world, that is, the time that has passed since the creation, has been calculated on the basis of the genealogies of Gen. 5 and 11, the result has been that the creation took place c. 4004 B.C. and the flood of Noah's time c. 2449-8 B.C. (so Ussher, given in most KJV Bibles). Historical, archeological and other studies have, however, given the result that there were notable cultures and kingdoms c. 4000 B.C. in Egypt and Mesopotamia. The age of the world must be much higher than c. 6000 years. How can this conflict be solved?

The chronology of Ussher (and other similar chronologies) is based on the assumption that the genealogies in Gen. 5 and 11 are complete, with no generations missing. This assumption, however, cannot be correct. Biblical genealogies are often incomplete, and their purpose is not to give all the successive generations. They mention only the persons who have had significance from the point of view of men's history with God. The genealogies in Gen. 5 and 11, as well as those in Mt. 1 and Lk. 3, show the line of men to which Christ belonged as to His human nature. E.g. Mt. 1:8 states that Joram begat Ozias (Uzziah), but from the OT genealogies we know that there were three generations between Joram and Uzziah. Ezra 7:3 speaks of Azariah as a son of Meraioth, but from 1 Chr. 6:7-9 we know that there were six generations between them. In the genealogy between Noah and Abraham, Lk. 3:35f. mentions Cainan, not listed in Gen. 11:1-13.

As we have already shown, in biblical language such terms as "begat," "son," "father," indicate descent in general, whether immediate or more or less distant.

The impossibility of the interpretation of the generations mentioned in Gen. 11 as successive, with no missing links, is seen from the fact that in that case Noah would have been living until Abraham was about 50 years old, and three of those who were born before the tower of Babel, Shem, Shelah and Eber, would have outlived Abraham. Eber would have died two years after Jacob arrived at Haran to work for Laban. According to Josh. 24:2, 14f. Abram's fathers had fallen into idolatry. It is not at all probable that Noah and Shem still lived in those times—they must have died a long time before. According to Ex. 6:20, Aaron and Moses were sons of Amram and Jochebed. But in Nu. 3:17-19, 27-28 we are told that "the family of Amramites," together with the families of Amram's three brothers (Izhar, Hebron and Uzziel) was in the days of Moses 8,600 males, from a month old and upward, and the total number must have been somewhere around 18000 persons. Such an increase within about one generation is impossible. Amram and Jochebed must have been ancestors of Aaron and Moses, and they must have lived 300-400 years earlier. This is again an example of how the words "bare," "begat," etc., often mean a more or less distant descent. Because of this, it is not possible to compute the age of the earth from the genealogies of the Bible.* It must be much older than c. 6000 years.

Scientists tried earlier to determine the age of the earth and its various geological formations by means of certain **geological methods.** It was estimated that the

---

* This question is discussed more fully e.g. in Morris-Whitcomb's **op. cit.,** pp. 474-483.

thickness of sediments in the continental shelves is c. 5,000 meters (this estimate, however, is probably too high), and their rate of accumulation in our time about 30 cm. in 800 years. On this basis, the continental shelves were calculated to be c. 14-15 million years old. Recent studies (by Scripp's Institution of Oceanography, led by Dr. Roger Revelle) have given the result that the thickness of sediments in ocean bottoms is ab. 200 meters which, according to the present rate of accumulation, represents c. 100 million years. These figures are, however, all too high, for at least at the time of the great universal flood the accumulation of sediments in ocean and shallow sea bottoms was thousands of times faster than now.

In recent decades scientists have used almost exclusively **"radioactive clocks"** for age determinations. Radioactive elements break down at definite rates. By determining these rates and the amounts of "parent" and "daughter" elements, the ages of minerals that contain them can be calculated. For the determination of **long ages**, millions and hundreds of millions of years, the disintegration of uranium and thorium into radium, helium and lead, and the breakdown of rubidium into strontium and of potassium into argon and calcium have been used. By means of these methods, the Paleozoic Era has been calculated to have started about 600-500 million years ago, the Mesozoic Era c. 200 million years ago, and the Cenozoic Era c. 100/60 million years ago. The evolutionists hold that these results have given strong support to the theory of evolution, and also provided sufficient time for it.

There are, however, **many uncertainties** in these age determinations. One of them is the unsolved question whether God in the beginning created the parent elements only or also some of the daughter elements. If He made a part of the daughter elements too, the radioactive elements' ages are **apparent but not real**—just as Adam, whom God probably created as a full-grown man, had an apparent but not a real age. The same was probably true of plants and animals. Another problem is the question of the **formation of sedimentary rocks**: numerous facts seem to indicate that they were formed in a short time in a **universal flood,** and not during 5-600 million years as the evolutionists assume. The radioactive minerals that have been found in sedimentary formations are in that case from the antediluvial (or, as it is usually called, from the Proterozoic and Archaic) time and have been enclosed in the sediments during the flood, and therefore do not show the age of these formation. One of the most serious arguments against the figures obtained by means of radioactive calculations is their immense **discrepancy with the ages obtained by means of geological methods.** Although—as already pointed out—even the latter are probably all too high, they are merely a small fraction of the radioactive figures. It is quite impossible that e.g. the sediments in continental shelves, ocean bottoms and river deltas would have been accumulating about 5-6 billion years.

One of the arguments set forth by Morris-Whitcomb (**op. cit., p.379f.**). against the radioactive ages is the fact of the falling of **meteoric dust** on the earth. It has been estimated that more than 14 million tons of it settles on the earth each year. If the earth has existed c. 5-6 billion years, the meteoric dust should form a layer of c. 54 feet thick over all the surface of the earth. No such layer, however, exists. And as this dust contains mostly iron and nickel, its accumulation during 5-6 billion years should have resulted in much larger amounts of these minerals in the crust of the earth than there actually are. These facts (Morris-Whitcomb mention several others, see pp. 380-391) force us to the conclusion that there must be something basically wrong in the results of radioactive calculations. The earth is obviously much younger than they seem to indicate.

On the basis of the assumption that the **moon** is about as old as the earth, scientists thought that its surface must be covered with a thick layer of dust, due to the "weathering" and disintegration caused by the changes of temperature. Recent pictures sent by a rocket landed on the moon have, however, shown that there is hardly any layer of dust on its surface. This shows that its age (and also the earth's) must be relatively short.

Age of Mankind

The age of mankind belongs for the most part to the time after the flood, or, as geologists usually call it, to the **Quarternary** period, which is divided to the **Pleistocene** (Ice Age) and **Holocene** (Recent, after the Ice Age) epochs. Several scientific methods, both geological and radioactive, have been used to determine its length. According to the usual uniformitarian theory (according to which geological processes have in general been slow and uniform, as they are in our time), the Pleistocene followed after the Tertiary, while the flood theory (held by many Christian scientists and others) holds that it came almost immediately after the flood. **Geological methods,** such as those based on the varves (annual or seasonable layers), the **recession of waterfalls** (particularly those of Niagara and the St. Anthony Falls at Minneapolis, Minn.), have given c. 15-14,000 years as the time from the greatest extension of the ice sheet to the present, and the time c. 6000 B.C. as the time when the Ice Age ended.

The **radiocarbon method** (based on the breakdown and decrease of carbon 14 in organic remains after their death) has given nearly the same time as the geological methods for the period after the recession of the ice sheets. According to this method, some grains of cultivated wheat and barley in Egypt are c. 6,400 years old; the first people who have left remains in North America lived here c. 9,000 years ago.

The **fluorine method** (based on the accumulation of fluorine in bones buried in the ground), has given c. 30-25,000 years as the time from the beginning of the Ice Age to the present time.

The **radioactive inequilibrium method** (based on the amount of excessive radium in ocean bottom sediments and its breakdown) has given the time c. 24,000 years ago for the start of the last (the only?) glaciation, and the time c. 14,000 years ago as the time when the ice started to retreat.

The times given by these various methods are not accurate, and there are differences between their results; but possibly they are of the right order of magnitude. The time of the Ice Age and after it (Pleistocene and Holocene) is according to the results of these methods c. 30-20000 years. When we add to this the time from the creation of the first men to the universal flood of Noah's time, possibly 1,500-2,000 years, we get the whole probable age of mankind. It is, however, possible that it is considerably shorter, maybe less than 20,000 years.

Literature on Creation and Evolution
Brief discussions:
Creation Research Society, 1966 Annual (P. O. Box 496, Freedom, Cal. The same, **Quarterly,** July 1966.

Frank Lewis Marsh, **Evolution or Special Creation?** (Review and Herald Publ. Assn., Washington, D. C. 1963).

M. L. Moser, **Creation or Evolution** (publ. by the author, Little Rock, Ark. 1966).

Larger books:
John W. Klotz, Genes, Genesis and Evolution (Concordia, St. Louis, 1955).

Henry M. Morris, The Twilight of Evolution (Baker Book House, Grand Rapids, Mich. 1964).

John Fred Meldau, **Why We Believe in Creation, Not Evolution** (Christian Victory Publ. Co., Denver 11, Colorado, 1964).

Byron C. Nelson, "After Its Kind" (Augsburg, Minneapolis, 1946).

For a more extensive list of literature, see **Bible-Science Newsletter** (P. O. Box 1028, Caldwell, Idaho, 83605), June 15, 1966.

2. Fall into Sin and the Serpent

Should we take the account of the first fall into sin in Gen. 3 as actual history or as a parable or myth that speaks of what is taking place in men in general, as the liberals commonly do? And how is it possible that a serpent could speak?

The NT speaks of Adam and Eve as real historical persons and of their fall as an actual historical event:

Lk. 3:38 says that Adam was the father of Seth ("Seth [son of] Adam") just as e.g. Jacob was son of Isaac or David was son of Jesse.

Paul writes in 1 Tim. 2:13f: "Adam was first formed, then Eve. And Adam was not deceived, but the woman being deceived was in the transgression."

The meaning of Paul is (as Jamieson-Fausset-Brown correctly explains): "Adam was not deceived—as Eve was **deceived** by the serpent; but was **persuaded** by his wife. Genesis 3:17, 'Hearkened unto... voice of... wife.' But Genesis 3:13, Eve says, 'The **serpent beguiled me.**' Being more easily deceived she more easily deceives... (2 Corinthians 11:3). Last in being, she was first in sin—indeed, she alone was **deceived.** ... She yielded to the temptations of sense and the **deceits of Satan;** he to **conjugal** love."

In Rom. 5:12-19 Paul, likewise, speaks of Adam as a real person and of his sin as a real historical event:

> "As by one man sin entered into the world, and death by sin; and so death passed upon all men, for that all have sinned... Death reigned from Adam to Moses, even over those whose sins were not like Adam's transgression, who is the type of the one who was to come... For if by one man's offence death reigned through that one man; much more those who receive abundance of grace and the gift of righteousness will reign in life by one, Jesus Christ..."

Adam is here presented as the first transgressor, because as the first man created he was the "head" and starting point of the human race and responsible for what happened. Adam and Eve are here probably considered as one in sinning, since they were "one flesh" (Gen. 2:24), so that, as to guilt, Eve is here included in Adam.

Men never sin in a "parable-manner," or "mythically," but in the actual "historical" life. The first people had a definite particular commandment (prohibition) of God which they transgressed. Why could it not be the prohibition to eat of the tree of the knowledge of good and evil? Why should it be something else?

It was not a natural serpent that beguiled Eve, but the devil, as the Bible clearly teaches, speaking of the devil as "that old serpent, called the Devil, and Satan, who deceiveth the whole world" (Rev. 12:9). But since beings of the spirit world, both good angels and evil angels or devils, must take a visible form in speaking to men, so the devil chose to take the form of a serpent. Why not this form as well as any other? He could not take the form of man since Adam was then the only man, and probably it would have been more difficult to deceive Eve in a human form.

If Adam and Eve were not real "historical" persons but "figureheads" of every man and every woman, then Paul's arguments in Rom. 5:12-19 and 1 Cor. 15:45ff. concerning the correspondence between the "first Adam" and "last Adam" lose their meaning. This correspondence, however, is fundamental in the biblical doctrine of salvation: As Adam's sin plunged mankind into sin and condemnation, so Christ's work opened to mankind salvation in free justification and new life in the Spirit. If the "first Adam" and his sin were not real, then it may be questioned whether the "last Adam" and His saving work were real either. If the "first Adam" and his fall was a mere symbol of "everyman" and his sinning, there may be some justification for the thought that the "last Adam" too is a symbol of "everyman" and his self-salvation. This is actually what many liberals teach.

If the tree of the knowledge of good and evil and the serpent were not real but mere symbols of forces that are struggling in everyman, the necessary conclusion is that already before the fall, men had something evil in their nature, whether as remnants of their animal stage, as the "theistic evolutionists" must think, or otherwise. In that case the biblical teaching that man was in the beginning good and righteous, an image of God, must be rejected. But such a view subverts the entire biblical teaching of creation, the nature of man, the fall, sin, and salvation. If man was originally not righteous and with God in a fellowship that was not disturbed by sin, how can he be "renewed in knowledge after the image of him who created him" (Col. 3:10), and be re-created "after God in righteousness and true holiness" (Eph. 4:24)? The scriptural teachings of creation, fall, and salvation are inseparable, and if one of them is changed or rejected, the others, too, will break down.

What happened in the first fall in Paradise is, naturally,

also a type or pattern of what happens in "everyman's" life. But it can be such only if it was a real "historical" event. The "old serpent" continues to use about the same methods and tactics as he used then. His main method continues to be to lead men to doubt the word of God and to give up faith in and obedience to it. In our time he is doing it particularly by means of liberal Bible criticism. And as he then led people to eat of the forbidden tree of the knowledge of good and evil in order to gain a better knowledge than they had from God, so also now he is leading people to "eat" of the "tree" of literature and teaching in which good and evil are mixed. Numerous believing people have lost their faith and fellowship with God when they have allowed themselves to be led to eat of the modernistic "tree of knowledge" which has led them away from a simple faith in the truth of God's Word and obedience to it.

3. The "NEPHILIM" of Genesis 6

Gen. 6:1-4 records that before the great flood "the sons of God saw the daughters of men that they were fair; and they took them wives of all whom they chose... The giants (Hb. NEPHILIM) were on the earth in those days, and also after that, when the sons of God came in to the daughters of men, and they bore children to them; these were the mighty men who were of old, the men of renown." Who were the "sons of God" and the "giants," NEPHILIM?

Some have explained that the "sons of God" were angels who had sexual intercourse with women. True, some pagan religions, such as that of Greece, have had mythological tales of "gods" who have had children with human women. But according to the Bible, angels (both good and evil) are asexual, as is seen from Christ's words in Mt. 22:30; they are spirits (Heb. 1:14) without material bodies ("a spirit hath not flesh and bones," Lk. 24:39), so that sexual intercourse between them and women is impossible. Angels have appeared to men in human form, without, however, having material body, which is necessary for sexual intercourse.

As Luther and many other leading interpreters (so also

Scofield, Gen. 6:4, and Jamieson-Fausset-Brown's Commentary) have explained, the "sons of God" were Sethites, the generation of God's children, and the "daughters of men" were women of the ungodly generation of Cain, who obviously were able to adorn themselves so as to look "fair" in the eyes of Sethite men. God has always wanted His children to observe the rule set down in 2 Cor. 6:14ff: "Be ye not unequally yoked together with unbelievers; for ... what part hath he who believeth with an unbeliever." This wall of separation broke down between the Sethites and Cainites, and the Sethite men "took them wives of all whom they chose," following their natural desires, unmindful of the will of God. This disregard of the divine prohibition to marry unbelievers on the part of the Sethites resulted in the spread of sin-corruption among them to the extent that finally Noah and his family were the only God-fearing and righteous people in the mankind of that time.

The Hebrew word NEPHILIM, translated "giants" (as Jamieson-Fausset-Brown's Commentary correctly explains), "implies not so much the idea of great stature as of reckless ferocity, impious and daring characters, who spread devastation and carnage far and wide." Because of this, "the earth was filled with violence" (6:11), and "all flesh corrupted its ways on the earth" (6:12). Mixed marriages between believers and unbelievers have always been a source of much calamity and curse on earth.

4. Animals in the Ark, The Great Flood

Gen. 6:19f. reports how God commanded Noah to take a pair of each (land) animal into the ark, but in Gen. 7:2f. we read that he had to take the clean beasts by sevens. How is this to be understood? — and how did Noah manage to get the animals into the ark?

The first of the referred passages reports the first general command that the Lord gave to Noah when He first directed him to build the ark. When the ark was ready, that is, after ab. 120 years, God gave him the supplementary order to take the clean beasts by sevens. This did not probably mean that he had to take 14 animals (7 males and

7 females), but that he had to take three pairs and one supernumerary, probably to be used for sacrifices after the flood.

The "kinds" of animals that Noah had to take into the ark probably were not the same as most modern taxonomists (scientists who classify animals and plants into the various groups, such as phyla, classes, families, species) have classified as different species. They were likely the basic forms which after the flood have diversified by way of microevolution into varieties, geographical races and in some cases into parallel related species (united by the taxonomists who have the polymorphic concept of species as variant forms of the same species). Since only land animals were to be taken, the total number did not need to be more than ab. 25,000, and the great majority of them were smaller than a cat. There was enough room for them on the three floors of the ark, and also for their food, which was needed for a little more than a year. Probably numbers of the animals passed much of this time in a state of hibernation ("winter sleep") and did not need food or care at that time. Almost all reptiles and mammals have at least a latent ability for it.

Animals have often a curious instinct to know that danger is coming and to flee. God, the Creator, obviously gave the animals such an instinct that they—the ones that had to come—came into the ark of their own accord, so that Noah did not need to seek and drive them into it. God also had His supernatural and natural means to take care of them in the ark.

Because of the (probable) water canopy before the flood and the consequent more even climate, the distribution of animals was not as scattered and diversified as it is now, so that most of the various kinds of land animals may have lived in a relatively small area and did not need to travel long distances to the ark (see Morris-Whitcomb, **op. cit.**, pp. 63-88). If Alfred Wegener's theory of the "continental drift" is true, the continents were at that time grouped together, and travelling to the ark was easier and distances shorter for this reason, too.

Both the animals and men that were outside the ark perished, except aquatic and amphibian animals, of which only a part were destroyed. The sedimentary beds that were formed in the flood (the "Paleozoic," "Mesozoic" and "Cenozoic" formations) contain a large part of the vegetation, animals and men of the antediluvian era in fossilized form, bearing witness to a universal flood. A great number of these natural facts show that the flood covered the whole earth and was not local, as some have assumed. Many of these facts also show that the flood could not last more than about a year, as the Bible reports. Scripture and the facts of nature agree well with regard to the flood.

On the flood and the facts of nature that bear witness to it, see Morris-Whitcomb, **op. cit.;** Byron Nelson, **The Deluge Story in Stone** (Augsburg Publ. H., Minneapolis, Minn., 1931); H. W. Clarke, **The New Diluvialism** (Science Publications, Anguin, Calif., 1946); George McCready Price, **Common Sense Geology** (Pacific Press, Mountain View, Calif., 1946); Dudley Joseph Whitney, **The Case for Creation** (Christian Evidence League, Malverne, N. Y., 1946); L. M. Davies, **Scientific Discoveries and Their Bearing on the Account of the Noachian Deluge** (Transactions of the Victorian Institute, LXII, London, 1930); Alfred M. Rehwinkel, **The Flood** (Concordia Publ. H., St. Louis, Mo. 1951).

5. Differences in Names and Numbers

We read in 2 Sam. 8:3 that David smote Hadadezer, but in 1 Chr. 18:3 the name is Hadarezer. In Gen. 10:3 the name of one of the sons of Gomer is Riphath, but in 1 Chr. 1:6 he is called Diphath (KJV has here too Riphath). How should we understand these differences?

Until about 1450 A.D. the books of the Bible were copied by hand. Although the copyists in general did their best, they made here and there mistakes. In some cases these errors were caused by their reading the text wrongly. In addition, the OT text has been once changed from one type of script (the old Hebrew) to another (the square script). Some mistakes probably crept into the text in this process. The original manuscripts are inerrant, not the copies and translations.

In the cases of Riphath-Diphath, Hadadezer-Hadarezer

the reason obviously is that in Hebrew square script the letters d and r are very alike, the only difference being that in d the angle is sharp, in r roundish, so that they are easily confused if not written carefully. Because of this, some early copyist has confused the two letters. The correct forms are Riphath and Hadadezer.

2 Sam. 8:4 reports that David took from the referred Hadadezer 700 horsemen, but in 1 Chr. 18:4 this number is 7,000.

2 Sam. 24:13 states that the possible famine was to last 7 years, but in 1 Chr. 21:12 it is 3 years.

1 Ki. 4:26 reports that Solomon had 40,000 stalls of horses, but according to 2 Chr. 9:25 he had only 4,000.

According to 1 Chr. 18:12, Abishai slew in the valley of salt 18,000 Edomites, but the heading of Ps. 60 says that Joab smote of Edom in the valley of salt 12,000 men. How are these differences to be explained?

The differences between the numbers 3 and 7, 4,000 and 40,0000 obviously are due to mistakes by copyists. In the case of the famine the correct number must be 3, for this was the number in the other two alternatives. In Hebrew 3 was written by the letter **gimel** and 7 by **zayin,** which are in Hebrew script so alike that they are easily confused if not written carefully. In the case of the number of Solomon's horses, the 4,000 is probably the correct number.

Numbers were written in Hebrew either in words or by using letters of the alphabet as numerals. Thus, the first letter, **aleph**, was one, the second letter, **beth**, was two, etc. The letters from **kaph** to **tsadi** represented tens from 20 to 90, the letters from **koph** to **tau** stood for the hundreds up to 400. Thousands were expressed by two dots over the proper unit letter. Thus, the letter **teth** alone stood for 9, but with two dots it stood for 9,000. When this method was used, errors in transcription occurred easily and preservation of numerical accuracy was difficult. Some numerical errors possibly also crept into the text at the time when the old Hebrew script was replaced by the square script.

The difference between 1 Chr. 18:12 and the heading of Ps. 60 is only apparent: 1 Ki. 11:15f. reports that Joab went to Edom to bury the slain, remaining there six months, and during that time he "cut off" (put to death) the males of Edom. This implies that a great number of men had been slain before he went there. The men whom he went to bury were obviously those whom the army led by his brother Abishai had smitten (doing it as his subordinate). The 12,000 mentioned in the heading of Ps. 60 were those smitten during the half a year which Joab himself was there.

2 Sam. 10:18 tells that David slew in the war against the Syrians 700 chariots and 40,000 horsemen, but according to 1 Chr. 19:18 he slew 7,000 chariots and 40,000 footmen. How is this to be explained?

The difference between 700 and 7,000 is obviously due to a copyist's error. That the 40,000 in one case are called horsemen and in another case footmen is probably due to the fact that they were used as both, as has been done in many other cases. The same men could, therefore, be called either horsemen or footmen.

According to 2 Sam. 24:9 Israel had 800,000 valiant men who drew the sword and in Judah 500,000 men, but in 1 Chr. 21:5 the corresponding numbers are 1,100,000 and 470,000. How can this discrepancy be accounted for?

These differences in numbers are probably due to different methods of counting, and we do not know what these methodical differences were. Scofield (2 Sam. 24:9) suggests that 2 Sam. 24:9 gives the total military strength, 1 Chr. 21:5 the number of men actually in array. We must leave the matter open.

Nu. 25:9 reports that "those who died in the plague were 24,000," but according to 1 Chr. 10:8 there "fell in one day 23,000." What is the reason for this difference?

Scofield probably gives the correct interpretation in noting that Nu. 25:9 gives the total number of the dead in the plague, while Paul speaks of the number of deaths in one day. The additional thousand people died after that one day.

According to Gen. 14:14 Abram pursued the kings of the east to Dan, smote them and rescued Lot and all that he had, but Judg. 18:27-29 reports that the city of Dan was built much later, and that the name of that place before that was Laish. How is this to be understood?

There are two possible explanations: First, the "Dan" to which Abram pursued the kings may have been another place, an earlier city in a different area, having the same name (there were also, e.g. two cities whose name was Bethlehem). Second, Gen. 14:14 may have had originally "Laish," but it was later changed to "Dan," since the city was then known by that name and the older name was no longer used. We do not know which of these explanations is correct.*

The lists of the Jews who returned from Babylon in Ezra 2:1-64 and Neh. 7:7-66 have several differences, although the total number in both is the same, 42,360. But when the numbers listed in the two records are added, the sum total is in Ezra 29,818 and in Neh. 31,089. How are these differences to be accounted for?

The differences may be due to copyists' errors: They have accidentally dropped some names and numbers, in Ezra somewhat more than in Neh., although the total number has remained the same. Another possibility is that both Ezra and Nehemiah have purposely omitted some names and numbers which they did not regard as important and gave the sum total. Such omissions are common in biblical genealogies, as we have shown.

1 Sam. 18:19 reports that Saul's daughter Merab was

---

* The "Amraphel" of Shinar who was one of the kings of the east (14:1), was not the Hammurabi of Babylon, the famous lawgiver, as sometimes has been assumed but an earlier king. Hammurabi (there were actually three contemporary kings who had this name) lived ab. 300 years later than the Amraphel of Gen. 14:1.

given to Adriel to wife, but 2 Sam. 21:8 speaks of Michal, another daughter of Saul, as Adriel's wife. According to 1 Sam. 18:27f. Michal was a wife of David. How can these discrepancies be explained?

Michal was the better known of Saul's daughters. Since the names of both daughters begin with the same letter and in Hebrew the other letters too somewhat resemble one another, some early copyist has written in 2 Sam. 21:8 Michal instead of Merab. This error is easily corrected on the basis of 1 Sam. 18:19.

6. Abraham's Age and Place of Calling

Gen. 11:26, 32 and 12:4 relate that Terah begat Abram, Nahor and Haran when he had lived 70 years. Terah died in Haran at the age of 205 years, and Abram was 75 years old when he departed from Haran after his father's death. But in Acts 7:4 we are told (Stephen): "After his father died, God removed him [Abram] from there [Haran] into this land." These passages seem to contain a conflict: If Terah was 70 years old when Abram was born and lived to the age of 205 years, Abram must have been 135 years old when he left Haran after his father's death. But according to Gen. 12:4 he was only 75 years old when he departed from Haran. How are these passages to be reconciled?

Gen. 11:26 does not obviously mean that Abram, Nahor and Haran were all born when Terah was 70 years old, for they were hardly triplets. It means that after Terah had become 70 years old these three sons were born to him, but at different times, possibly several years between. That Abram is mentioned first does not necessarily mean that he was the oldest. It may be due to the fact that he was the most important of them, the one whom God chose to be the receiver of His revelation and the father of the chosen nation. The firstborn were not usually chosen by God. Abraham may well have been the youngest of the three sons of Terah, born when he was 130 years old. In that case he was 75 years old when his father died and he left Haran. If understood in this manner, there is no discrepancy between the referred passages.

We read in Gen. 12:1f. that the Lord said to Abram after the death of his father Terah: "Go from thy country ... to the land that I will show thee"; but Stephen says in Acts 7:2f., that God appeared to Abraham "in Mesopotamia, before he dwelt in Haran, and said to him, Depart from thy country..." How should we understand these apparently conflicting passages?

There is no real conflict between these passages. Abraham obviously received from God the **first** call in the Ur of the Chaldeans, and it was because of this that he moved to Haran; but he stopped there and did not go on to Canaan. He had to receive a **new** order from God before he went on to the promised land. We have a reference to the first call in Gen. 15:7: where God says to Abraham: "I am the Lord who brought thee from Ur of the Chaldees..." Had Abraham not received a revelation and commandment from God in Ur, the Bible would hardly say that the Lord brought him from there.

The same is usually the case with men in general: God's first call does not commonly lead them all the way from the world into His kingdom. Another call is needed, and maybe even more. Thus, there is nothing strange in the fact that God called Abram first in Ur and then in Haran. Gen. 12:1f. and Acts 7:2f. are not contradictory but supplementary.

7. The Israelites' Stay in Egypt, Confirmation of the Covenant

Gen. 15:13 records God's words to Abram: "Know of a surety that thy descendants will be sojourners in a land that is not theirs, and will be slaves there, and they will be oppressed, four hundred years." In Ex. 12:40 we read: "Now the time that the children of Israel dwelt in Egypt was 430 years." Paul writes in Gal. 3:17: "The law, which came 430 years afterward, cannot annul the covenant that was previously confirmed by God, so as to make the promise void." We may understand the 400 years in Gen. 15:13 as a "round number" that means "about 400 years." Ex. 12:40 gives the more accurate length of time. But how can we explain the statement in Gal. 3:17 that the interval between the confirmation of the promise given to Abraham and the exodus from Egypt and giving of the law was 430 years? The time from the giving of the promise to Abram to Jacob's arrival at Egypt was about 215 years. If we add to this the 430 years that the Israelites were in Egypt, the time between the giving of the promise and the giving of the law was ab. 215 years longer than the 430 years given by Paul. How should this be understood?

True, Paul writes in Gal. 3:17 of the promise and blessing to Abraham and his seed. But Paul does not speak here of the **making** of the covenant but of its **confirmation,** and this was done to Jacob when he was in Beersheba on his way to Egypt. The Bible makes a clear distinction between the **making** of the covenant with Abraham and its **confirmation** to Jacob. We read of this in Ps. 105:9f. and 1 Chr. 16:16f:

> "The covenant which he made with Abraham..., which he confirmed to Jacob..."

Paul counts the 430 years from the confirmation of the covenant to Jacob in Beersheba, not from its making with Abraham.

According to 1 Ki. 6:1, Solomon began the building of the temple in the 480th year after the departure from Egypt, which was 967 B.C. When we count from this year 480 years backward, we get the year 1447 B.C. for the year of the exodus from Egypt. 430 years from 1447 B.C. backward is 1877 B.C., which is the year when God confirmed the covenant to Jacob.

We have inserted in Gen. 15:13 a comma before the words, "four hundred years," because the Hebrew Masoretic text has here a punctuation mark that corresponds to our comma. It is here necessary, for the 400 includes the entire period spoken of in this verse, and not only the time when the Israelites were oppressed.

8. Marriages of Brothers and Sisters

In Lev. 18:9, 29 marriages between brothers and sisters

are forbidden at the pain of death, but according to Gen. 20:11f. Sarah, Abraham's wife, was his sister, of the same father but of different mother. How is this to be understood?

God had not prohibited marriages between brothers and sisters before Moses, and they were therefore not sin. For Adam's and Eve's sons and daughters such marriages were the only possible ones. Gen. 5:4 reports that Adam and Eve had several daughters. Cain married one of his sisters, and Seth did the same. At that time people were so healthy and normal that marriages between brothers and sisters had no harmful effects on the offspring. But after sin had corrupted and weakened mankind, so that they had degenerative genes, such marriages became dangerous, since a brother and sister may both have the same harmful gene which in such a case would be fatal to the offspring. God knew this and for the good of men prohibited such marriages.

Lev. 20:21 forbids a man to marry his brother's wife, but Deut. 25:5f. (cp. Mt. 22:24) ordains to the Israelites that in case brothers live together and one of them dies without offspring, his surviving brother must take the widow and raise offspring to him. The firstborn son was to be counted as a son of the brother who had passed away, in order that his name would not be blotted out from Israel. How should these apparently conflicting ordinances be reconciled?

Exception confirms the rule. Lev. 20:21 gives the general rule, but an exception of it was to be made in the described case. This was, however, not compulsory (Deut. 25:7ff.).

9. Was Isaac Abraham's Only Son?

Gen. 22:2 and Heb. 11:17 speak of Isaac as Abraham's only son, but according to Gen. 16 and 25:6 Abraham also had other sons, namely, Ishmael of Hagar and several sons of Keturah. How is this to be explained?

Paul writes in Rom. 9:7f: "Not that all are children of Abraham because they are his descendants, but 'In Isaac shall thy descendants be called.' This means that it is not the children of the flesh who are the children of God; but the children of the promise are counted as seed" (descendants). Among the children of Abraham, Isaac was the only "child of the promise" who was counted as his "seed." He was the only one of the line through whom God's revelation was carried on and of which Messiah, Christ, was to be born. From this point of view, Isaac was Abraham's "only son."

10. Number of Jacob's Family and Their Burial Places

Gen. 46:27 reports that "all the persons of the house of Jacob who came into Egypt were seventy," but Stephen states in Acts 7:14 there were 75 souls in the kindred of Jacob. How should we explain this discrepancy?

Stephen obviously used the Septuagint version which had in Gen. 46:20 the addition: "Manasseh had sons from his Syrian concubine Marik. Marik gave birth to Galad. The sons of Ephraim, brother of Manasseh, were Sutalam and Tam. Sutalam's son was Edom." When the members of Jacob's "kindred" mentioned in LXX, but not in the Hebrew text, are counted the sum total is 75. Thus, both numbers, 70 and 75 are correct, depending on whether the descendants of Manasseh and Ephraim are counted or not. The possible reason why the descendants of Manasseh and Ephraim are mentioned in LXX is that they were born during the life time of Joseph, but they did not exist at the time when Jacob moved to Egypt. At that time the number of his family was 70, but it increased after that, during Joseph's life.*

According to Gen. 50:13 Jacob's sons carried his body to Canaan and buried it in the cave of Machpelah, which Abraham (Gen. 23:17f.) had bought from Ephron the Hittite. Josh. 24:32 reports that, after having settled in

---

* Scofield explains that the difference between Gen. 46:27 and Acts 7:14 is due to the fact that in the latter passage the wives of Jacob's sons are included in his "kindred." This cannot be the right solution, for the 12 sons of Jacob must have had more than five wives.

Canaan, the Israelites buried the bones of Joseph in Shechem, in the parcel of land which Jacob had bought from the sons of Hamor the father of Shechem. But Stephen states in Acts 7:15f: "So Jacob went down into Egypt and died, he and our fathers, and were carried back to Shechem and laid in the tomb that Abraham had bought... from the sons of Hamor." How are these statements to be reconciled?

The words of Stephen do not necessarily mean that Jacob was also buried in Shechem. "Our fathers," the sons of Jacob, were buried there. True, the OT tells only of the burial of the bones of Joseph at Shechem, but the Jews had a tradition (whose reliability we have no reason to doubt) that the other sons of Jacob were also buried there.

More difficult is the statement of Stephen that Abraham had bought the parcel of land in Shechem whereas Josh. 24:32 reports that it was bought by Jacob. The following solution has been suggested: According to Gen. 12:6, Shechem was one of the localities where Abraham dwelled. Although Gen. does not mention it, it is possible that he bought there a parcel of land. When he moved away and did not return, the piece of land fell into the hands of the former owners and their descendants. When Jacob came to the place ab. 185 years later, the descendants of Hamor did not acknowledge him as the owner. He did not want to quarrel, and purchased to himself the same piece of land. Stephen knew the tradition about this.

Another possible explanation (given by R. A. Torrey, **Difficulties in the Bible,** Moody Press, pp. 93f.) is as follows: The two sepulchres mentioned in Gen. 23:17f. and Acts 7:16 are not the same. Possibly Abraham purchased another sepulchre, at another place, in addition to the one mentioned in Gen. 23:17f., and Jacob bought later "the parcel of field" in which the sepulchre was. Josh. 24:32 informs that the bones of Joseph were buried in the parcel ground which Jacob bought, and which presumably contained the sepulchre that Abraham had bought at an earlier date. These are, of course, only assumptions, but they show that we have no reason to think that there is a real discrepancy between the referred passages. We merely do not know all the facts.

11. Horses of Egypt and Passage through Edom

Ex. 9:3-6 reports that the cattle of Egypt, horses included, died of murrain, but no cattle of Israel died. Ex. 14:9, however, tells that the Egyptians pursued the Israelites, all the horses and chariots of Pharaoh, and his army. If the horses of the Egyptians died in the murrain, where did they get horses so soon?

Ex. 9:3 states expressly that the horses and cattle that were **in the field** died of the murrain. Pharaoh's war horses were probably largely in stalls, and they did not die. Besides, the Egyptians could take horses from the Israelites if they needed them.

Nu. 20:14-21 relates that the Edomites refused to grant Israel passage through their land, and therefore the Israelites turned away from Edom. But Moses tells in Deut. 2:3-7 that the Israelites passed through the territory of the children of Esau; they were, however, not allowed to "contend with them," but they had to buy food and water when they needed them. How can these passages be reconciled?

Deut 2:8 also reports that the Israelites passed by from the children of Esau. Num. 20:23, etc., indicates that the Israelites journeyed on the road that was along the eastern border of Edom. In doing so, they had to travel to some extent also in the area of Edom. Although the Edomites threatened them with sword they did not dare to attack them, because they feared them (Deut. 2:4). Thus, the Israelites did not journey across the land of Edom, but they travelled partly on its territory and avoided all that could have provoked strife. There is no real conflict between the referred passages.

12. Daughter of Jephthah and the Course of His Life

We read in Judg. 11:30-39 how Jephthah, a Gileadite, vowed to the Lord that if He would give the Ammonites into his hands, whoever would come forth from the doors of his house to meet him when he would return as victor, should be the Lord's. After he had defeated the Ammonites and returned home, his daughter came to meet him, his only child, and he offered her to the Lord. Was this kind of human sacrifice right?

God did not command the Israelites to sacrifice their children. In the case of Abraham, Scripture tells expressly that the Lord tempted (=tried) him. Through Moses the Lord gave the Israelites a strict prohibition against sacrificing their sons and daughters as burnt-offerings (Deut. 12:31). Jephthah gave his vow inconsiderately, without asking the will of God, probably forgetting this prohibition of the law of Moses or being ignorant of it. When he saw that his daughter came to meet him, he should have asked God for pardon of his thoughtless vow. Instead, he committed another error and misdeed in offering her. The Bible does not pronounce any judgment on his action, but lets the event speak for itself.

In writing about monastic vows, Luther shows how it is wrong to fulfill a vow that is in conflict with God's Word. The divine ordinances have supreme authority, and they should not be transgressed, even if a vow has been given. Scripture reports the case of Jephthah and his daughter in order to caution against inconsiderate vows and promises.

Liberals have asserted that there is a conflict between Judg. 11:1-3, which states that Jephthah was son of a harlot and was driven away by his brothers, sons of the legitimate wife of Gilead, after which he became a bandit, and 11:34 which reports that he was a respected house owner in Mizpah. This indicates, the critics say, that the writer of Judg. 11 used two source documents, the "J" and "E." How should these passages be explained?

The fact that Jephthah was driven from his home and was for some time a bandit did not hinder him from settling down later in Mizpah and owning a house there. There is no conflict between the two passages, and the talk of the two source documents is just liberal imagination.

13. Last Phases of King Saul's Life

According to 1 Sam. 22:23 and 23:6, Abiathar, a priest of Nob, fled to David, when Saul let the priests of Nob be put to death. Abiathar took with him the priestly ephod and the Urim and Thummim that belonged to its breastplate and that were used for inquiring the will of God. 1 Sam. 28:6 reports that Saul inquired of the Lord, but He did not answer him, neither by dreams, nor by Urim, nor by prophets. But 1 Chr. 10:13f. says that Saul died for his transgression, because he did not obey the Lord and consulted one who had a familiar spirit (a "medium"), and did not seek guidance from the Lord. How should we understand the apparent contradiction that one of the passages states that Saul did not seek guidance from the Lord, but another one says that he inquired of the Lord, but the Lord did not answer him?

After Abiathar had fled to David, Saul probably appointed somebody else to serve as high priest and had another ephod with Urim and Thummim prepared. He inquired of the Lord by means of them, but did not receive answer because he merely wanted help for his own plans, without true repentance and submission to the will of God. Therefore the Lord did not accept it as a genuine enquiring of Him. He only accepts as true enquiring such asking which takes place in the right frame of mind and which aims at the doing of His will, and is not merely seeking help for one's own carnal desires and plans.

1 Chr. 10:4 states that Saul committed suicide, casting himself on his own sword, but according to v. 14 the Lord slew him. How should these passages be reconciled?

The Lord uses means in accomplishing His works of judgment and salvation. He slew Saul by letting him cast himself on his own sword.

1 Sam. 31:3f. relates that Saul, being sore wounded, took a sword and fell upon it, but according to 2 Sam. 1:2-10 an Amalekite told David that he had slain Saul at his own request. How can these two reports be reconciled?

There are two possible explanations. One is that the Amalekite lied to David, and the Bible merely records what he said, having related before how Saul's death actually took place. Another one is that Saul, being badly wounded, cast himself on his own sword but did not die, and rose again; when he was leaning on his spear, the Amalekite came, and Saul asked him: "Slay me; for anguish hath seized me, and yet my life still lingers." He was close to death, and at his request the Amalekite gave the final stroke. This may be implied in the Amalekite's words to David: "So I... slew him, because I was sure that he could not live after he had fallen." There is no real conflict between the two reports.

14. Did Absalom Have Sons?

According to 2 Sam. 14:27, three sons and a daughter were born to Absalom, but 2 Sam. 18:18 tells that Absalom reared up for himself a pillar, saying: "I have no son to keep my name in remembrance." How is the apparent discrepancy between the two passages to be solved?

There are two possibilities: Either Absalom reared the pillar prior to the birth of the sons, or else, his sons died in their youth without leaving offspring, and therefore he, in his vanity, reared up a memorial pillar for himself.

15. Who Moved David to Number Israel?
Price for the Threshingfloor

We read in 2 Sam. 24:1: "Again the anger of the Lord was kindled against Israel, and he incited David against them to say, Go, number Israel and Judah." But in 1 Chr. 21:1 we are told that "Satan stood up against Israel and incited David to number Israel." How should we understand these conflicting passages?

Scripture states many a time how God has executed His deeds of punishment or mercy either through angels or men, or through evil spirits. He has done this either by commandment or by permission. He destroyed Samaria and the kingdom of Israel in 722 B. C. by means of the army of Assyria, and in 70 A.D. He destroyed Jerusalem through the agency of the Roman army led by Titus. In Mt. 22:7 Jesus speaks of the army that was to destroy Jerusalem as God's army. God allowed Satan to destroy Job's property, and yet Job said: "The Lord gave, and the Lord hath taken away" (Job 1).

The numbering of Israel obviously took place so that God's wrath was kindled against Israel because of its sins, and He wanted to punish it. He did it by letting Satan move David to order the numbering. This action of vanity and pride was then punished. God "moved" David by letting Satan do it.

In general, Satan cannot do to God's people more than God permits, and He allows only things that He sees needful to His people for chastening, humbling, etc. The two passages, 2 Sam. 24:1 and 1 Chr. 21:1, set forth the two sides of the same event, and only together they give the complete picture.

2 Sam. 24:24 reports that David paid for the threshingfloor of Araunah (Ornan), where he offered sacrifices, 50 shekels of silver, but according to 1 Chr. 21:25 the price for the place was 600 shekels of gold by weight. How can these two passages be reconciled?

2 Sam. 24:24 states that David paid 50 shekels of silver for the threshingfloor (Hb. GOREN), but according to 1 Chr. 21:25 he paid 600 shekels of gold for the place (Hb. MAKOM) or area, on which was later built the temple with its spacious courts. David obviously first bought only the small threshingfloor, but soon after it bought the whole place, about a hundred times larger than the threshingfloor. 2 Sam. 24 reports only the purchase of the threshingfloor, 1 Chr. 21 combines the two purchase transactions.

16. Contents of the Ark of the Covenant

We read in 1 Ki. 8:9 that "there was nothing in the ark except the two tables of stone, which Moses put there at Horeb," but in Heb. 9:4 we are told: "The ark of the covenant... contained a golden pot that had manna, and Aaron's rod that budded, and the tables of the covenant." How can these passages be reconciled?

The difference is probably due to the fact that the pot of manna and Aaron's rod that were in the ark at early times were no longer there when the ark was taken into the temple built by Solomon. The ark had many "fortunes," and one of them was that it was for some time in the hands of the Philistines. In some phase the pot and rod had been removed from it. Possibly the words, "there was nothing in the ark except the tables of stone..." imply that there had been other things in it before, but they were no longer there at that time.

17. Removal of High Places by Asa. Relations between Asa and Baasha

1 Ki. 15:11, 14 relates that king "Asa did what was right in the eyes of the Lord...But the high places were not taken away." 2 Chr. 14:2ff, however, tells that Asa "took away...the high places, and broke down the images." How should we understand these apparently conflicting passages?

2 Chr. 15:17 reports the same thing as 1 Ki. 15, that the high places were not taken away. Asa wanted to remove them and gave an order to that effect, and many of them were actually removed, but the people adhered to them so stubbornly that many of the destroyed ones were taken into use again, and many others were not removed. This is in general the case when a government attempts to abolish something that has become the custom of the people. The statements both in 1 Ki. and 2 Chr., that the high places were not taken away imply "between the lines" that attempts were made to remove them.

Note: Scofield, 1 Ki. 15:14 and 3:2, explains that Asa destroyed the idolatrous high places but not the Jehovistic ones, those that were used for worshipping the Lord of Israel, and that the altars on high places were not evil in themselves. The prohibition in Deut. 12:11-14 came into effect only after the building of Solomon's temple. — This interpretation cannot be right, for, as we have seen, Josh. 22 shows that the prohibition to offer sacrifices on other altars except on the one in the Tabernacle was already then in force. All the altars on high places (except the temporary altars built at God's special orders) were transgressions of the divine law. The altar on the high place of Gibeon, on which Solomon offered sacrifices at the beginning of his reign, was the one in the tabernacle, which at that time was there (1 Ki. 3:4; 1 Chr. 16:39: 21:29; 2 Chr. 1:3), and it was therefore the right place for sacrifices.

1 Ki. 15:16 tells that Asa, king of Judah, and Baasha, king of Israel, had war between them all their days, but in 2 Chr. 14:4ff. we read that Asa's kingdom was quiet before him, and he built fenced cities in Judah, for the land had rest, and there was no war in those years. Only somewhat later did Asa have war with Zerah the Ethiopian and with Baasha. How should we understand these apparently conflicting passages?

It is customary in our time to speak of a "cold war" and a "hot war." There was enmity between Asa and Baasha all the time, that is, "cold war," which later became a "hot war." Asa built fenced cities in the years he had no "hot war" but only "cold war."

18. Service Age of Levites

We read in Nu. 4:3, 38f. that the Levites were counted from 30 years up to 50 years old to do the work in the Tabernacle, but Nu. 8:24 states that the Levites had to serve in the Tabernacle from 25 years old and upward. 1 Chr. 23:3, 24, 27 reports that the Levites were numbered from the age of 30 years and upward, but they served in the sanctuary from the age of 20 years and upward. How should these passages be understood?

Both according to Nu. 4 and 1 Chr. 23, the Levites from the age of 30 years upward were numbered. Nu. 8:24 says that they had to serve in the age of 25-50, but David lowered the start of the service age to 20 years. Why the age used in numbering was higher than the age when they had to start their service is not known to us. We have here no discrepancy, but it is a question of different ordinances at different times.

19. Dates of Kings. Elisha and Ben-hadad

1 Ki. 16:8 reports that Elah, son of Baasha, began to reign over Israel in the 26th year of Asa, king of Judah,

but according to 2 Chr. 16:1, Baasha went against Judah in the 36th year of Asa—which should have been about a decade after Baasha's death, if we count his life according to 1 Ki. 16:8. How can these discrepancies be explained?

There are two possible explanations. First, 2 Chr. 16:1 may have a transcription error: An early copyist has written 36 instead of 26. If so, Baasha died in the same year when he went against Judah. Second, the time in 2 Chr. 16:1 is counted from the division of the kingdom. If so, Baasha's attack against Judah took place in the 15th year of the reign of Asa. In this case 2 Chr. 16:1 should be translated: "In the 36th year, while Asa reigned, Baasha king of Israel came up against Judah..."

We are told in 2 Ki. 8:26 that Ahaziah became king when 22 years old, but 2 Chr. 22:2 says that he was 42 years old when he began to reign. How can this be explained?

2 Chr. 22:2 obviously has a transmission error made by an early copyist, and the correct number is the one given in 2 Ki. 8:26, namely, 22 years.

According to 2 Ki. 15:30, Hoshea killed Pekah and became king of Israel in the 20th year of Jotham king of Judah, but a few verses later (33) we read that Jotham reigned only 16 years in Jerusalem. How is this to be understood?

Jotham's father Uzziah had leprosy in the last years of his life. Although he was formally the king, his son Jotham took care of the government, and his father lived in a separate house (2 Ki. 15:5; 2 Chr. 26:21). The 20 years in 2 Ki. 15:30 are counted from the beginning of his regency (or maybe from the time when he became coregent with his father), not from the time of the death of Uzziah.

We read in 2 Ki. 15:30 that Hoshea became king of Israel in the 20th year of Jotham, but 2 Ki. 17:1 states that Hoshea began to reign in the 12th year of Ahaz of Judah. Since Ahaz started to reign in 736 B.C., the year of Hoshea's ascension was in reality the 4th or 5th year of Ahaz. How should this problem be solved?

It is not possible that the same writer would have in the original autograph given conflicting statements like these. The conflict must have entered the text through a copyist's error: an early copyist must have written 12 instead of 4 or 5. This could easily happen when letter-numerals were used instead of writing out the numbers with words.

If Hezekiah, son of Ahaz, succeeded his father in 716 B.C., how can this be reconciled with the statement in 2 Ki. 18:1 that Hezekiah began to reign in the third year of Hoshea king of Israel? As mentioned above, Hoshea began to reign in 732 B.C.

Before we can suggest a solution of this problem, we must consider the question of the chronology of the kings of Israel and Judah in general.

Note: Chronology of the Kings of Israel and Judah

E. R. Thiele prepared at the Oriental Institute of the University of Chicago his doctor's dissertation on the chronology of the kings of Judah and Israel in the period 900-600 B.C. entitled, **The Mysterious Numbers of the Hebrew Kings** (2nd ed., Eerdmans, Grand Rapids, Mich. 1965). Thiele shows that in figuring out the times when the kings of Judah and Israel reigned the following things should be observed:

1. In Israel or the Northern Kingdom the regnal year began in the month **Nisan** (or Abib, the first months of the sacred and the seventh of the civil year, answering to a part of our March and April), while in **Judah** it began in the month **Tishri** (or Ethanim, the seventh month of the sacred and the first of the civil year, answering to parts of our September and October).

2. During the period of the divided kingdom, **Judah** reckoned the years of its kings so that the fraction of the year when a king began to rule was regarded as his accession year, but not his first year. His first year was counted from the beginning of the month Tishri following his accession to the throne. In **Israel** the year when a king began to reign was reckoned as his first year, and his second year began with the first of Nisan following his accession.

3. Both in Israel and Judah, when the years of the other country's kings were counted, the method of counting in the own country was followed, not the neighbor's method.

HATH GOD SAID?

4. Both in Judah and Israel coregencies were used, and in such cases the years of the king were usually reckoned from the beginning of the coregency. These factors often explain the apparent conflicts in the lengths of the reigns of the kings. By taking them into consideration and by using other factors which harmonize the biblical accounts, Thiele came to the conclusion that the chronological data of the kings of Israel and Judah harmonize well. In some cases—as in the ones mentioned above—the discrepancies are obviously due to mistakes in transcription.

In dealing with Hezekiah's reign, Thiele (p. 140) assumes that the author of 2 Ki. committed an error. He holds that 715 B.C. was the time when Hezekiah began to reign, and that there is a mistake in 2 Ki. 18:1, which affirms that his rule began in the third year of King Hoshea of Israel. Hoshea began to reign in 732, and this would point to 728 as the beginning of Hezekiah's reign, or about 13 years before 715 B.C. 2 Ki. 18:9, 10 states that Shalmaneser of Assyria began his siege of Samaria in the fourth year of Hezekiah and captured it in his sixth year. Since Samaria fell in 722 B.C., this means that the reign of Hezekiah began in 728 B.C. But in conflict with this 2 Ki. 18:13 states that Sennacherib invaded Judah in the "fourteenth year" of Hezekiah's reign. Since the Assyrian invasion is firmly datable in 701 B.C., this would point to 715 B.C. as the commencement of Hezekiah's rule. In his review of the second edition of Thiele's book **(Christianity Today,** April 15, 1966, pp. 34-36) Professor Gleason L. Archer offers a plausible solution of this problem. He suggests that in the original spelling of the numerals **fourteen** and **twenty-four** in Hebrew, a scribal error in copying a single letter, substituting **he** for a **mem,** would cause "twenty-four" to become "fourteen." If this textual emendation is accepted, there is no difficulty in reconciling this statement with the rest of the data in 2 Ki. If the 24th year, according to the emended reading, is reckoned from 725 B.C., the year of the death of Hezekiah's father Ahaz (with whom he was coregent for three years), the result is 701 B.C., the date of Sennacherib's invasion.

Thiele (p. 120) also assumes an error in 2 Ki. 17:1, which states that Hoshea of Israel began his rule in the 12th year of Ahaz, since this would involve a 12-year coregency with his father Jotham. Prof. Archer explains that "if Hoshea's reign began in 732, and this year was both the twelfth year of Ahaz (II Kings 17:1) and the twentieth year of Jotham (II Kings 15:30), the co-regency would amount to only seven or eight years, for Jotham ceased ruling in 736/5, and apparently lived in retirement until 732. If he began as co-regent with his father, Uzziah, in 751 (as Thiele maintains), then Jotham's sixteen years (II Kings 17:1) of rule ran from 751 to 736/5, and Ahaz began as co-regent with Jotham in 743. Since Ahaz reigned for sixteen years, this means that he ended his active career in 728/7, although he lived on for three more years (cf. II Kings 18:1), until 725. By this interpretation all the data can be harmonized, and there is no need to assume that any of the statements made in Second Kings are erroneous, apart from the one point (II Kings 18:13), that seems to require the textual emendation suggested above (and this is not chargeable, of course, to the original manuscript itself)."

Thiele offers a convincing solution of the puzzling data of Pekah, who reigned, according to 2 Ki. 15:27, twenty years, beginning his rule in the 52nd year of Uzziah, that is, in 739 B.C. The difficulty is that Menahem ruled in Samaria in 752-742, and his successor Pekahiah ruled until 740/39. Since Pekah's successor Hoshea began to rule in 732, this would give only about 7 or 8 years for Pekah's rule. Thiele's solution of this problem is as follows: Pekah had set up a rival dynasty in Gilead back in 752 and spent his earlier years there (2 Ki. 15:25), but did not succeed in overthrowing Menahem or Pekahiah until 740/39. Hence it is accurate for 2 Ki. 15:27 to state that Pekah began his rule (that is, as sole ruler of all Israel) in the 52nd year of Uzziah, that is, 739 B.C. It was only natural for Pekah to maintain that he had always been the only legitimate king of Israel, even from 752, once he had established himself as supreme over the whole realm.

We read in 2 Ki. 6:22f. how the king of Israel, at the counsel of Elisha, prepared a great meal for the army of Syria which had been led into the city of Samaria by the prophet. The effect of this act of kindness was that the Syrians made no more raids to Israel. But the following verse reports that Ben-hadad king of Syria mustered his whole army and besieged Samaria, capital of Israel. How can these passages be reconciled?

The writer would hardly have given conflicting information in successive sentences. His meaning is obviously that the kind treatment experienced by the raiding army in Samaria had the effect that for a while the Syrians made no raids on Israel. But after some time the Syrian king's lust for war awakened again, but then he came with his whole army. When understood in this manner, the text has no discrepancy.

20. Standing Still of Sun and Moon. Returning of Shadow in Sun Dial.

Hare that Chews Cud. Jonah in the Belly of a Whale.

Josh. 10:12ff. tells us how the army of Israel fought against the five kings of the Amorites, and how Joshua said in the midst of the battle: "Sun, stand thou still at Gibeon; and thou Moon, in the Valley of Aijalon. And the sun stood still, and the moon stayed, until the people had taken vengeance on their enemies." In practice this should have meant that the rotation of the earth stopped for several hours, and likewise the movement of the moon. Scientists say that such an event would have upset the earth to the extent that the waters of oceans would have flooded the continents, and the upheavals would have been so great that hardly any living creatures would have survived, at least in the land areas. Isn't this story of the Bible impossible?

The Bible tells that Joshua spoke of the matter to God and gave his orders to the sun and moon according to God's instructions. God is the almighty Creator, and the earth is before Him as a small grain of sand. If He saw it fit to stop the movements of the earth and moon for several hours, He could do it so that no disturbances took place in and on the earth. The powers of nature are fully in His control, who created them. Whatever was the manner in which He accomplished the miracle of Gibeon and Aijalon, it was not difficult for Him. A Christian believes the Word of God as it is, for he believes in the mighty God whose Word is truth.

We read in Is. 38:7f. and 2 Ki. 20:8-11 how God gave king Hezekiah the sign that the shadow returned in the sun dial of Ahaz ten degrees. Isn't this impossible? The earth should in that case have returned almost a half of its daily rotation!

The Scripture does not say here that the earth turned backward in its rotation, but that the shadow in the sun dial was brought backward ten degrees. God has made greater miracles than this, and we have no reason to doubt that He did at the time of Isaiah and Hezekiah what His Word says.

Lev. 11 speaks of the animals that the Israelites were not allowed to eat, and among them (vv. 5f.) were "the coney (ASV and RSV: rock badger) because it cheweth the cud but doth not part the hoof ... And the hare, because it cheweth the cud, but doth not part the hoof." We know from biology that neither the coney (or rock badger) nor the hare are ruminants. How should we understand this passage?

There are two possible explanations: First, the names of the animals in the Hebrew text are misunderstood, and neither coney nor hare are really meant. Second, the word "chew the cud" may not be used here in the biological sense, but means merely that these animals move their cheeks in a somewhat similar manner as the ruminants. Whichever of these interpretations is right, we are not justified to charge the Bible with an error.

The book of Jonah relates how the prophet was cast into the sea, and how the Lord prepared a great fish to swallow him. After three days and nights in the belly of the fish, he was vomited by it upon the dry land. How can such a thing be possible?

Christ speaks of the factuality and historicity of this event in Jonah's life in Mt. 12:40: "As Jonah was three days and three nights in the belly of the whale, so shall the Son of Man be three days and three nights in the heart of the earth." Thus, if we deny the historicity of this event in Jonah's life, we deny the truth of Christ's words. Many liberals deny either thing in the cited statement of Christ, both Jonah's getting out of the whale's belly after three days and night, and Christ's resurrection from the "heart of the earth" after three days and nights. This is, ultimately, a question of faith and unbelief.

Professor W. Arndt discusses the question of Jonah quite thoroughly in his book **Bible Difficulties** (Concordia Publ. H., St. Louis, Mo., 1953, pp. 127-131). He admits that the "whalebone whales" have so narrow a throat that they are not able to swallow a man. But certain kinds of the sperm or toothed whales (cachalots) have a gullet which, according to a manager of a whaling station, "can take lumps eight feet in diameter," and it is this very whale that is found in such subtropical waters as the Mediterranean. The skeleton of a shark 16 feet long has been found in the belly of a sperm whale, and bodies of octopus (8-armed cuttle-fish), far larger than the body of man, have been found in its stomach. It has the habit of swimming "with its lower jaw hanging down and its huge gullet gaping like some submarine cavern. Only too easy to be swallowed by it."

This whale has enough air in its stomach for a man to breathe. Its gastric juice cannot digest living matter, for otherwise it would digest its own stomach. There are reliably recorded instances in which the sperm whale has swallowed men, who have come out alive from their gruesome prison. There is, therefore, nothing impossible in the story of Jonah.

We should, however, remember that the events of Jonah's life were no mere natural incidents, but they were specially arranged by God, who took care of him. God was able to keep him alive and cause the whale to vomit him upon dry land, just as He was able to keep the three friends of Daniel alive in the fiery furnace—which was a much greater miracle.

But a miracle almost still greater is required for a

Christian young man to survive spiritually alive during the three-year brain-washing of a liberal theological seminary.

The main thing in the book of Jonah is the three-fold truth set forth in it: (1) God loves sinners, even the heathen, and sends messengers to them to call them to repentance, in order that they would be converted and saved. (2) Jonah's stay in the belly of the whale was a type of Christ's stay in the tomb, and Jonah's emergence from it alive a type of Christ's resurrection. (3) As the conversion and salvation of the Ninevites through the preaching of Jonah was followed by his emergence from the whale's belly, so the conversion and salvation of great numbers of heathen through the preaching of the Church, body of Christ, has followed His resurrection from the "heart of the earth."

21. Genealogies of Jesus and His Virgin Birth

There are great differences in the genealogies of Jesus in Mt. 1 and Lk. 3. That the Gospel of Matthew begins with Abraham and the Gospel of Luke with Adam is, of course, no "conflict," but is due to the fact that the former was written for the Israelites, Abraham's descendants, and the latter for the Gentiles, or mankind in general, the descendants of Adam. But how should we understand the fact that the two genealogies are entirely different from David to Joseph: Mt. proceeds from David through Solomon to Joseph and Jesus, but Lk. goes on from David through his other son Nathan (the prophet Nathan was a different person) to Heli, Joseph and Jesus?

According to OT prophecies, the Messiah was to be the heir of the throne of His "father" David, belonging to the legal Davidic line of kings (Is. 9:6f. — Lk. 1:32), but He was also to be David's natural descendant, "a shoot out of the stump of Jesse" (Is. 11:1 — Rom. 1:3).

As we read in Jer. 22:30, king Jehoiachin (=Coniah), who belonged to the official Davidic line, was "written as childless" in the sense that "no man of his offspring shall succeed in sitting on the throne of David." Thus, the Messiah was to be a member of the Davidic line through Jehoiachin, but He could not be his natural descendant; yet, he was to be a descendant of David in the natural sense.

The only manner in which these two lines of prophecies could be fulfilled was that Joseph, Jesus' foster father and as such His "legal" father, was heir of the Davidic throne in the legal line, and that He was David's natural descendant through His mother Mary.

According to an Israelite tradition, the son-in-law was counted as a man's son if he had no male heir (cp. Deut. 25:5 — Mt. 22:24), and the son of this son-in-law with his daughter was counted as his lawful "seed" or descendant.

The genealogy of Mt. wants to show that Jesus was the legal heir of David's throne through Solomon—Jehoiachin—Joseph. The genealogy of Lk. intends to show that He was a natural descendant of David through His mother Mary. Heli, who in Lk. is given as the father of Joseph, was not his natural father (such was the Jacob mentioned in Mt. 1:16) but his father-in-law, the father of Mary, his wife. Lk. does not say that Heli **begat** Joseph, but simply that he was "of Heli" (the word "son" is an addition by the translators, and is not in the Greek text). The necessary interpretation is that he was Heli's son-in-law (thus e.g. Scofield, Jamieson-Fausset-Brown, and F. Davidson, **The New Bible Commentary,** IVF, 1963, Lk. 3:23).

Many liberal theologians hold that a virgin birth is impossible, against the laws of nature, and that therefore Jesus could not be born of a virgin, but was a natural son of Joseph and Mary. The "virgin birth" is merely a figurative or mythical manner to say that He was more than a mere man. What should we think of this?

"Virgin birth" is not impossible among men. Medical science estimates on the basis of its observations that about one child in a million is actually "virgin-born." All such children are necessarily girls. However, in the case of Jesus, the virgin birth was not the main issue, but the essential thing was His conception of the Holy Spirit. His virgin birth was the necessary consequence of this. Had He been virgin-born in a natural sense, He would have been a mere man. The fact that He was God and Man in the same person was due to His being begotten of the Holy Spirit, as the words of the angel Gabriel show:

> "The Holy Spirit shall come upon thee, and the power of the Most High shall overshadow thee; therefore also the holy One born of thee shall be called the Son of God" (Lk. 1:35).

Mt. 1:18, 20 likewise records that an angel revealed to Joseph that the child who was to be born of Mary was begotten of the Holy Spirit.

If we do not believe these plain statements of the Bible concerning the conception and birth of Jesus, how can we believe anything else that the Bible teaches?

22. Cyrenius the Governor. Accounts of Jesus' Infancy

Lk. 2:2 records that Cyrenius (Lat. Quirinius) was the "governor" of Syria at the time of Jesus' birth. Josephus, however, informs that Cyrenius was governor of Syria in 6 A.D., or about a decade later. The list of Roman governors of Syria in the last years of Herod the Great does not include Cyrenius. How should we explain this?

Lk. 2:2 does not say that Cyrenius was "governor" of Syria, but that he was commander or leader (Gr. **hegemoneuontos**) of Syria. We know from secular sources that Varus was the governor of Syria, but Cyrenius, too, was in the east at that time. He was a military man, probably the military commander of the Roman forces in those areas. As such the burden of carrying out of the imperial order concerning the census for taxation rested mainly on him.

The census that is mentioned in Acts 5:37 was held in 6 A.D. The Romans took a census every 14 years, and going back 14 years from 6 A.D. takes us to 8 B.C. It was obviously at this time that the first census was started, but it took time before it could be organized in the distant provinces, especially since it was the first one, and the necessary machinery had to be set up. It is therefore quite understandable that a couple of years passed before it could actually be accomplished in Syria-Palestine. Herod the Great died in 4 B.C., and Jesus was probably born either in 6 or 5 B.C. A mistake of several years was later made in counting the beginning of the Christian era.

Some critics have tried to disqualify Luke's account by appealing to the Roman system, according to which people had to register in the city or town where they lived, and not in their ancestral locality. This was, however, no exceptionless rule. The Romans were shrewd rulers, and they adapted themselves in the various lands, as far as possible, to the local customs and traditions. Some documents that have been discovered have shown that in Egypt people had to go for census to their ancestral towns. If so in Egypt, why not in Palestine, where the tradition of the people required a similar method?

According to Mt. 2, the wise men from the east came to Bethlehem, and after their departure, at the direction of an angel, Joseph took his family to Egypt. After the death of Herod the Great, they returned to their own land and settled down in Nazareth. The Gospel of Lk., however, tells nothing of the wise men and the sojourn in Egypt. Instead, it relates how, after the days of Mary's purification (that is, 33 days after the birth of Jesus, Lev. 12:6f.), Jesus was taken to Jerusalem where He was presented before the Lord, and the sacrifices that the Mosaic law required were offered. While in the temple, Simon blessed them, and Anna, a prophetess, also spoke of Jesus. After this, they returned to Galilee, to their own city Nazareth. How can the accounts of Mt. and Lk. be reconciled?

Luke wrote his Gospel later than Matthew (Lk. 1:1-3), and he obviously wanted to supplement Mt., telling (partly) of different things. The course of events was probably as follows:

Joseph and Mary stayed with Jesus in Bethlehem until the days of purification were fulfilled. Having performed in the temple what was required by the law of Moses, they returned to Nazareth, where they had their home and where the angel had appeared to Mary and Joseph, revealing to them the coming birth of Jesus, the Savior (Lk. 1:26ff., Mt. 1:18ff.). From there, they soon moved to Bethlehem, planning to live in this ancestral city of the family of David. While there the second time, the wise men from the east came to worship Jesus. After their departure, they went to Egypt, and returned from there after Herod's death, according to the directions by an angel. The statement in Mt. 2:22 that Joseph was afraid to go to Judea because Archelaus was ruling there seems to imply that his intention was to go to Judea, probably to Bethlehem, to reside there, since they had been living there before going to Egypt. Having received new directions from an angel, they "turned aside" and went to Galilee, settling down in Nazareth. That Herod ordered all male children of Bethlehem and its surroundings, two years old and under, to be slain seems to indicate that the visit of the wise men took place more than a year after Jesus' birth. Thus, there was enough time for the holy family to go to Nazareth, to dwell there several months, to return to Bethlehem and to live there for some time before the arrival of the Magi. Understood in this manner, the accounts of Mt. and Lk. do not contradict but supplement each other.

23. Beginning of Jesus' Public Ministry

According to Mk. 1:14, Jesus went to Galilee after John the Baptist had been put into prison and preached there the Gospel of the kingdom of God. But in Jh. 3:22 we are told that Jesus was active in Judea, where He made disciples and baptized (through the agency of His disciples, Jh. 4:1f.). John the Baptist preached and baptized at the same time at Aenon near Salim, for he was not yet cast into prison. How are these apparently conflicting accounts of the beginning of Christ's public ministry to be explained?

True, Mk. is silent of Jesus' activity in Judea, but he does not deny it. He merely starts his record with Jesus' activity in Galilee, while Jh. tells of His work in Judea before

He began it in Galilee. Prior to it, He had, however, had a short activity in Galilee, having been, among others, at the marriage feast in Cana (Jh. 2). While Jesus was on his way back to Galilee, He stopped for a couple of days at Sychar, where many people believed in Him (Jh. 4:1-42). After this He began His actual work in Galilee. There is no conflict between Mk. and Jh., they merely supplement each other.

Lk. 3:1ff. reports that John the Baptist began to preach and baptize in the 15th year of Tiberius Caesar. We know from general history that Augustus died in 14 A.D., and that Tiberius was his successor. The 15th year of Tiberius was 29 A.D. After John had been active for some time, Jesus, being about 30 years old, came to him to be baptized (Lk. 3:23). Since He was born ab. 6-5 B.C., He was "about 30 years old" some years before 29 A.D. In the 70 year-week prophecy of Daniel (9:24-27), the 70 year-weeks began in 457 B.C., and the beginning of the 70th year-week (7 years) was in 27 A.D. The middle of it was 30 A.D., when the OT sacrifices ceased (to be in force before God) through the all-sufficient sacrifice of Christ. Other facts, too, point to the year 30 A.D. as the time when Christ was crucified, rose again, and when the Christian Church was born. How are these things to be explained?

Tacitus and Suetonius, two Roman historians, report that Tiberius was co-ruler with Augustus from the year 11 or 12 on. Lk. obviously counts the 15 years from the time when Tiberius became co-ruler. From that time, there was 15 years to 26-27, when John began his public ministry.

Lk. 3:2 states that Annas and Caiaphas were high priests at the time when God's word came to John and he began to preach baptism of repentance. How is this to be understood, for according to the Mosaic law there was to be only one high priest at a time?

Annas became high priest in 7 A.D., but the Romans deposed him in 14 A.D. One of his sons was high priest before Caiaphas, who was his son-in-law. Four sons of Annas were high priests after Caiaphas. Even after his removal from office, Annas was highly respected by the Jews, and he was still spoken of as high priest. The Jews regarded his deposition as illegal, for according to the Mosaic law the office of the high priest was for life. Lk. 3:2 is, therefore, to be understood to mean that Annas was the high priest according to the divine law, while Caiaphas was the high priest who was appointed by the Romans.

24. Temptations of Jesus

The "Synoptics," Mt., Mk., and Lk., relate that after His baptism Jesus was led by the Spirit to the wilderness where He was tempted by the devil. But Jh. tells that, after having been in touch with John the Baptist, Jesus called Andrew, Simon Peter, John, Philip and Nathanael to be His followers. After that, on the third day, He was at the marriage feast of Cana. How can these accounts be reconciled?

Jh. 1:32 implies that Jesus had been baptized by John before the events recorded here. The visit of the messengers of the Jews, mentioned in vv. 19ff., had also taken place after His baptism by John. Thus, the record of John starts at a different point of time than those of Mt., Mk., and Lk., namely, after the baptism and temptation of Jesus. There is no conflict between them. Jh. 2:1 speaks of the third day after the recorded events, not of the third day after Jesus' baptism.

According to Mt. 4:1ff., the Spirit led Jesus to the wilderness to be tempted by the devil, and after He had fasted for 40 days and nights He was hungry. Then the devil came to Him and urged Him to turn stones into bread. But in Lk. 4:2 we read that Jesus was "forty days tempted by the devil," eating nothing during that time. After the forty days, when Jesus was hungry, the devil said to Him: "Command this stone to become bread." How can these accounts be harmonized?

The statement in Mt. 4:1, that Jesus was led by the Spirit into the wilderness to be tempted by the devil implies that He was tempted all the time, possibly at first inwardly. After the forty days, the series of three temptations took place, recorded both in Mt. and Lk. There is no discrepancy here. That the devil, according to Mt., spoke of stones in plural, and, according to Lk., in singular, of one stone, is a trifle. Maybe the devil said something like this: Command this stone, and this, and this to become bread. Lk. shortened this, taking only the first part, and Mt. contracted it by using plural. Whatever may be the case, this is an insignificant bagatelle.

How should we understand the fact that in Mt. the temptation of the pinnacle of the temple is the second in order, while it is the third one in Lk.?

Neither Mt. nor Lk. says that the temptations took place in the order they tell of them. This question has hardly any significance. There are numerous cases in the biblical records in which the events are not recorded in their chronological order, but in the order determined by the contents or meaning of them. This may also be the case with regard to the order followed in Mt. and Lk. **Matthew** wrote his Gospel record primarily for the Jews, whose special temptation was false religion and seeking high places in the congregation, symbolized by the pinnacle of the temple. The Jews also wanted, as the devil's agents, to get Jesus down from the supreme place that belonged to Him, doing it by appealing to the Holy Scriptures. This attempt of the Jews was, in a sense, anticipated by the devil who appealed to what was written in trying to get Jesus to jump down from the pinnacle of the temple. **Luke** wrote his Gospel record for the Gentiles, the Romans, and their special temptation was the seeking of the glory and power of the kingdoms of the world. A regard to the readers may have determined the order of the last two temptations in Mt. and Lk.

25. Use of Wine in Prov. 31 and in the Wedding of Cana

We read in Prov. 31:4-5: "It is not for kings..., it is not for kings to drink wine; nor for princes strong drink;

lest they drink, and forget the law, and pervert the judgment of any of the afflicted." But the following verses say: "Give strong drink to him who is ready to perish, and wine to those who are of heavy hearts (or, bitter distress). Let him drink, and forget his poverty, and remember his misery no more." Prov. 20:1 warns of wine, and 23:31ff. does it still more strongly: "Look not at wine when it is red... At last it bites like a serpent..." Isa. 5:22 pronounces woe to those who are heroes at drinking wine, and according to 1 Cor. 6:10 drunkards will not inherit the kingdom of God. How should we understand these apparently conflicting statements, and the fact that Jesus changed water into wine in the wedding feast of Cana, thus providing wine for drinking?

Prov. 31:4-5 plainly warns of drinking wine, which leads kings and princes to forget the law and pervert justice. Verses 6 and 7 do not encourage to use strong drink and wine in general, but only in cases of extreme physical weakness and despondency, when the man is "about to perish." A person in such a condition can be stimulated by the wine, lifted up from his depression. This passage is related to 1 Tim. 5:23, in which Paul counsels Timothy to use a little wine (as medicine) for his stomach troubles and weakness. Both passages speak of the use of wine as medicine, either in extreme weakness and despondency or in stomach trouble, not otherwise. Even in our time many doctors prescribe wine, possibly with some other ingredients, in cases like these. The Bible does not prohibit the use of wine as medicine, but it prohibits its use as intoxicant.

In the wedding feast of Cana Jesus came to the rescue when the wine failed. But there is not a hint that the wine He made was intoxicating. New-made wine is never intoxicating, and such was the wine Jesus made. Wine becomes intoxicating only after some time, when the process of fermentation has set in. It was, as the steward (KJV: "governor") admitted, better wine than they had been drinking, but this did not imply that it was intoxicating. Even if some of the guests were already drunken, or had drunk freely (Jh. 2:10, KJV: "have well drunk," ASV and RSV: "have drunk freely") of wine that may have been intoxicating, it was only good for them that Jesus substituted it with good quality unintoxicating fresh wine.

Another thing to be noted is that the Bible uses wine as a symbol of the grace of God that gives true joy in the heart. In Isa. 25:6, which is part of a prophecy of the new covenant and its salvation, "wines on the lees well refined," is used in this sense, and so is the word "wine" used in Isa. 55:1. This kind of application can be used for both Prov. 31 and Jh. 2.

26. Centurion and His Servant

Mt. 8:5-13 tells us of a centurion in Capernaum who came to Jesus and asked Him to come and heal his servant, but according to Lk. 7:1-10, he did not come to Jesus himself but sent Jewish elders to Him. How can these accounts be reconciled?

An old principle states: "He who acts through another, acts himself" (Lat: **Qui fecit per alium, facit per se**). The Bible has a number of examples of actions done through representatives, which are dealt with as having been done by the persons (God or men) themselves. Gen. 32:28 states that Jacob strove with God, but Hosea 12:4 tells us that "he strove with the angel, and prevailed." Jh. 3:22 reports that Jesus baptized, but in Jh. 4:1f. we are told that His disciples performed the baptisms, that is, Jesus baptized through their agency. The centurion asked Jesus to heal his servant, presenting his request through the agency of certain Jews. We should note that in Lk., too, the centurion speaks in the first person, although he does it through his Jewish friends. There is no real discrepancy between the accounts of Mt. and Lk. In Mt. the events are recorded more briefly, in Lk. in more detail, probably because the case of the Roman centurion naturally was of special interest to the Romans for whom Luke wrote his Gospel record.

27. Ahimelech and Abiathar. "Zechariah Son of Barachiah"

Mk. 2:26 relates how Jesus told to the Pharisees (who

charged His disciples with a transgression of the sabbath law when they plucked ears of grain and ate the grain), how David in the time of Abiathar the high priest went into the house of God and ate the showbread which was not lawful for any but the priests to eat. However, according to 1 Sam. 21:1-6, it was Ahimelech who was the priest who gave David the showbread. How should we understand the conflict between these passages?

When we read the following chapter in 1 Sam. we see that Abiathar, son of Ahimelech, was the only priest of Nob who escaped when Saul had the priests of this city slain. He fled to David, taking the ephod with him (23:6). Abiathar was called priest, just as Ahimelech was, and he was later a high priest. Thus, when David went to Nob, both Ahimelech and his son Abiathar were there. It was therefore just as right to say that the event took place in the time of Abiathar as to say that it took place in the times of Ahimelech. Abiathar is possibly mentioned in Mk. 2:26 because he was a much more prominent person and better known than his father Ahimelech. We should also note that Jesus does not say in Mk. 2:26 that Abiathar gave David the showbread, but merely that this took place in his time, and this was the case.

The translation of ASV and RSV, "When Abiathar was high priest," is not quite accurate. KJV has a more accurate translation: "in the days of Abiathar the high priest." The Greek **epi Abiathar archiereos** means: "in the time of A. the high priest."

Note: 2 Sam. 8:17 speaks of Ahimelech son of Abiathar, who was priest in the time of David. There are two possible explanations: Either Abiathar had a son who had his grandfather's name, or an early copyist has written here by mistake "Ahimelech son of Abiathar" instead of "Abiathar son of Ahimelech."

Mt. 23:35 records that Jesus spoke of Zechariah son of Barachiah as having been slain between the sanctuary (temple) and the altar, but according to 2 Chr. 24:20ff. Zechariah was son of Jehoiadah. How is this to be explained?

There are four possible solutions:

1. Jehoiadah was also called Barachiah. This was either his second name or an honorary title (meaning "Blessed of the Lord/Yahweh") given him because of the great services that he accomplished for his people.

2. Barachiah was Zechariah's grandfather or ancestor. We have seen how the Bible in many cases uses the phrase "son of N." when this "N." actually is an ancestor (as e.g. Jesus is called "son of David," Zacchaeus "son of Abraham," etc.).

3. The words "son of Barachiah" may not have been in the original autograph of Matthew but has been erroneously added to the text by an early copyist. **Codex sinaiticus (Aleph*)**, which is one of the oldest manuscripts (from c. 325-350 A.D.), does not have the words "son of Barachiah" in the original text, but someone has added them to it later. Th. Zahn and some others have thought that the writer of Aleph* deliberately omitted the phrase in order to "correct" the passage, and that the person who later added it to the text did it on the basis of older manuscripts. This is, however, a mere assumption. It is possible, if not likely, that while writing this passage an early copyist recalled either the prophet Zechariah son of Berechiah (Zech. 1:1) or the "Zechariah son of Jeberechiah" of Is. 8:2 (Berechiah/Barachias and Jeberechiah were variants of the same name), erroneously identified him with the Zechariah meant by Jesus, and inserted to the text the words "son of Barachias." If so, these words are an early error of a copyist, and do not belong to the inspired text.

4. The possibility has been also suggested that either the prophet Zechariah son of Berechiah or Zechariah son of Jeberechiah was killed between the altar and sanctuary, and that Jesus referred to this event, known to the Jews from their tradition, although not mentioned in the OT.

We must leave undecided which of these solutions is right.

28. Names of Some Apostles

The lists of the twelve apostles in Mt. 10 and Lk. 6 are otherwise alike, except that they have two different names: Mt. has Lebbaeus, surnamed Thaddaeus, and Simon Canaanite; Lk. has Judas [son] of James (KJV has "brother of," but "son of" is probably right), and Simon called Zealot. How is this to be understood?

The word "Canaanite" is formed of a Hebrew or Aramaic word that means "zealot." Lk. translates this word, Mt. leaves it untranslated. Lebbaeus (Thaddaeus) is obviously the same person as Judas [son] of James. He had two names (plus his surname Thaddaeus), which he probably used at different times, just as Paul used earlier his Hebrew name Saul and later his Latin name Paul(us), and as Mark is also known by his other name John. Possibly Judas [son] of James at one time used his name Lebbaeus to avoid confusion with another Judas (Iscariot) among the apostles.

29. Supplies to be Taken for Missionary Journey

Mt. 10:9f. reports how Jesus gave His apostles, on sending them to their first missionary journey, the instruction that they should not provide for it gold or silver or brass, or two coats or shoes or staves, etc., but according to Mk. 6:8f. He said that they had to take a staff only, be shod only with sandals, and not put on two coats. How can these passages be reconciled?

According to Mt. 10:9f., Jesus told His apostles that they should not **provide** a staff or shoes for themselves. According to Mk. 6:8f., they were allowed to **take** a staff and sandals (Gr. ktesesthe—airosin). This meant: If they had a staff, they could take it along and use the sandals they had, but they should not go to acquire a staff or additional shoes. There is no discrepancy between the two passages, they merely supplement each other.

30. The Unrighteous Steward

Jesus tells in Lk. 16:1-14 of an unjust steward who wasted his master's goods and then reduced the amounts that the debtors of his master owed to him in order that they might receive him into their houses. According to KJV, we read in Lk. 16:8: "And the lord commended the unjust steward, because he had done wisely: for the children of this world are in their generation wiser than the children of light." Jesus went on to say: "I say unto you, Make to yourselves friends of the mammon of unrighteousness; that, when ye fail, they may receive you into everlasting habitations." How could Jesus commend such a scoundrel as the unjust steward was and hold him up for imitation to His disciples?

We should first of all notice that Jesus does not commend his dishonesty. On the contrary, He says right after speaking of this man: "He who is faithful in that which is least is faithful also in much; and he who is unjust in the least is unjust also in much. If therefore ye have not been faithful in the unrighteous mammon, who will commit to your trust the true riches." In these words Jesus severely warns of dishonesty and exhorts to faithfulness. In His parable, too, Jesus shows that an unjust steward is once required to give account of what he has done.

The second thing that Jesus says is that "the children of this world are in their generation wiser than the children of light." He makes here a clear distinction between the children of this world, unbelievers, and the children of light, believers. The former are wiser in the sense that they use their utmost ingenuity and efforts to make present opportunities count for the future needs. The children of light, whose hearts are not after the worldly mammon (or, at least, should not be) do not use similar energy and ingenuity for the business and other affairs of this world.

Jesus does not exhort His disciples to follow this example of the children of this world. Rather, His point is this: If the children of this world use all their ingenuity and energy to procure for themselves a secure future in this short life, how much more should the children of light make effort to use the opportunities that they have to secure for themselves, and for others too, a happy eternity?

Third, the statement, "And the lord commended the unjust steward, because he had done wisely," does not mean that the Lord Jesus commended him, but that the lord (ASV and RSV use here the word "master") of the steward commended him, that is, acknowledged that he had been clever in his efforts to secure for himself the favor of his master's debtors. He naturally did not approve of his dishonesty.

Fourth, Jesus exhorts in this parable His disciples to make themselves friends by means of the mammon of unrighteousness in order that, when it will fail, they may receive them into everlasting habitations (thus ASV).

Jesus means: His disciples should use their temporal means (which He calls "the mammon of unrighteousness" in contrast to the true riches) for helping their fellow men both in their physical and spiritual needs. If they do so, the people whom they have thus helped will testify for them in eternity, saying something like this: These people helped us during our earthly life in our needs. They supported the work of the Gospel with their temporal means, and so we too heard it and were saved. All this shows that they should be accepted into the everlasting habitations, for they have shown by their works that they have believed in Christ as their Savior and Lord and followed Him.

In other words, Jesus set forth in a new and striking form what He had taught many other times, namely, that we should not selfishly keep our money to ourselves and hoard it, but we should spend it for doing good, particularly to God's needy ones, and so invest in heavenly and abiding securities. Paul says essentially the same thing when he writes 1 Tim. 6:17-19:

> "Charge those who are rich in this world not to be haughty, nor trust in uncertain riches, but in the living God...; that they are to be good, be rich in good works, ready to distribute, willing to be generous; laying up in store for themselves a good foundation for the time to come, that they may lay hold on the life which is life indeed."

Thus, when understood aright, according to the intention of Jesus, the passage in Lk. 16:1-14 does not contain any difficulties but gives important teachings to His followers.

31. Violence to God's Kingdom and Its coming

Mt. 11:12 records the words of Jesus: "From the days of John the Baptist until now the kingdom of heavens suffereth violence, and the violent take it by force." What is the meaning of this statement?

Jesus speaks of the same thing in Lk. 16:16: "The law and the prophets were until John; since that time the kingdom of God is preached (Gr. **euangelidzetai**=the Gospel of the kingdom of God is proclaimed), and every man presseth into it" (so KJV; ASV: "entereth violently into it"; RSV: "enters it violently"). The Greek word **biadzetai**, used both in Mt. and Lk., is probably a translation of the Hebrew and Aramaic word PARAZ (from which is derived PHAREZ, name of a son of Judah, Gen. 38:29), whose basic meaning is to **divide, tear, break through,** but which also means: **to ask earnestly, to plead, and so to get through, to constrain by that means, to urge.** The word is used in this meaning in 1 Sam. 28:23, in which KJV has: "But his servants, together with the woman, compelled him; and he hearkened unto their voice." ASV has here: "...constrained him," and RSV: "...urged him." Jesus' meaning in the quoted passages, when the word **biadzein** is understood according to its probable Hebrew and Aramaic original, is: The penitent sinner who earnestly pleads for mercy and admission into God's kingdom and thus "constrains" Him, gets it to himself, is accepted into it. The Greek translation of the word PARAZ does not make the meaning of Jesus as clear as the Hebrew and Aramaic does, when understood according to its OT usage.

Jacob was an example of this kind of "violence" when he took hold of the angel who wrestled with him and said: "I will not let thee go, unless thou bless me" (Gen. 32:25f.), and so was also the sinful woman in Simon's house, who wept at Jesus' feet and gained the kingdom when Jesus forgave her sins to her (Lk. 7:36-50). Such was also the Philippian jailer who trembling fell down before Paul and Silas and said: "Sirs, what must I do to be saved?" (Acts 16:29f.) He too entered it through faith in the Gospel.

There are those who use the wrong kind of violence in order to grab the kingdom of God to themselves, but they never get it. The Jewish leaders wanted to take the "vineyard" to themselves by having the Son of the Owner of the vineyard killed, but the consequence was that the kingdom was taken and given to the Gentiles (Mt. 21:33-43). The "times of the Gentiles" began in the time of the apostles (not with the captivity of Judah under Nebuchadnezzar, as Scofield explains, Lk. 21:24), and they end after the war of Gog and Magog, when God pours out His Spirit upon Israel, so that it will be converted to Christianity (Ez. 37-39; Zech. 12; Joel 3; Rom. 11). Then the old city of Jerusalem will go under the rule of Israel (Lk. 21:24). The Roman Church has claimed that God's kingdom belongs to it, that it is the kingdom, and it has used violence against those who have not acknowledged this. At the end-period of the present age the great harlot church, Babylon the Great (the World Church that will be the end result of the ecumenical movement, led by the final great Antichrist who will sit on seven mountains, i.e. in Rome, the Pope), will make the final great effort to take the kingdom of God by force. She will practice such violence against the Bible-believing Christians, members of the true kingdom of grace, who do not submit to her rule, that she will be drunk with the blood of saints (Rev. 17:6). But this attempt will end in catastrophe, when the scarlet beast (red world power) and its ten horns (satellite states) will turn against the harlot World Church and destroy her (Rev. 17:16). Carnal violence will never succeed in its attempt to take the kingdom of God. The only "violence" that succeeds in it is a penitent sinner's pleading for mercy: "A broken and contrite heart, O God, thou wilt not despise" (Ps. 51:17).

* * *

Jesus says in Mt. 16:28: "Verily I say to you, There are some standing here who will not taste death, before they see the Son of Man coming in his kingdom." In Mk. 9:27 Jesus says the same thing in partly different words: "There are some of those who stand here who will not taste of death, before they see the kingdom of God come with power." In Lk. 9:27 we have the words: "There are some standing here who will not taste death, before they see the kingdom of God." How should we understand this statement of Christ in its slightly different variations?

The kingship of Jesus and the kingdom of God are inseparable, since Christ is the King of God's kingdom. The coming of Christ in His kingdom means therefore the same as the coming of the kingdom of God. Jesus' words, originally spoken in Aramaic, have been translated into Greek in slighty different ways in the three Gospels, but their meaning is the same.

The kingdom of God has two "parts," the kingdom of grace here in this world, with God's believing children as its members, and the kingdom of glory in the invisible world, with departed saints and angels as its members. In speaking of the kingdom of God or kingdom of heavens, Jesus in most cases means the kingdom of grace. His words to Pilate, "My kingdom is not of this world" (Jh. 18:36), apply both to the kingdom of grace and the kingdom of glory.

The kingdom of God in the sense of the new covenant kingdom of grace came with power on Pentecost, when God sent His Spirit upon those who believed in Jesus. It was then that Jesus came in His kingdom, and when His spiritual kingdom came with power into the hearts of His disciples and then to thousands and thousands of others.

Many Christians have had difficulties with regard to the quoted passages for the reason that they have misunderstood them to mean the second coming of Christ, whereas in reality they speak of the spiritual coming of His kingdom on Pentecost and then in the Christian Church.

32. Was Jesus Mistaken as to the Time of His Second Coming?

Jesus says in Mt. 24:34: "This generation shall not pass away, till all these things be accomplished" (cp. Lk. 21:23). Jesus speaks before these words of the last events and His second coming. They did not take place during that generation. Was Jesus mistaken as to the time of His return?

Jesus spoke only what God gave Him to speak (Jh. 8:28, etc.). He is the true God (1 Jh. 5:20), and everything that He spoke was absolute truth. He could not make any mistake in the quoted statement. We have a clue to the right understanding of His words in what He says in the previous verse:

> "From the fig tree learn its parable: as soon as its branch becometh tender and putteth forth its leaves ye know that the summer is near; even so also, when ye see all these things ye know that he (or, it) is near, at the doors."

In Lk. 21:30-31 Jesus says:

> "Behold the fig tree, and all the trees: as soon as they shoot forth, ye see and know of your own selves that the summer is near. Even so also, when ye see these things coming to pass, ye know that the kingdom of God is near."

The things or events which show that the coming of Christ and of the kingdom of God (in its new millennial phase) is near like the budding and coming out in leaf of the fig tree and other trees shows that the summer is near are the ones spoken of by Christ before: wars, earthquakes, false teachers and prophets who lead many astray, great tribulation, and finally, after the tribulation, darkening of the sun, moon, etc. "This generation" is obviously the same time as the one symbolized by the budding and shooting forth of the branches of the trees, or the time when these events take place. The generation which will see the beginning of these events will not pass away till Christ comes, sending out His angels to gather His elect and to take them up to Him in the clouds. In other words, the last events which in a special sense are signs of the times and omens of

His coming will be accomplished within one generation (probably the life span of man, according to Ps. 90:10, 70-80 years), the last one, not the generation which lived when Jesus spoke these words.

When understood in this manner, Jesus' words in Mt. 24:34 and Lk. 21:30f. contain no particular difficulty.

It is generally understood that Israel is the "fig tree" of which Jesus speaks here. Its time of hardening and dispersion, and the corresponding "times of the Gentiles," has been like winter time for a fig tree. The first signs that showed that the branches of the Israel fig tree were "becoming tender" appeared toward the end of the past and the beginning of the present century when something like an invisible force began to draw Jews to their own land and the Zionistic Movement was born. The first "putting forth of leaves" started in the fall of 1917, when the Allied army, led by General Allenby, freed Palestine from Turkish rule, and when the British government gave the so-called Balfour Declaration, according to which Palestine was to be made the national home of the Jews. The "dead bones"—as Ez. 37 describes the scattered Israelites among the nations—began to gather together to their ancient land in ever larger numbers. When the British mandate rule ended in the May of 1948, the Jews in Palestine declared that they had formed the independent state of Israel. The bones thus formed a "body" which has "flesh, sinews and skin." In the "body" of the state of Israel the prophecies in Is. 11:11-13 and Ez. 37:15-22 have come true: there is no longer division between Judah and Israel ("Ephraim") but they form one nation. The next turning points in the last-generation history of Israel will be the war of Gog (obviously Soviet Russia, for it is the only great power in the "uttermost parts of the north," looked at from point of view of Israel, and to it also point the names Rosh-Russia, Meshech-Moscow and Tubal-Tobolsk), after which God will pour out His Spirit on Israel, so that will be converted to Christianity (Ez. 38-39; Zech. 12; Joel 3). It seems obvious that the events of the last generation in Israel began to be fulfilled in 1917, and a part of the prophecies concerning them have already been fulfilled.

About the time of the war of Gog and Israel's conversion, when the "times of the Gentiles" end, the old city of Jerusalem will cease to be "trodden down by the Gentiles" (Lk. 21:24): it will be transferred from Jordan to Israel, together with other areas that belonged to it in the time of David and Solomon. The converted Jews will then be a blessing to other nations, too (Zech. 8:13; Rom. 11:12, 15). The conversion will take place after the war of Gog, some time before the time of the Antichrist, not after the battle of Harmageddon and Christ's second coming (as e.g. Scofield explains, Zech. 12:1, etc.).

Jesus mentions in Lk. 21:29 "other trees" in addition to the fig tree. The last events are universal, concerning all the nations of the earth in one way or another. There are, however, two particular "other trees" whose budding and bursting into leaf are signs that the last generation before Christ's second coming has set in. The first of them is the ungodly political world power which blasphemes God and makes war with His saints. It is symbolized in Dan. 2 by the two feet of the great image and in Dan. 7 by the last beast or horn that at first is little but then becomes large than any world power that has existed previously. In Rev. 13 and 17 this blaspheming and persecuting political world power is symbolized by the scarlet-red beast that has ten horns.

The second "tree" whose budding and putting forth of leaves is a special sign which shows that men are living in the last generation before Christ's coming is the second beast of Rev. 13:11ff. that has two horns like a lamb but which speaks like a dragon, and the great harlot or Babylon the Great of Rev. 17, which obviously both typify the Antichrist-led apostate World Church of end time.

The fulfillment of the prophecies concerning the ungodly blaspheming and persecuting political world power whose characteristic color is scarlet or red began in the fall of 1917, or about the same time as the fulfillment of the end-time prophecies concerning Israel set in. The biblical prophecies on the scarlet-red beast of the last time apply with such accuracy to the red or communistic world power of our time that only a spiritually blind person can fail to see it. As in the history of Israel, so also in the development of the scarlet beast, the year 1948 was a turning point: In that year Czechoslovakia went under red rule, and the communist-led Chinese government was formed. The red beast started then its great expansion, whose result was that soon more than one third of mankind was under its rule. In these events the biblical prophecies on its structure came true: As the great image of Dan. 2 has two feet with ten toes, and as the beast of Rev. 13 and 17 has ten horns, so the red world power has two main parts, Soviet Union and Red China, and they have together ten communistic satellite states on the Eurasian continent (1. Poland, 2. East Germany, 3. Czechoslovakia, 4. Hungary, 5. Rumania, 6. Bulgaria, 7. Albania, 8. Outer Mongolia, 9. North Korea, 10. North Viet Nam. Yugoslavia is not counted, for it does not belong to the "satellites" of the Soviet Union and Red China, although it is communistic).

The apostate World Church, symbolized by the great harlot and Babylon the Great, and which will sit on seven mountains, is obviously the united World Church which is being built by the ecumenical movement and its central organization, the World Council of Churches. When it reaches its goal, the merger of most Protestant, Greek Orthodox, Eastern Orthodox and the Roman Church into one united World Church, its seat of government, and the seat of its head, the Pope (who will be the final great Antichrist) will be in Rome, the city of seven mountains. The development is quite obviously now going in that direction with an increasing speed.

According to Rev. 13:12 the second beast has two horns like a lamb but it speaks like a dragon. The two horns symbolize the Antichrist's claim to be the vice-regent of the Lamb of God, the visible head of the Church, as Christ is its invisible Head. That it speaks like a dragon means that its doctrine and ordinances (orders) are not biblical but represent a falsified gospel that originates in the laboratory of Satan. That this beast will exercise the authority of the first beast, or the red world power, in its presence and make the earth and its inhabitants worship the first beast, means that there will be cooperation between the communistic world power and the Antichrist-led world church. The former will authorize the World Church to carry on its work and rule in its own sphere, and the World Church in turn will serve as a propaganda agent of the red world power to convince people that it is God-given for the happiness of nations and a representative of God.

Rev. 17:3 describes the great harlot sitting on the scarlet colored beast. This is another picture of the cooperation between the political and ecclesiastical world powers of end time. Their cooperation will probably last three and a half years (Dan. 7:25; Rev. 11:2; 12:6, 14; 13:5), which will be the time of great tribulation for the true Church: the red beast will continue to make war with the saints, the chosen and faithful of Christ (Rev. 13:7; 17:14), and the great harlot church will be drunken with the blood of saints and the witnesses (martyrs) of Jesus (Rev. 17:6).

The red beast and its ten satellites, however, hate the harlot church all the time, being atheistic and materialistic, and have cooperation with it only for a while for tactical reasons, in order to have its support. After they have sufficiently solidified their power, the red beast and its ten horns turn against the harlot church, "make her desolate and naked, and devour her flesh and burn her up with fire" (Rev. 17:16). The Pope, the Antichrist, will, however, remain the leader of falsified christianity and continue his alliance with the red world power. He is after this called "the false prophet," because he is no longer the official head of the World Church (which has ceased to exist). When the red beast after this gathers its forces against the true Church and tries to get other states of the world for its allies in this last satanic endeavor, the false prophet is its ally (Rev. 16:12-16). This war and battle will obviously be world-wide, but its focal point will be Israel, which after its conversion to Christianity is, in a sense, the heart of Christendom. Because of this, it is called the battle of Harmageddon (Har=mountain, Mageddon=Megiddo). In Zech. 14:1 Jerusalem is spoken of as its focal point. At the time of this "midnight" (Mt. 25:6) of an utterly hopeless situation Christ will appear, take up His true Church and destroy the powers of evil: The red beast and false prophet will be seized and cast into the lake of fire, and their armies will be slain. Soon after this, after the marriage feast of the Lamb (which will probably last only several hours or a few days), Christ will come with His risen saints, the bride-Church that has become wife-Church, and establish on earth His thousand-year rule (Rev. 19:20f.; 20:1-6; Zech. 14:1-9; Jude 14). This event is symbolized in Dan. 2 by the stone that smites the great image at its feet and toes of iron and clay, becoming a great mountain that fills the whole earth. In Dan. 7 it is described as the coming of the one like a Son of Man in the clouds of heaven, receiving dominion, glory and kingdom under the whole heaven, so that all peoples, nations and tongues will serve Him. When the Lord will come with all his saints, we read in Zech. 14, His feet will stand on the Mount of Olives, and He will then become the king over all the earth.

As we have shown, the budding and putting forth of leaves in the "trees" of Israel and the scarlet beast started decisively in 1917. The foundations of "Babylon the Great" were laid about the same time: the first ecumenical organization (World Alliance for Promoting International Friendship) was founded in 1915 and the second one (International Missionary Council) in 1921. It seems that the last generation of which Jesus speaks in Mt. 24:34 started in 1917, and 70-80 years from it will be 1987-97. About that time, according to the plan of **Wycliffe Bible Translators,** the Bible will also be available in all the languages of mankind, so that Christ's words in Mt. 24::14 will come true.

Jesus did not make any mistake in speaking of the last generation.*

---

* For a fuller account of the biblical end-time prophecies, see U. Saarnivaara, **ARMAGEDDON — Before and After (1967).**

33. Did Paul Expect Christ's Second Coming in His Lifetime?

Paul writes in 1 Thess. 4:15-17: "This we say to you by the word of the Lord, that we who are alive, who are left to the coming of the Lord, shall in no wise precede those who are fallen asleep. For the Lord himself will descend from heaven with a shout, with the voice of the archangel and with the trump of God; and the dead in Christ will rise first; then we who are alive, who are left, will together with them be caught up in the clouds to meet the Lord in the air; and so we shall be ever with the Lord." Don't these words indicate that Paul expected Christ to come in his life time, and that he consequently was mistaken as to its date?

The words of Paul in 2 Thess. 2:1-12 show that he did not expect Christ's coming at any moment. There were things that had to take place first, and only after that was Christ's coming to take place. He writes:

> "Now concerning the coming of our Lord Jesus Christ and our gathering together to him [that is, the "rapture" of the true Church], to the end that ye be not ... troubled ..., to the effect that the day of the Lord is just at hand ... ; for it will not come unless the falling away (apostasy) come first, and the man of sin (or, lawlessness) be revealed, the son of perdition, he who opposeth and exalteth himself against all that is called God or that is worshipped; so that he sitteth in the temple of God, setting himself forth as God ... And now ye know that which restraineth (Gr. **to katechon**=the restraining thing), that he may be revealed only in his appointed time. For the mystery of lawlessness is already at work; only there is one who restraineth (Gr. **ho katechon**=he who restrains), until he be taken out of the midst (Gr. **ek mesou**). And then shall be revealed the lawless one, whom the Lord Jesus will slay with the breath of his mouth, and bring to nought by the manifestation of his coming **(te epiphaneia tes parousias autou)**: whose coming is according to the working of Satan with all power and signs and wonders of falsehood, and with all deceit of unrighteousness for those who perish, because they received not the love of the truth that they might be saved; that all may be judged who have not believed the truth, but have taken pleasure in unrighteousness."

There is a falling away or apostasy in Christendom

(pagans cannot "fall away," because they have not been in) before the coming of Christ, and this apostasy is a horrible reality in our time, as we have seen. The final outcome and climax of this apostasy, which has worked a long time in secret, will be the appearance of the "man of sin" (or, lawlessness), the Anti-christ. But there are two factors that restrain his appearance, an impersonal (**to katechon**=the restraining thing) and a personal one (**ho katechon**=he who restrains). It seems obvious that the impersonal restraining factor is the division of Christendom into numerous independent churches. When the ecumenical movement will have reached its goal, a united World Church, this restraining factor is removed. The personal restraining factor is Spirit-enlightened Bible-believing leadership in churches. When the spirit of apostasy (Bible criticism, falsified gospel in its various forms, ecumenism) has imbued the majority of ministerial and lay leaders of churches, then the personal restraining factor is away "from the midst" of Christendom, and the way is open for the appearance of the man of sin, the Antichrist. He will take his seat in the "temple of God," the united World Church, as its supreme leader. This temple will not be the rebuilt old covenant temple of Jerusalem. It will never be rebuilt, for at the time when the state of Israel will get the old city of Jerusalem and the temple area under its rule (after the war of Gog when the times of the Gentiles come to end), the Israelites will be converted to Christianity and have then no need or desire to rebuild the temple and start again its sacrificial worship. The "temple of God" in which the Antichrist will sit as its supreme ruler will be the united World Church built by the ecumenical movement, called in the Bible the "great harlot" and "Babylon the Great" (Rev. 17:1-9). The **Lutheran Confessions** hold the correct view that the Antichrist will be the head of the future World Church, not a political ruler. They state:

> "In describing the Antichrist in his letter to the Thessalonians Paul calls him 'an adversary of Christ who opposes and exalts himself against every so-called god or object of worship, so that he takes his seat in the temple of God, proclaiming himself to be God'

(2 Thess. 2:3, 4). He speaks therefore of one who rules in the church and not of the kings of nations, and he calls that man 'an adversary of Christ' because he will devise doctrines which conflict with the Gospel and will arrogate to himself divine authority" **(Treatise on the Power and Primacy of the Pope, 39)**.

"The kingdom of Antichrist is a new kind of worship of God, devised by human authority in opposition to Christ... the papacy will... be a part of the kingdom of Antichrist..." **(Apology XV: 18)**.

The words that the papacy, that is, the Church of Rome, will be a part of the kingdom of Antichrist implies the presumption that other churches also belong to it, and that it will be the united World Church of end time. Since the great Babylon harlot, the united apostate World Church, led by the Antichrist, will sit on seven mountains (Rev. 17:9), it is obvious that the seat of the Antichrist will be in Rome, and that the Pope will be the final great Antichrist, as he is the greatest of the preparatory ones.

These events, spoken of in 2 Thess. 2, were far ahead in Paul's time. Since he emphatically explained that Christ's coming and the gathering of His saints to Him would take place only after the time of the "man of sin," it is obvious that he did not expect it in his life time. Phil. 1:21ff. and 2 Tim. 4:6ff. show that Paul expected his death to take place before Christ's second coming through martyrdom. That he spoke of the taking up of the saints (the "rapture") in the first person plural ("we") was merely a manner of expression which did not imply that he actually expected to be alive at the time of Christ's second coming, as we see from his other statements. This manner of speech is often used in the Bible in cases when the speaker obviously is not contemporary with the event. Isaiah says in 53:2-3 of Christ: "when we see him, there is no beauty that we should desire him. He was despised..., and we esteemed him not." John writes in 1 Jh. 3:2 of the second coming of Christ: "When he appears we shall be like him, for we shall see him as he is." We have therefore no reason to conclude from Paul's words in 1 Thess. 4:17 that he expected to see Christ's second coming in his lifetime.

The rather common idea of an "any moment imminent coming of Christ," which is often connected with the view that Paul expected Christ's coming at any moment, is not biblical. Scripture teaches plainly that His second coming will take place only after the events that shall precede it will be fulfilled.

34. Blind Men Near Jericho

We are told in Mt. 20:29-34 that Jesus healed **two** blind men **after** having left Jericho, but Mk. 10:46-52 speaks of only **one** blind man. Lk. 18:35-43 tells of the healing of one blind man while Jesus was **approaching** Jericho. How can these accounts be reconciled?

One possibility is that the cases in which Jesus healed one blind man and in which He healed two blind men are two different events, both of which took place in the neighborhood of Jericho. If the three Gospels speak of the same event, the mentioning of only one blind man in Mk. and Lk. does not deny that there was another man, too. Bartimaeus, the more active of the two, is especially mentioned by Mk. A possible reason for giving his name may also be that he was an active and well known member in the church. We have no certainty on which of these interpretations is correct, and we must leave the matter open.

Archeology has brought solution to the problem why Mk. reports the healing of the blind man as having taken place when Jesus went out of Jericho, and Lk. when He came near Jericho: There were two Jerichos at that time, the old city, and the new city that was built by Herod the Great a short distance from the old city. Jesus obviously healed the blind man between the two cities, and it was equally right to say that He healed the blind man when going out of the (old) Jericho, as to say that He did it when coming near (the new) Jericho.

35. Peter's Denials and the Crowings of the Cock

Mt. 26:34, Lk. 22:34 and Jh. 13:38 relate how Jesus said to Peter that he would deny Him thrice before the cock would crow. But according to Mk. 14:30, Jesus said to Peter that the cock would crow twice before his threefold denial. Accordingly, Mk. 14:68-72 tells that the cock crew the first time after Peter's first denial and the second time after his third denial. When the cock crew the second time, Peter remembered Jesus' words: "Before the cock crows twice, thou wilt deny me thrice." How can these accounts be reconciled?

The probable explanation is that in speaking to Peter of his coming denials Jesus spoke twice of the crowing of the cock. We may imagine that the discussion went on something like this: Jesus said first to Peter, "This night, before the cock crows, thou shalt deny me thrice." As Peter assured that he would rather die than deny Him, Jesus repeated His words and added a detail: "Before the cock crows twice, thou wilt deny me thrice." The first time Jesus only paid attention to that crowing of the cock which Peter would notice, the second time also to that crowing to which Peter would pay no attention. Mt., Lk., and Jh. report the events more briefly and mention only the last crowing, which took place after the three denials; Mk. also mentions the first one which did not yet awaken Peter.

36. Judas Iscariot's Betrayal and Death. Aceldama.

We read in Lk. 22:3-7 of how Satan entered Judas Iscariot, and how he went and conferred with the chief priests and captains concerning a betrayal of Jesus. But in Jh. 13:27 we are told that Satan went into Judas at the last supper, after Jesus had given him a dipped morsel (sop). How are these accounts to be reconciled?

Both of these passages speak of the influence of Satan on Judas and on his yielding to the evil one. His betrayal had two phases: First, he made an agreement with the chief priests and captains, and second, committed the actual deed of betrayal in the garden of Gethsemane. In either case Scripture speaks of Satan entering him. These accounts do not contain any discrepancy. A parallel, though opposite, case was the twofold infilling of the Holy Spirit in the Early Church: The disciples were filled with the Spirit on Pentecost, but they were filled with the Spirit again when they were praying together at the time of persecution (Acts 2 and 4).

* * *

According to Mt. 27:5-10, Judas cast the money that he received for the betrayal into the temple, and then went away and hanged himself. The chief priests took the money and bought with it a potter's field for a burial place of foreigners. But Peter reports in Acts 1:18ff. that Judas himself purchased a field with the reward of his iniquity, and falling headlong, he burst open in the middle, and all his bowels gushed out. The field was called Aceldama, the field of blood. How can these accounts be reconciled?

Judas probably hanged himself on the edge of some cliff in the outskirts of Jerusalem and fell headlong in this process. Possibly the rope broke so that he fell headlong into the precipice and burst open. There is no conflict at this point.

The question of the purchase of the field is more difficult. Since both Matthew and Peter were in Jerusalem at that time and closely followed the events, and since there were numerous Christians who could "check" the reports, it is impossible that there can be any real discrepancy in them. We merely do not know all the facts.

Possibly the events ran somewhat like this: Judas bought a potter's field with his betrayal money, but repented of it soon, cancelled the deal, cast the money into the temple and hanged himself. The chief priests then bought the same field (which was again "for sale") with the money that Judas had returned. The field that was bought first by Judas and then by the chief priests was called Aceldama, Field of Blood.

* * *

Mt. 27:9f. ascribes to Jeremiah the words which speak of the purchase of the potter's field for thirty pieces of silver, but it is actually Zech. 11:12f. that speaks of thirty shekels of silver. How should we understand this?

Mt. 27:9f. does not give a direct quotation, and no quotation marks should therefore be used in it. In reality it contains allusions to two prophetical passages, one of them being Jer. 32:6-15 and the other Zech. 11:12f. The referred passage of Jeremiah speaks of the purchase of a field and the potter's earthenware, and the passage in Zechariah deals with thirty pieces of silver and the potter. The OT had numerous events, persons, and things that were no direct prophecies of Christ and the NT realities, but were "shadows" or types that pointed toward them in a symbolical manner (Col. 2:17; Heb. 8:5; 10:1), and have had or have their fulfillment in Christ and the Christian Church. The purchase of the field in Jer. 32 is used in Mt. 27:9f. as a historical type ("shadow") that had its fulfillment in the purchase of the field in connection with Judas' betrayal. Whether Zech. 11:12f. is a direct prediction or a type, is hard to say.

Since the main thing in Mt. 27:9f. is the purchase of the field, reference is made to Jeremiah, for Zech. 11:12f. speaks nothing of such a purchase, although it speaks of thirty pieces of silver. It is therefore natural that Mt. mentions the passage in Jeremiah, which contained the main "shadow" of the event in question.

It has been suggested that the word "Jeremiah" in Mt. 27:9 may be an early error of a copyist: The text had originally "Zechariah," but the copyist changed it by mistake into "Jeremiah." This assumption is not necessary, since the main OT type in this case was in Jeremiah.

37. How Long Was Jesus in the Grave?

According to Mt. 12:40, Jesus said that He would be "in the heart of the earth" "three days and three nights," but actually He was not that long in the grave: He was buried toward the evening on Friday, and He rose from the dead on Sunday morning, being in the grave one whole day and parts of two other days. How should we understand this?

We must find out what in the biblical language is the meaning of the phrase "three days and three nights."

1 Sam. 30:11-15 tells of a certain Egyptian who had "eaten no bread nor drunk water for three days and three nights." But soon after we read how this man explained, "I fell sick three days ago." This shows that actually he had been without food and drink from the third day previously. This indicates that in Israel the phrase "three days and three nights" did not mean three full days and nights but a time to which belonged one full day and parts of two other days. According to Mk. 8:31, Jesus said that He would "after three days rise again," and in Mt. 16:21 we have His statement that He would "be raised again on the third day." This shows that the phrases "after three days," "on the third day," and "after three days and three nights," meant the same thing. It is not right to take some biblical phrases in their literal form without paying attention to what these phrases meant in the language of that time. This is no true "literal interpretation" of the Bible, but a true literal and grammatical interpretation requires that the meaning of words and phrases in the language of that time, and in the context in which they are used, is carefully observed.

E.g. the Germans say: **"Heute über acht Tage,"** literally = today over eight days, but this phase means: after a week, after seven days, and not: after eight days. Just as it would be wrong to take this German phrase literally, without finding out what it means, so it is wrong to take literally the statement "three days and three nights," disregarding the fact that in Israel this phrase meant the same as "on the third day."

38. Inscription of the Cross

We read in Mt. 27:37 how Pilate set up over the head of Jesus on the cross "the charge against him, which read, THIS IS JESUS THE KING OF THE JEWS"; but in Mk. 15:26 we are told: "The inscription of the charge against him read, THE KING OF THE JEWS," in Lk. 23:38, the "inscription over him" was [some manuscripts add: "in letters of Greek and Latin and Hebrew"]: "THIS IS THE KING OF THE JEWS," and in Jh. 19:19 that the inscription was, "JESUS OF NAZARETH, THE KING OF THE JEWS." How are these differences to be understood?

The meaning of all the Gospel accounts at this point is about the same. None of the Evangelists gives the entire inscription, but they all shorten it in one way or another. All of them have the words, THE KING OF THE JEWS. Luke adds, THIS IS, Matthew and John add the word JESUS, and John the words OF NAZARETH (more exactly: THE NAZARENE, Gr. ho nadzoraios). When we combine the accounts we get the whole inscription: THIS IS (Mt. and Lk.) JESUS (Mt. and Jh.) OF NAZARETH (the Nazarene, Jh.) THE KING OF THE JEWS (all). As we have seen, it is usual that whenever the Bible has two or more parallel accounts of the same thing they supplement one another and only together give the whole picture. This holds true of the account concerning the inscription on the cross as well.

It may also be possible that the inscription was partly different in the three languages, Hebrew, Greek and Latin, and that the various Evangelists give, at least in part, the different versions.

39. Thieves on the Cross

According to Mt. 27:44 and Mk. 15:32, both thieves on the cross reviled Jesus, but in Lk. 23:39f. we read that one of them repented and even rebuked the other criminal for reviling Him, asking Jesus to remember him when He would come into His kingdom. How should we explain this apparent conflict?

It is obvious that both thieves reviled Jesus at first and for some time, but later on one of them changed his mind (or rather, God worked a change in it) and repented. Mt. and Mk. report only what they did at first, and Lk. only that one of them repented, and that Jesus had mercy on him. The different accounts supplement one another.

40. Times of the Last Supper and Crucifixion

According to the Synoptics, Mt. Mk. and Lk., Jesus ate the passover meal with His disciples on the Thursday night of the Holy Week (Mt. 26:17ff. & par.), but in Jh. 18:28 we are told that the Jewish leaders early on **Friday** morning did not go into the praetorium ("hall of judgment") of Pilate "so that they might not be defiled, but might eat the passover." This shows that the passover meal was still ahead on the Friday morning. How should this be understood?

We know from Jewish literature that the Pharisees and Sadducees of Jesus' time disagreed on the time of the passover meal: The Pharisees interpreted the OT ordinances to mean that this meal was to be eaten then on Thursday night, whereas the Sadducees held that it was to be eaten on Friday, on the eve of the Sabbath. As the high priest and other chief priests were Sadducees, and the passover lambs were to be killed in the temple, the Pharisees and the people who followed them ate their passover meal on Thursday night without the lamb. The killing of the lambs took place on Friday afternoon, and the Sadducees ate them on Friday night. Thus, Jesus and His disciples ate their passover meal on Thursday night without the lamb. The "passover lamb" of the new covenant, Jesus, died on the cross at the very time when the OT passover lambs were slaughtered in the temple on Friday. God obviously led the matter so.

The word "passover" that is used in this connection means (1) the Easter festival in general, (2) the Easter meal whether with or without the lamb, and (3) the lamb. The disciples prepared the passover meal in the upper room without a lamb. The statement in Mk. 14:12, "killed the passover" (so in KJV; ASV: "sacrificed the passover"; RSV: "sacrificed the passover lamb"; Gr. **pascha ethyon)** means here preparing the passover meal, whether with a lamb or not. Jesus was crucified on the 14th of Nisan, or Friday, and the last meal was thus on Thursday night, which, according to the Jewish counting, belonged to Friday (from 6:00 p.m. on) the 14th.

Since the passover lambs, according to the law (Deut. 16:12), could be killed only in the sanctuary, the majority of the Jews, who could not come to Jerusalem, had to eat their passover meals without the lamb, and there was therefore, even from this point of view, nothing uncommon and strange in the fact that Jesus and His disciples did it that way on Thursday night.

Note: R. A. Torrey (op. cit., pp. 103ff.) explains that Jesus was crucified and buried on Wednesday, and that His body was in the grave from about the sunset of Wednesday to about the sunset of Saturday, that is, fully three days and three nights. Torrey appeals to astronomic calculations according to which the Passover day in the year 30 A.D., which is the commonly accepted year of Christ's crucifixion, was on Thursday, April 6th, and not on Friday.

This explanation is not possible, for according to Mk. 15:42, Lk. 23:54 and Jh. 19:31 Jesus' crucifixion and burial took place on the day before Sabbath, that is, on Friday. The fact that, according to astronomic computations, the Passover was in the year 30 A.D. on Thursday fits well into the interpretation that we have given: The Pharisees held that the Passover meal was to be eaten on the evening of the full-moon day, that is, on Thursday night (as we count the days), but the Sadducees who controlled the temple and the slaughtering of the lambs held that it was to be eaten on Friday night. Jesus and His disciples followed the interpretation of the Pharisees, and so did the great majority of the Jews. Torrey's explanation is not necessary, for as we have shown, the Bible speaks of Jesus' resurrection on the third day and after three days and three nights, which in the Jewish phraseology meant the same thing.

* * *

Mk. 15:25 reports that Jesus was crucified about the third hour (9:00 a. m.), but according to Jh. 19:14, Jesus was still before Pilate about the sixth hour. How is this to be understood?

We have a clue for the solution of this problem in Jh. 20:19: Jesus appeared to His disciples "on the evening of ... the first day of the week," that is, on the evening of the day of resurrection. According to the Jewish counting of time, that evening did not belong to the first day of the week, but to its second day, for their day began at 6:00 p. m. This method of counting is also seen in the creation account of Genesis, which in the case of each day states: "And there was evening and there was morning, the second day," etc.

The fact that John speaks of the evening of the first day of the week shows that he follows the **Roman** reckoning of time, according to which the day began at midnight. Several Roman authors (e.g. Plutarch, Pliny, Gellius) report that the Romans counted a day from midnight to midnight. We have inherited this method from them. Thus, the sixth hour when Jesus, according to Jh. 19:14, was before Pilate, was ab. 6:00 a. m., since the Roman reckoning of time is used here. But since Mk. uses the Jewish method, the "third hour" when Jesus was crucified (Mk. 15:25), was ab. 9:00 a. m. It took ab. three hours before the crucifixion took place, after Jesus was before Pilate. Thus, there is no conflict between Mk. and Jh.; they merely use different methods of reckoning the time.

41. Events after Jesus' Resurrection

According to Mt. 28:1-10, in the morning of the first day of the week (Sunday), or the Easter morning, Mary Magdalene and the other Mary came to see the tomb of Jesus. But in Mk. 16:1-11 we are told that the persons who went to the sepulchre were Mary Magdalene, Joanna and Mary [mother] of James. Jh. 20:1-18 mentions Mary Magdalene alone. How should we explain these differences?

All three Gospels mention Mary Magdalene, and Mk. and Lk. mention Mary [mother] of James—called in Mt. "the other Mary." The word "we," used by Mary Magdalene in Jh. 20:2, implies that she was not alone at the tomb, although the names of the others are not mentioned. No Gospel record has a complete list of the women, but they supplement one another. There is no real conflict between them at this point.

Mk. tells that the women came to the tomb very early "when the sun had risen" (ASV), but according to Jh. 20:1, Mary Magdalene "came to the tomb early, while it was dark, and saw that the stone was taken away." How can these reports be reconciled?

Mary Magdalene and the other women obviously left for the tomb when it was still dark. They had to walk some distance, and when they arrived at the tomb, the sun rose. The fact that Mary saw the stone had been taken away shows that it was no longer dark when they arrived at the tomb. Thus, there is no real conflict between the two records: Jh. speaks from the point of view of the situation when the women left and were on their way, and Mt. from the point of view of their arrival at the tomb. The ASV translation of Mk. 16:2 is not quite accurate. KJV has here: "at the rising of the sun.." The form in the Greek text, **anateilantos** (aor. part.) means that they came to the tomb at the very moment when the sun rose. Mt. has here, "as it began to dawn" (KJV and ASV), "toward the dawn" (RSV). The Greek **epiphoskouse** (pres. part.) means: when the light was in the process of beginning to shine.

* * *

How should we explain the fact that, according to Mt. and Mk., the women saw one angel in the tomb, but Lk. and Jh. speak of two angels?

A carefully reading and comparison of the Easter accounts of the four Gospels shows the following facts:

Mt. reports that an angel rolled the stone from the tomb and sat on it. He said to the women that Jesus had risen, and that they should go and tell of this to His disciples, and that He would go before them to Galilee. Mark's account is shorter and does not contain all the details that are in Mt., but it has the addition that the message was to be also taken to Peter.

According to the record of John, the two angels appeared to Mary Magdalene when she was at the tomb the **second time,** after having told to the disciples what she had seen at her first visit to the tomb. Thus, Jh. speaks of a different event than Mt. and Mk.

The main difference between the accounts of Mt. and Lk. is that the former speaks of one angel, while the latter speaks of two. But when we read Matthew's account carefully we see that he does not say whether there was one angel or two. He merely relates that **the** angel who rolled the stone from the door of the tomb told the women: "Fear not . . ."

In telling of these events, Lk. mentions two angels, but the words spoken by an angel to the women are different from the ones recorded in Mt. Only the words, "He is risen," are the same. A possible explanation is that both angels spoke to the women, and that Mt. reports the words of one of them, Lk. of the other.

* * *

According to Mt., the women left the tomb quickly with fear and joy, running to bring the word to the disciples, but in Mk. we read that the women went out quickly from the tomb, trembling and being amazed to the extent that they said nothing to anybody. How can these passages be reconciled?

Mk. obviously tells of the first phase of the events; Mt. skips over this and tells what they did after recovering from their terror. The women were at first so frightened that they were not able to tell anybody what they had seen and heard. However, the angel had commanded them to tell the disciples of the resurrection of Jesus, and they would have been disobedient if they would not have done so. After a while they obviously recovered from their fright and told the disciples what the angel had commanded them to tell. Mt. reports this, but does not mention how they at first were not able to speak anything.

The original Gospel of Mark ends with the words: "for they were afraid." What this Gospel originally said after this, we do not know. Its original end section has been lost by some accident, and the end part that we have now (vv. 9-20) has been added to it later. Since this end part is quoted by Irenaeus and Hippolytus in the second century, it has been added to it probably late in the first century or in the early part of the second century. The end section of Mk., as we have it now, is as reliable as the rest of the Gospel, but it does not contain the same words as the original ending has had. Probably the original text told how the women soon recovered from their fright and delivered to the disciples the message that the angel had sent them to bring to them.

* * *

According to Mt. 28:16f. and Mk. 16:7, Jesus directed His disciples to go to Galilee, where they would see Him. Mt. tells that the eleven went to Galilee, and that they saw Jesus there on the mountain that He had appointed to them for that purpose. There He gave them the commission to make disciples (KJV has here a wrong translation, "teach all nations"; the Greek **matheteuete** means never "teach," but, "make disciples"; ASV and RSV have the correct translation) of all nations, baptizing and teaching them. But in Jh. 20:19-23 we read that Jesus appeared to His disciples on the Easter day evening behind closed doors, greeted them and said to them: "Receive the Holy Spirit. Whose soever sins ye forgive, they are forgiven to them; and whose soever sins ye retain, they are retained."* After a week Jesus again appeared to His disciples in Jerusalem, and then Thomas also was with them, confessing his faith in the risen Lord: "My Lord and my God." Only after this, in the following chapter, Jh. tells of Jesus' appearance to His disciples in Galilee, but it took place at the sea of Tiberias, not on a mountain. How do these accounts fit together?

Mt. does not deny that Jesus appeared to His disciples in Jerusalem, neither does Jh. deny that He also appeared to

---

* Jesus repeated in these words in a plainer manner what He had said to His disciples before (Mt. 16:19; 18:18). The power to retain sins or to bind to them is the same as the task to proclaim the law for the knowledge and conviction of sins and to call sinners to repentance. The power and task to forgive (remit) sins or to loose from them is the task and authority to proclaim forgiveness of sins in Jesus' name and blood to repenting sinners (see Lk. 24:47). This twofold task is the main part of the ministry of reconciliation (2 Cor. 5:18f.) or the spiritual priesthood of believers (1 Pet. 2:5, 9). It is actually Christ, the Head of the Church, who thus speaks through the mouth of His believers, using them as His "ambassadors."

HATH GOD SAID?

them on a mountain in Galilee. They simply tell of different events, supplementing each other. Lk. reports how Jesus in addition appeared to His two disciples on the road to Emmaus and in Emmaus. Mk. has on this only a short reference (16:12). The different Gospel records supplement one another, although we do not in all cases know the exact sequence of events. Paul mentions in 1 Cor. 15:5-8 some appearances of Jesus that are not recorded in the Gospels (specially to Cephas, to more than 500 brethren, then to James). We may be sure that there would be no difficulties in these matters if all the facts were known.

When we combine the four Gospel accounts, the sequence of events after the resurrection of Christ seems to be as follows:

1. Mary Magdalene, Mary [mother] of James, Joanna and Salome and some other women went to the tomb of Jesus early in the morning on the first day of the week with sweet spices to anoint His body. They found the stone rolled away, saw two angels, one of them sitting on the stone, and both of them spoke to them, sending them to tell the disciples of the resurrection of Jesus and to give them the direction to go to Galilee, where they would see Him. When they were on their way, Jesus met them and repeated to them the direction to go to Galilee (Mt. 28:1-10; Mk. 16: 1-8; Lk. 24:1-10).

2. When the women brought the message to the disciples, Peter and John ran to the tomb, went into it and saw it empty, with the linen clothes in order, and believed (Lk. 24:12; Jh. 20:2-10).

3. After Peter and John had left the tomb, Mary Magdalene came back to it and stood there, weeping. When she stooped to look into the tomb, she saw two angels who asked her why she was weeping. Mary answered that she wept because they had taken away her Lord, and she did not know where they had laid him. Mary did not yet perceive that Jesus truly had risen **bodily,** although angels had told it to her, and Jesus had appeared to her and the other

women. Jesus and His resurrection had again become unreal to her, and she did not comprehend that Jesus' body had truly risen (His human soul and Divine Nature were alive all the time and did not need resurrection) and become a glorified resurrection body. Then Jesus appeared to her again, but this time she was not sent to tell the news of resurrection, as had been the case the first time, but her message was to be of His ascension: "I ascend to my Father, and to your Father" (Jh. 20:11-17).

4. Jesus appeared to Peter some time during the day (Lk. 24:34; 1 Cor. 15:5).

5. He appeared to two disciples on the road to and in Emmaus (Lk. 24:13-33; Mk. 16:12).

6. He appeared to more than 500 disciples (1 Cor. 15:6).

7. He appeared to James (1 Cor. 15:7).

8. He appeared to His disciples behind closed doors (Lk. 24:36-49; Jh. 20:19-23).

9. After a week He appeared to them when Thomas was with them (Jh. 20:24-29).

10. He appeared to them in Galilee, at the sea of Tiberias (Jh. 21).

11. He appeared to them on a mountain in Galilee (Mt. 28:16-20).

12. He appeared to His disciples in Jerusalem, led them to the Mount of Olives to Bethany, and ascended to heaven (Lk. 24:50-52; Acts 1:6-12).

Note: Liberal critics have made much of the variant details in the Gospel narratives of what happened after Christ's resurrection, holding that there are irreconcilable inconsistencies and conflicts between them. As we have shown, this is not true, although we do not know all the facts. The reports are fragmentary and incomplete, but they are true and supplement one another. On the liberal views, and the Bible-believing position, see Otten, **op. cit.**, pp. 104-118; W. Arndt, **Does the Bible Contradict Itself?** (Concordia Publ. H., St. Louis, Mo., 1951), pp. 79-87.

42. When Did the Disciples Receive the Holy Spirit?

We read in Jh. 20:22 that Jesus appeared to His disciples on Easter evening, breathed on them and said: "Receive the Holy Spirit." But according to Lk. 24:49 and Acts 1:4, 5, 8 Jesus directed His disciples to wait in Jerusalem for the fulfillment of the promise of the Holy Spirit, and according to Acts 2, this promise was fulfilled on the Pentecost, fifty days after the resurrection of Jesus. How do these passages fit together?

When Jesus, according to Jh. 20:22, breathed on His disciples and said: "Receive the Holy Spirit," this must be understood—in the light of the other passages of the Bible —as a reference to what was to take place on the Pentecost. The disciples did not receive the Holy Spirit on Easter evening. Jesus wanted then to show to them that after having received the Holy Spirit they had to serve their fellow men for their salvation—for leading them to repentance and faith—by forgiving sins (proclaiming the Gospel of forgiveness) to penitent sinners and retaining them (proclaiming them to be retained, unforgiven) to impenitent sinners. This was to be the office of Holy Spirit, who was to be necessary for this ministry of reconciliation. Without the Holy Spirit they should not presume to do it.

43. Infilling with the Spirit and Speaking in Tongues

According to Acts 2:4-8, the Holy Spirit was poured upon the disciples of Jesus, and they began to speak in other languages, so that people from different lands said: "Behold, are not all these who speak Galilaeans? And how hear we every man in our own language wherein we were born? Parthians and Medes and Elamites, and the dwellers in Mesopotamia, ... in Pontus, ... in Egypt, ... and sojourners from Rome, ... and Arabians, we hear them speaking in our own tongues the mighty works of God." But when Paul writes of speaking in tongues, he says in 1 Cor. 14:2, 5, 14: "He who speaketh in tongues speaketh not to men, but to God; for no man understandeth; but in the Spirit he speaketh mysteries, ... except he interpret, that the church may be edified ... For if I pray in a tongue, my spirit prayeth, but my understanding is unfruitful." How should we understand these apparently conflicting passages on speaking in tongues?

The NT shows that there are two kinds of speaking in tongues. The first of them is spoken of in Acts 2, which relates how the Holy Spirit on the first Pentecost miraculously gave the disciples the ability to proclaim the Gospel in the languages of the people who had come to Jerusalem from different countries and were present. The other kind of speaking in tongues is the one spoken of in 1 Cor. 12 and 14: It is no human language, but something that no one understands, unless the person himself or someone else has the Spirit-given gift of interpreting it. The person who speaks in tongues in this manner does it by the influence of the Holy Spirit, and he speaks in the Spirit mysteries to God, not to men. He is in a sort of trance in which his "understanding is unfruitful," but he is edified by it himself. Both kinds of speaking in tongues belong to the miraculous gifts of the Spirit, and both of them exist in Christendom even today. However, the second kind of tongues is much more common than the first one.

Since the second type of speaking in tongues, as to its outward appearance, is made up of uttering sounds that cannot be understood, Paul gives the rule that it should be allowed in the meetings of a congregation only when the person himself or somebody else has the gift of interpreting it. A person who has the gift of tongues should pray for the gift of interpretation in order that he may edify the congregation by his gift. Another rule is that in one meeting or service two or at most three should be allowed to speak in tongues, and the same limitation applies to the speaking of the prophets. If there is no interpreter, those who have the gift of tongues should remain silent in the church service (1 Cor. 14:27-29).

We have in Mk. 16:17 the word of Christ: "These signs will follow those who believe: In my name they will cast o demons; they will speak in new tongues; they will take up serpents; and if they drink any deadly thing, it will not hurt them; they will lay hands on the sick, and they will recover." But Paul writes in 1 Cor. 12:30: "All don't speak with **tongues.**" (The translation, "Do all speak with tongues?" is not accurate, for the Greek text has here the negative **me**= not). Jesus says that those who believe speak in new tongues, but Paul says that they do not all speak with tongues. How should we explain this?

In order to understand this matter aright we should note that the Bible speaks of three groups of workings and gifts of the Holy Spirit:

The **first** group is made up of the **general saving and sanctifying works** of the divine Spirit, such as conviction of sin and repentance, faith in and knowledge of Christ, regeneration, knowledge of truth, sanctification of life, and power to witness (Jh. 16:4-14; 1 Pet. 1:2; Acts 1:8, etc.). To this group also belongs the inner witness or earnest (seal) of the Spirit (Rom. 8:16; 2 Cor. 1:21f.; Eph. 1:13f.), the guidance of the Spirit (Rom. 8:14), His help in prayer (Rom. 8:26f.; Jh. 4:23f.), the fruits of the Spirit, such as love, joy, peace, gentleness, self-control, etc. (Gal. 5:22).

The **second** group of the gifts and workings of the Spirit are those mentioned by Paul in Rom. 12:5-8: Ministry (service), teaching, exhortation, giving, leadership (KJV: ruling; so also ASV; the RSV has here: "he who gives aid, with zeal"; the Greek verb used here, **proïstamenos,** from **proïstemi,** does not mean "give aid," but "place before," "set over," "preside," "lead," "rule"). This group of gifts is made up, in the main, of **Spirit-sanctified natural gifts** for the building up of the Church.

The **third** group is made up of such **miraculous gifts** of the Spirit as "gifts of healing," "working of miracles," "prophecy," "discerning of spirits," "the interpretation of tongues," etc. (1 Cor. 12:9f.).

The **first** group of the workings and gifts of the Spirit is—in greater or smaller measure—given to **all Christians.** But of the **second** and **third** groups Paul says in 1 Cor. 12:

11: "All these are worked by the same Spirit, who divideth (apportioneth) to each one individually as he will." And in vv. 28-30 in the same chapter the apostle writes:

> "God hath set (appointed) in the church first apostles, second prophets, third teachers, then miracles, then gifts of healings, helps, gifts of administration, various kinds of tongues. All are not apostles! All are not prophets! All are not teachers! All are not workers of miracles! All do not possess the gifts of healing! All do not speak in tongues! All do not interpret."

The various gifts of the Spirit mentioned by Christ in Mk. 16 and by Paul in 1 Cor. 12, 14, etc. are present in the true Church and follow or accompany true believers at all times; but every one does not have every gift, and the Spirit divides or apportions them to Christians individually as He wills. Just as all Christians do not have the gift of prophecy or healing, so all of them do not have the gift of tongues. None of these gifts is **the** gift that is **the** special sign that a person has received the Holy Spirit or been filled with the Spirit. There are numerous Christians who are filled with the Spirit but who never speak in tongues, never have the gift of prophecy, or of healing, etc. They may, however, have e.g. the gift of serving and helping, or the gift of leadership, or of exhorting, or of teaching, or giving (contributing). Indeed, the gift of teaching, or exhortation, or leadership, is much more valuable for the edification of the Church than e.g. the gift of tongues, or "taking up serpents" (which is seldom needed, but is occasionally, as in the case of Paul at Malta, Acts 28:3-6). True, Paul says, "I would that ye all spoke with tongues" (1 Cor. 14:5), but he does not encourage to seek particularly this gift, since it does not edify the Church (unless it is accompanied by the gift of interpretation). He, rather, counsels Christians to desire earnestly the best or higher gifts (1 Cor. 12:31), the ones that build up the Church. However, in order that some Christians would not try to hinder and suppress the gift of tongues, he writes: "Forbid not to speak with tongues; but all things should be done decently and in order" (1 Cor. 14:39f.).

Thus, speaking in tongues is not **the** special gift that shows that one has received the Spirit. Inwardly, such a special sign is the "earnest" or seal (assurance) of the Spirit (Eph. 1:13f.; 2 Cor. 1:21f.). The outwardly recognizable sign which shows that a person has received the Holy Spirit is **love** "The love of God is shed abroad in our hearts by the Holy Spirit, who is given to us" (Rom. 5:5). Jesus says: "By this will all men know that ye are my disciples, if ye have love one to another" (Jh. 13:35). Paul cautions: "Though I speak with tongues...and have not love, I am become as sounding brass or a tinkling cymbal" (1 Cor. 13:1).

All the gifts of the Spirit are really His **gifts**, particularly the third group of them, the miraculous gifts. The Spirit-sanctified natural gifts (the second group) can be developed by exercise (cp. 1 Tim. 4:14ff.), but the miraculous gifts, tongues and others, can never be attained by any exercises. They can be desired and prayed for (1 Cor. 12:31; 14:1), but the Spirit apportions them to each Christian as He wills. If the gift of tongues is obtained by certain exercises, it is a self-made skill and as such usually harmful, tending to work self-exaltation, weakening of love, withdrawal from other Christians, slackening in fruitbearing for the building up of the Church, etc. It belongs to the category of "will worship" (Gr. **ethelothreskeia),** or self-planned and self-made worship, which is "of no value" but is "for the satisfying of the flesh" (Col. 2:23). Just as there is self-made prophesying, so there is self-made speaking in tongues. To both of them apply the Lord's words to Ezekiel (13:17): "Set thy face against the daughters of thy people, who prophesy out of their own hearts." Genuine Spirit-wrought prophecy and speaking in tongues is a blessing, but man-made conterfeits of both are a curse, condemned by God's word.

* * *

According to Acts 2:4, the disciples were "filled with the Holy Spirit," but in Acts 4:31 we read that they—at least many of them were the same people—were again "filled with the Holy Spirit." How should we understand this?

Paul writes to the Ephesian Christians (1:13f.): "After that ye believed, ye were sealed with that Holy Spirit of promise (promised Holy Spirit), who is the earnest of our inheritance." But he writes later (5:18) to the same Christians: "Be filled **(present passive,** repeatedly or continually filled) with the Spirit." In 1 Cor. 12:13 he writes: "By one Spirit are we all baptized into one body, ... and we have all been made to drink of one Spirit." Jesus says in Jh. 3:5f. that those who have entered the kingdom of God have been "born of the Spirit."

These Bible passages show that all true Christians who are members of the body of Christ, the true Church, have been "born of" the Spirit, received the "baptism" of the Holy Spirit, "sealed" with the Spirit, made to "drink" of the Spirit (cp. Jh. 7:37-39). All true believers have, as Heb. 6:4f. states, "tasted of the heavenly gift and ... been made partakers of the Holy Spirit." But such believers can again be filled with the Spirit, and indeed, are exhorted to be repeatedly or continually filled with the Spirit. Thus, there is one "baptism," "sealing," "birth of" the Holy Spirit, but there may be, and should be, subsequent "infillings" of the Spirit.

The effects of a renewed infilling of the Spirit are seen from the record in Acts 4:31ff: Those who were anew filled with the Spirit (1) "spoke the word of God with boldness," and "with great power gave ... witness to the resurrection of the Lord Jesus"; (2) they were "of one heart and one soul," being strengthened in mutual love and fellowship; (3) "none said that any of the things which he possessed was his own," but gave their possessions to the use of the Lord and His Church. The effect and sign of this renewed infilling with the Spirit was not speaking in tongues, but the more important and fruitbearing effects of the Spirit. Of course, the gift of tongues or some other gifts **may** be received in connection with such an infilling.

44. Reports of Paul's Conversion

According to Acts 9:7, the men who journeyed with Saul (Paul) to Damascus heard the voice but saw no man, when Christ appeared to him, but in Acts 22:9 Paul says that his companions saw the light, but they did not hear the voice of Christ who spoke to him. How can these passages be reconciled?

In Acts 9:7 the Greek word **phone**=voice, sound, is in genitive and implies that Paul's companions heard some sort **of sound,** but "they did not hear **the voice (phone** in accusative) of him who spoke" (Acts 22:9) to Paul. His companions saw the **light,** but they did not see Christ ("no man"); only Paul saw Him. There is no conflict between these two passages.

Something similar takes place even now. There are numerous people who hear a sort of "sound" when the Gospel is preached, and they may see in it some kind of "light" (moral, etc.), but they do not hear the "voice" of Christ to themselves, neither do they "see" Him as their own Savior and Lord.

45. Does God "Repent"?

We read in Nu. 23:19: "God is not man, that he ... should repent." But in Gen. 6:6 we are told that "it repented the Lord that he had made man." How can these passages be harmonized?

We read in Jer. 18:7-9: the words of the Lord:

> "If at any time I speak concerning a nation or a kingdom, to pluck it up, and to pull down, and to destroy it; if that nation, concerning which I have spoken, turns from its evil, I will repent of the evil that I thought to do to it. And if at any time I speak concerning a nation or a kingdom to build and plant it; if it do evil in my sight, that it obey not my voice, then I will repent of the good, with which I said I had intended to do to it."

God is both holy and merciful. In His holiness He hates sin and punishes those who love sin and continue in it; but He has mercy on the penitent. He deals with men according to this eternal rule which is based on His own nature, which is holiness and love.

The word "repent" has different meanings, just as many other words have, and the context shows in each case what it means. The statement in Nu. 23:19 means that God does not "repent" in a human manner: He cannot repent of sin, for He has no sin; neither can He repent of error, for He does not commit mistakes.

When the Bible uses in reference to God the word "repent" (Hb. SHUB=turn around, change one's mind, be converted), it means that, in a certain sense, God "changes His mind," doing it relative to the attitude men take to Him and His word, as He Himself says in the quoted passage.

Nineveh in the time of Jonah was an example of the "repentance" of God mentioned first in the said passage: He threatened to destroy that city after 40 days, but when the people of Nineveh humbled themselves to repent of their sins, God "repented" of His threat and recalled it, having mercy on its people.

What happened to David's descendants on the throne of Israel and Judah is an example of the last mentioned "repentance" of God. He gave David the promise, which, however, was conditional: "If thy sons take heed to their way, to walk before me in faithfulness with all their heart and with all their soul, there shall not fail thee ... a man on the throne of Israel" (1 Ki. 2:4). God, however, "repented" of this promise because of the ungodliness of many descendants of David, since they did not walk before Him in faithfulness, and so there was no man on the natural throne of Judah after 586 B.C. The promise to David has been fulfilled in a higher supernatural sense in Christ, who occupies the "throne of David" in the spiritual kingdom of God (Lk. 1:32f.; Jh. 18:33-37; Acts 15:16). Another example of the same thing is in Jesus' parable of the unmerciful servant: The servant was forgiven his huge debt, but the king retracted his forgiveness when the servant subsequently refused to forgive his fellow servant his small debt (Mt. 18: 23-35).

It "repented God" that He had created man in the sense that He decided to destroy men from the earth because of their wickedness, sorrowful on account of it; but He gave them 120 years during which Noah had to serve as a "preacher of righteousness" among them in order that they would repent, turn from their evil ways, and be pardoned, for His "heart" is seen from His words in Ez. 33:11:

> "As I live, saith the Lord God, I have no pleasure in the death of the wicked; but that the wicked turn from his way and live; turn ye, turn ye from your evil ways; for why will ye die...?"

46. Election and Responsibility. Eternal Security and Backsliding

Jesus says in Jh. 6:37, 39: "All that the Father giveth me will come to me; and him who cometh to me I will in no wise cast out... And this is the will of him who sent me, that of all that he hath given me I should lose nothing, but should raise it up at the last day." In Jh. 10:27-29 Jesus says: "My sheep hear my voice, and I know them, and they follow me; and I give them eternal life, and they shall never perish, and no one shall snatch them out of my hand. My Father who hath given them to me is greater than all; and no one is able to snatch them out of the Father's hand." Paul writes in the same tone in Rom. 8:30, 38, 39: "Whom he foreordained, them he also called; and whom he called, **them he also justified**; and whom he justified, them he also glorified... I am persuaded that neither death, nor life, nor **angels**, nor principalities,... nor any other creature will be able to separate us from the love of God, which is in Christ Jesus our Lord." But on the other hand Jesus says in Lk. 13:34: "How often would I have gathered thy children together, as a hen gathereth her own brood under her wings, but ye would not." And Paul warns in 1 Cor. 10:1-12, using the illustration of what happened to the Israelites, that people who once are saved may fall and be lost. "Wherefore, let him who thinketh he standeth take heed lest he fall." In Gal. 5:4 he writes to the Galatians who once were in Christ: "Ye are severed from Christ, ye who would be justified by the law; ye are fallen away from grace." And 2 Pet. 2:20-

22 speaks of people, who once through the knowledge of Christ have escaped the defilements of the world, but may be again entangled in them, so that their last state becomes worse than the first. Isn't there conflict between these two groups of passages?

An apparent conflict, to be sure, exists here, and this has caused doctrinal tensions in the Christian Church. There was such a conflict among the Lutherans in the 1550's - 1570's, and another one in the Reformed church in the 17th and 18th centuries, between the Arminians and Calvinists. The former took onesidedly the passages that speak of the responsibility of man both in conversion and preservation; the latter appealed as one-sidedly to the passages that speak of salvation and preservation by grace alone, teaching the unfailing conversion and eternal security of the elect: The truly converted can never be lost; once saved always saved.

The Bible teaches both, and we cannot reconcile them in a rational and logical manner. We should not even attempt it, but let both sets of statements be as they are. The Bible teaches, on the one hand, that all those whom the Father draws to Jesus come to Him. And in Acts 13:48 we read: "As many as were ordained to eternal life believed." Sinners are saved by grace, through faith; not by their own doing but by the gift of God (Eph. 2:8f.). "It is not of him who willeth, nor of him who runneth, but of God who hath mercy" (Rom. 9:16). But on the other hand, Scripture emphasizes man's responsibility, as in the quoted word of Jesus in Lk. 13:34. In Ez. 33:7-16 the Lord speaks emphatically about how the man who is warned and called to repentance is responsible for his death if he does not heed, and the righteous is likewise himself guilty if he sins and falls away. Heb. 3 and 4 quotes twice the OT words: "Today, if ye hear his voice, harden not your hearts," admonishing Christians to take care that no one would have an evil, unbelieving heart that falls away from the living God. King Saul was truly born again: God gave him a new heart, and His Spirit came upon him (1 Sam. 10:9f.). But when he disobeyed God and did not repent, the Spirit of God left him, and an evil spirit troubled him (1 Sam. 16:14). A born-again child of God, who once has been enlightened and tasted the heavenly gift, becoming a partaker of the Holy Spirit and tasting the good word of God and the powers of the age to come, can fall away to the extent that he cannot be restored to repentance (Heb. 6:4-8; cp. 10:26-30). The Christian is guarded for salvation by the power of God, through faith (1 Pet. 1:5), but he may also fall and be cut off (Rom. 11:22). Even a Christian worker, unless he watches and prays, mortifying his flesh by the Spirit, after preaching to others, can be rejected (1 Cor. 9:26f.; Rom. 8:13).

It has always been harmful for the Christian faith to take onesidedly either one of these two groups of passages. They should be taught and believed with equal emphasis and earnestness, without attempting to fit them together in a rational manner. A living faith lives in the tension between the two. They are in conflict when taken according to natural human logic, but they are not discrepant when taken in faith; rather, both of them belong necessarily to the Christian preaching and teaching of the way of salvation and to the believer's good fight of faith. Although we cannot reconcile them according to human logic, we recognize them as belonging to the divine wisdom which is foolishness to the natural reason, but through which God saves those who believe (1 Cor. 1:20-25).

The modern doctrine of "eternal security" ("once saved always saved") is a variation of the old doctrine of predestination, another attempt of the human reason to follow with a straight human logic a line that does not exist in the Bible alone, but always in tension with another line, the one that emphasizes man's responsibility. Since God has joined these two together, let no man put them asunder, whatever are the difficulties from the point of view of human logic.

47. Attitude toward Enemies

According to Deut. 20:16ff., the Lord gave the Israelites the order to destroy utterly the peoples of Canaan, that they would not lead them astray to idolatry and other abominations. But in Prov. 25:21 the Israelites were instructed to do good to their enemies: "If thy enemy is hungry, give him bread to eat; and if he is thirsty, give him water to drink; for thou shalt heap coals of fire upon his head, and the Lord will reward thee." Jesus commands in Mt. 5:44 and Lk. 6:35f. us to love our enemies, pray for them and to do them good. But in many psalms the psalmists pray God to avenge and even destroy their enemies (e.g. Pss. 5:9-11; 10:15; 17:13; 137:8f.). How can we reconcile these apparently conflicting passages?

God is not only love; He also is a holy God, whose wrath is revealed from heaven against all ungodliness and unrighteousness of men, who hold the truth in unrighteousness (Rom. 1:18). When Israel went to conquer the land of Canaan, "the iniquity of the Amorites" who dwelled there was "full" (Gen. 15:16), and so God's wrath was revealed against their wickedness in their destruction through the Israelites. The iniquity of Sodom and Gomorrah was full in the time of Abraham, and so they were overthrown by means of fire and brimstone. The same had been true when God had destroyed the inhabitants of the earth by means of the great flood, with the exception of Noah and his family.

God uses different means for "cutting off" the people who incur His wrath because of their wickedness and impenitence. One of them is to deliver them into the hands of their enemies. This was the means that God used in destroying large numbers of the peoples of Canaan, and He used the same means for punishing the Israelites themselves when they turned to iniquity.

We have no right to murmur, when God's judgments fall upon men because of their wickedness, for His works are righteous. We should, rather, search ourselves, lest there is any wicked way in us, and repent of our own sins, seeking God's mercy, in order that we may not also fall under His judgment.

God has time and again given certain men the task of executing His judgments, and these men have had to obey, whatever have been their human feelings; otherwise they have drawn God's wrath upon themselves. The Israelites were punished by God by means of the Canaanites whom they did not "cut off" as He had ordered them to do. King Saul incurred God's wrath when he disobeyed His order to destroy all the Amalekites (1 Sam. 15).

As we have no right to murmur on account of God's temporal punishments, so we have no right to complain because of His eternal punishment in hell, as the liberals have frequently done. "We are sure that the judgment of God rightly falls upon those who commit such things...; who will render to every man according to his deeds... To those who are self-willed and do not obey the truth, but obey unrighteousness, indignation and wrath, tribulation and anguish upon every soul of man who doeth evil" (Rom. 2:2, 6, 8f.).

When the psalmists prayed punishment upon their enemies who were, first of all, enemies of God in their carnal mind, they did not do it according to the mind of flesh. It was the Holy Spirit who in this manner pronounced judgment on impenitent sinners, in order to turn them to repentance. We have a complete misunderstanding of these psalms if we regard them as expressions of human vindictiveness. In reality they are divine proclamations of judgment through the agency of these men, in other words, God's law in order to work knowledge and conviction of sin in sinners. Without such law and the conviction worked through it the proclamation of God's grace and forgiveness would be futile.

48. Does God Originate Evil?

Deut. 32:4 says of God: "He is the Rock; his work is perfect, for all his ways are justice; a God of truth and without iniquity, just and right is he." But in Am. 3:6 we read: "Will there be evil in a city, and the Lord hath not done it?" And in Is. 45:6f. the Lord Himself says: "I am the Lord... I form the light, and create darkness; I make peace, and create evil." How can these passages be harmonized?

Bible passages like these are to be understood in the

light of the divine law of holiness and mercy, set forth e.g. in Jer. 18:7-11 (quoted before). The "evil" that God "creates" is in Hb. RA' or RA'AH, and this word means woe (so it is translated in Is. 45:7 in RSV), sorrow, adversity, calamities, **not** moral wrong, sin. God "creates" woes and calamities as punishments and chastisements because of sin, in order to turn to repentance those whose measure of sin is not yet full, and in order to destroy those who have hardened their hearts and committed "sin to death" (1 Jh. 5:16). God never "creates" evil in the sense of sin and wrong, but only in the sense of woe, sorrow, calamities, etc. as punishments of sin. "He who is often reproved, yet hardeneth his neck, shall suddenly be destroyed, and that without remedy" (Prov. 29:1).

49. Peace or Conflict?

The coming Messiah, Christ, is called in Is. 9:6f. "the Prince of Peace," in whose kingdom peace will have no end, and the angels sang after His birth: "... on earth peace among men of good pleasure" (so literally; ASV: "in whom he is well pleased"; RSV: "with whom he is pleased," Lk. 2:14). But in Lk. 12:51ff. and Mt. 10:34f. Jesus says:

> "Suppose ye that I have come to give peace on earth? I tell you, Nay; but rather division; from henceforth there will be five in one house divided, three against two, and two against three. The father will be divided against the son, and the son against the father ..."

> "Think not that I have come to bring peace on earth; I came not to bring peace, but a sword. For I have come to set a man against his father, and the daughter against her mother... And a man's foes will be those of his own household."

How can these different statements be reconciled?

Christ gives inward peace through forgiveness of sins and free justification in His blood to those who repent of their sins and accept Him as their Savior and Lord. But most people do not repent and accept the Gospel, but are in their carnal mind aroused to anger by the call to repentance and faith, beginning to hate and persecute Christians, particularly witnessing believers. Jesus says:

> "The servant is not greater than his lord. If they have persecuted me, they will also persecute you ... all these things they do to you for my name's sake, because they know not him who sent me" (Jh. 15:20f.).
>
> "Blessed are ye, when men will revile you and persecute you and say all manner of evil against you falsely, for my sake" (Mt. 5:11).

Paul writes in 2 Tim. 3:12: "All who will live godly in Christ Jesus will suffer persecution." True believers are "peacemakers" (Mt. 5:9), but not between truth and falsehood, right and wrong, God and the devil, the ungodly world and kingdom of God. The condition of peace is always repentance of sin, acceptance of the Gospel of Christ, and submission to the obedience of faith—never without these. Since most people refuse to accept these God-given conditions of peace, no peace is possible between believers and unbelievers. The believers, on the one hand, cannot let the unbelievers go on in their evil way without warning and calling to repentance, and the unbelievers, on their part, cannot but hate believers because of this. There are, of course, good-natured unbelievers who let Christians alone, and also those who in their conscience feel that they are right, and therefore may even be friendly to them. But the general rule is the one set forth by Christ in Jh. 15:19:

> "If ye were of the world, the world would love its own; but because ye are not of the world, but I have chosen you out of the world, therefore the world hateth you."

50. Paul and James

Paul writes in Rom. 3:28 that "man is justified by faith apart from the works of the law," but James writes (2:24), that "man is justified by works and not by faith alone." How can these passages be reconciled?

The Bible teaches a two-fold righteousness:

1. Justification by faith, which takes place when a sinner repents and receives in faith the Gospel-promise of forgiveness of sins in the name and blood of Jesus, trusting

in Him alone as his righteousness, as a hymnist writes: "Nothing in my hands I bring, Simply to thy cross I cling."

2. Righteousness of life or sanctification, the new obedience which is worked by the Holy Spirit in those who believe in Christ.

These two, forgiveness and renewal, justification and creation of a new heart and mind, make up together the new birth or regeneration, and when this is real, good works in love necessarily follow.

A person cannot be justified by grace, for Christ's sake, through faith, unless the righteousness of life or sanctification follows. He is not justified because and on the basis of the renewal and his sanctified life, but the sanctification of life is a proof and evidence that justification through faith has really taken place, and is no mere sham and empty words. And a person cannot lead a righteous life in obedience to God's word and in love unless he has been first justified by grace and born again of the Holy Spirit.

Both Paul and James teach these two kinds of righteousness, the imputed righteousness of Christ that is accepted as a free gift without works, and the righteousness of life that is a fruit of faith and the work of the indwelling Spirit. Paul writes:

> "A man is not justified by the works of the law, but through faith in [Greek: of] Jesus Christ... For in Christ Jesus neither circumcision availeth any thing, nor uncircumcision; but faith which worketh by love" (Gal. 2:16; 5:6).

> "Sin shall not have dominion over you; for ye are not under the law, but under grace... Being then made free from sin, ye became servants of righteousness... But now being made free from sin, and become servants to God, ye have your fruit unto sanctification, and the end everlasting life" (Rom. 6:14, 18, 22).

> "For by grace ye are saved through faith..., it is a gift of God; not of works, that no man should glory. For we are his workmanship, created in Christ Jesus for good works, which God hath before prepared, that we should walk in them" (Eph. 2:8-10).

James writes:

> "Of his own will he brought us forth by the word of truth, that we should be a kind of firstfruits of his creatures... But be ye doers of the word, and not hearers only... What doth it profit, my brethren, though a man say he hath faith, and have not works?... If a brother or sister is naked and in lack of daily food, and... ye give them not those things which they need for the body; what doth it profit? Even so faith by itself, if it hath not works, is dead" (Jas. 1:18, 22; 2:14-17).

As a good tree brings good fruit, so a person who has become a new creature through faith is active in good works of love. But if one claims to be a believer and justified by grace, but his life does not give evidence of true faith in love and good works, this shows that he has a "dead faith," a mere profession of it, but not the reality, a mere lamp, but no oil. Jesus says: "By their fruits ye will know them" (Mt. 7:16, 20). Paul and James teach the same thing on these basic issues of Christianity.

51. Law of Love, False Teachers, and Christian Unity

In Mt. 5:44f. and Lk. 6:35 Christ says that we should love our enemies and be friendly to all men, and Paul teaches the same thing in Rom. 12:17-21. However, Jesus spoke to His opponents, the Pharisees and scribes, very sternly and severely, saying to them many times:: "Woe to you..." (Mt. 23). And He said to His disciples: "Beware of false prophets, who come to you in sheep's clothing, but inwardly they are ravening wolves" (Mt. 7:15). Paul gives Christians several severe injunctions to avoid heretics (e.g. Rom. 16:17f.; Tit. 3:10). John forbids Christians even to receive into their houses those who do not have the doctrine of Christ (2 Jh. 9ff.). Don't these instructions contradict one another?

False prophets and false teachers, in other words, representatives of various kinds of heresy and apostasy, have, in one way or another, forsaken the truth of God's Word and oppose it. They are "wolves" who destroy the Church. As Satan's agents they try to lead astray the followers of Christ, or, then, attempt to hinder people from obeying the truth and becoming His disciples.

False teachers should not, of course, be hated or treated in an unfriendly manner. "The servant of the Lord must not strive; but be gentle to all men, apt to teach, patient, in meekness instructing the opponents; if God perhaps may grant them repentance that they will come to know the truth, and that they may recover from the snare of the devil..." (2 Tim. 2:24ff.). In Rev. 2:15 Jesus said that He hated the doctrine of the Nicolaitanes, and commended the angel (leader) of the church in Pergamos for doing the same. False doctrine must be hated, but not the people.

False doctrine and error is never "innocent." It is always due to the person's refusal to submit to the teachings of the Bible in their simple literal sense. Its basic source is the carnal mind's revolt against the divine authority. The errorist looks for views and interpretations that in one way or another satisfy the "itching ears" of his flesh. As long as he follows this perverse way and refuses to submit in a simple childlike trust and obedience to the authority of God's Word, he is at the mercy of his sinful prejudices, a slave of the depraved paths of his carnal thinking and feeling, the opinions of men, the propaganda of the time, popular catchwords, etc. He is, as Paul writes, "tossed to and fro and carried about with every wind of doctrine, by the trickery of men, by craftiness in deceitful scheming" (Eph. 4:14).

False teachers are not only deceived themselves, but they are deceivers who lead others astray, as Paul writes in 2 Tim. 3:13: "Evil men and deceivers (impostors) will go on from bad to worse, deceiving, and being deceived."

Christian love does not require fellowship and cooperation with false teachers, for true love "rejoiceth not in iniquity (ASV: in unrighteousness; RSV: at wrong, Gr. **adikia**), but rejoiceth in truth" (1 Cor. 13:6). There cannot be true fellowship, unity and cooperation without faith in and obedience to God's truth in the Bible. The contrast of "being tossed to and fro, and carried about with every wind of doctrine, by the sleight of men," is "following the truth in love" (Gr. **aletheuontes en agape**="truthing in love").

All attempts to build up fellowship and cooperation between truth and falsehood, Bible-believing children of God and false teachers is strictly prohibited by the word of God, for such a fellowship would merely lead to confusion and the loss of truth. If healthful milk and deadly poison are mixed together, the milk will not make the poison healthful, or even neutral, but the poison makes the milk lethal. Therefore Scripture, out of love and concern for the salvation of men and maintenance of divine truth, directs Christians to admonish errorists, and if they do not heed, withdraw from them and refuse fellowship and cooperation with them:

> "A man who is a heretic after the first and second admonition reject (RSV: have nothing to do with him); knowing that he who is such is perverted and sinneth, being self-condemned" (Tit. 3:10f.).
>
> "Mark those who cause division and offences contrary to the doctrine which ye have learned; and avoid them. For such ones serve not our Lord Christ, but their own belly; and by good words and fair speeches deceive the hearts of the simple" (Rom. 16:17f.).
>
> "Whoever goeth onward [beyond what is written in God's word], and abideth not in the doctrine of Christ, hath not God . . . If there come any to you, and bring not this doctrine, receive him not into your house and greet him not. For he who greeteth him is partaker of his evil deeds" (2 Jh. 9-11).

An attempt to build up fellowship and unity between believers and unbelievers, Bible-believing Christians and apostates from the truth of God's Word, in reality means to try to reconcile Christ and the devil. Paul writes in 2 Cor. 6:14-18:

> "Be not unequally yoked with unbelievers; for what fellowship have righteousness and iniquity? or what communion hath light with darkness? And what concord hath Christ with Belial? or what portion hath a believer with an unbeliever? . . . Wherefore, Come ye out from among them and be ye separate, saith the Lord, and touch no unclean thing; and I will receive you, and will be to you a

Father, and ye shall be to me sons and daughters, saith the Lord Almighty."

We are living in a time when the watchword is fellowship and unity. In wide "Christian" circles the statement, "Be ye separate" is regarded as something out of place in these times. However, there is no real conflict between these words of Paul and the prayer of Christ in Jh. 17:11, 17, 21-23:

> "Holy Father, keep them in thy name whom thou hast given me, **that they may be one**, even as we ... Sanctify them in the truth; thy word is truth ... Neither for these only do I pray, but for those also who believe in me through their word; **that they may all be one;** even as thou, Father, art in me, and I in thee, that they also may be in us; that the world may believe that thou didst send me. And the glory which thou hast given me I have given them; **that they may be one** even as we are one; I in them, and thou in me, **that they may be perfected into one.**"

We have emphasized in this quotation the words of Christ in which four times He prays for the unity of His own. But He also prays for the fulfillment of the conditions, the nature, and fruits of this unity. They are:

1. The unity is between those whom God has given to Jesus, and who believe in Him through the word proclaimed by Christians.

2. It is unity between those who believe in God's word as truth, and who want to be sanctified in this truth, that is, be renewed inwardly and outwardly into harmony with this word.

3. It is a unity between those who are in God and in Christ and in whom is Christ (through faith in their hearts), and who are partakers of His glory (in grace and in fellowship with Him).

4. The pattern of this unity is the unity between the Father and the Son: As they are one God, but different persons, so Christians are different persons, but they are one in faith and love and as members of the one body of Christ, the true Church.

5. "That the world may believe" is directly dependent on that "they may be in us," that is, on the Christians' being in Christ and in God, their close communion "upward"—and only secondarily on their unity among themselves, or their "horizontal" communion.

When the ecumenists of our time again and again use the words of Christ, "that they may all be one," they usually tear it from its context, and leave off the words that are between this statement and the words, "that the world may believe,"—as though Christ's words were: "That they may all be one, that the world may believe." But if we take the immediate context of these words, they are: "That they ... may be in us, that the world may believe. "The world" (those whom God takes from it) believe the word of those who are in Christ and God.

Christ teaches here unity between His Bible-believing disciples who live in communion with Him and with God, wanting to be sanctified in the truth of God's word. He speaks of them in distinction from the world, which hates them, but in whose midst they are as His witnesses and ambassadors. This is something entirely different from the church-political merger of external church bodies, which is the goal of the ecumenical movement. The result of this movement will not be a unified body of Christ, but the great harlot church, the Great Babylon of Rev. 14, 17-19, which will be drunk of the blood of saints and of the witnesses of Jesus.

The true unity of Christians is the unity of the "holy remnant," the little flock to which the Father gives the kingdom (Lk. 12:32). It is this unity that the Christian Church confesses in the Apostles' Creed:

> "I believe the holy universal Church, the communion of saints";

And in the Nicene Creed::

> "I believe one holy, universal and apostolic Church,"

This one universal Church is built on the divine truth revealed through the apostles and prophets, Christ Jesus Himself being the chief cornerstone (Eph. 2:19f.). Without a wholehearted faith in and obedience to this revealed truth, recorded in Scripture, true unity is impossible. The **Formula of Concord** of the Lutheran Confessions sets forth the conviction of the entire Bible-believing Christendom in stating:

> "Such a peace and unanimity which is in conflict with the truth and which is aimed at its downfall will not be permanent at all, and still less such a one that is designed for the falsification of pure doctrine and for the embellishment and veiling of overt, condemned heresies" (II:11).

Those who regard external unity and organizational bigness and power as more important than faithfulness to the divine truth will succeed in building up a World Church colossus. But God is doing His work of salvation and sanctification through His faithful remnant, the "little flock." Dr. Martyn Lloyd-Jones writes in his excellent book **The Basis of Christian Unity** to the point:

> "Unity must ... never be thought of primarily in numerical terms, but always in terms of life. Nothing is so opposed to the biblical teaching as the modern idea that numbers and powerful organization alone count. It is the very opposite of the biblical doctrine of the 'remnant' ... God has done His greatest work throughout the centuries through remnants, often even through individuals ... Reformation and Revival go together and cannot be separated. He is the 'Spirit of truth,' and He will honour nothing but the truth. The ultimate question facing us these days is whether our faith is in men and their power to organize, or in the truth of God in Christ Jesus and the power of the Holy Spirit" (pp. 63f.).

An outward ecclesiastical unity and external greatness in a united World Church will never lead the world to believe. Conversion and true faith is the work of the Holy Spirit, and the divine Spirit works only where men honor God's Word and in the power of the Holy Spirit rightly divide this Word of Truth.

X. SOME FAULTY TRANSLATIONS

The translators of King James Version (1611) tried to be true to the original text, and most of the faults of this version are due to the fact that the Greek text of the New Testament that they used was late and contained numerous errors made by copyists. The American Standard Version (1901) is the most accurate version available, but even it contains mistakes. The Revised Standard Version (1946-52) is more fluent and modern in its use of English but it is not nearly as reliable as ASV: In numerous cases the translators have put into the text their own ideas of what the text should mean, and have not followed its exact grammatical meaning. In certain cases these translations of RSV contain ideas prevalent among the theologians of the liberal trend. Our purpose is not to take up all false renderings of the various versions but only a few selected disturbing and misleading ones (in addition to the cases already dealt with before).

Judges 15:19: Spring at Lehi.

KJV renders this passage: "But God clave an hollow place that was in the jaw, and there came water thereout; ... where he [Samson] called the name thereof En-Hakkore, which is Lehi..." **Lehi** means **jaw**, but here it is the name of the locality. Both ASV and RSV have corrected the translation of this passage and have: "hollow place that is in (at) Lehi."

2 Ki. 6:25: Price of "dove's dung."

KJV, ASV and RSV translate here that the fourth part of a kab (cab) of "dove's dung" cost five pieces of silver in Samaria during its siege by the Syrians. Bible interpreters are rather unanimous that the Hebrew word HIRJONIM used here was the name of a plant (Matthew Henry: "fitches, or lentils, or some such coarse corn, then called dove's dung"; Jamieson-Fausset-Brown: "a kind of pulse or pea";

Francis Davidson: "more likely some weed of which this was the popular name"). The translation "dove's dung" is wholly misleading. Since there is no certainty on what plant is meant, the best rendering may be, "kab of hirjonim plants."

2 Ki. 23:29: Pharaoh Neco and king of Assyria

Both KJV and ASV translate here: "Pharaoh-neco king of Egypt went up against the king of Assyria to the river Euphrates; and king Josiah went against him." It may be asked: Why did Josiah go against Neco when he was on his way against Assyria, the archenemy of Judah at that time? A clay tablet has solved this problem: The united armies of Babylonia and Media were attacking Assyria, and its capital, Nineveh, had already fallen. Pharaoh Neco went to help the remnants of the Assyrian army, and Josiah wanted to prevent him from giving aid to Assyria. This was the reason why he went against Neco. The Hebrew preposition 'al used here means: **on, upon, above, because of, for the sake of, on behalf of.** RSV translates here: "to the king of Assyria." In order to make the meaning clear this passage should be translated either as it is in RSV or, "on behalf of the king of Assyria." The rendering of KJV and ASV is the very opposite of the meaning of the text.

Ps. 2:11: "Kiss the Son," or, "kiss his feet"?

Both KJV and ASV render the words in Ps. 2:12: "Kiss the Son, lest he be angry...," but RSV has here: "kiss his feet lest he be angry..." The translation of KJV and ASV is correct, for the word BAR means **son**, never "feet." This word is the first part of the names **Barsabbas** (son of Sabbas, Acts 1:23), **Barnabas** (son of exhortation, Acts 4:36), **Barabbas** (son of father, Mt. 27:16ff.), Bartimaeus (son of Timaeus, Mk. 10:46), etc.

Prov. 8:22-25: "Possessed" or "created"?

KJV and ASV translate here: "The Lord [Jehovah] possessed me in the beginning of his way, before his works of old... Before the mountains were settled, before the hills I was brought forth." RSV renders this passage: "The

HATH GOD SAID?

Lord created me at the beginning of his work, the first of his acts of old ..." The rendering of KJV and ASV is correct. The Hebrew QANA' never means "create" (the Genesis 1-2 account of creation never uses this word, but the words BARA' and ASA'). The word QANA' means **to buy, to acquire, to possess.** The word DEREK means **way,** never "work," as RSV translates it. The translation of RSV seems to be influenced by the liberal denial of the deity of Christ. Jehovah's Witnesses, who also deny Christ's deity, naturally like the RSV rendering because it gives support to their doctrine. God **had** or **possessed** the Wisdom (which here obviously refers to Christ called in Jh. 1:1 LOGOS, WORD) from the beginning of His **ways.** He did not **create** Him at the beginning of His **works.** The Hebrew word QEDEM means **before,** as KJV and ASV correctly translate it, not "the first of" as RSV renders it. Thus, when translated correctly this passage gives no support to those who deny the deity of Christ.

Eccl. 3:19-21: The fate of men and beasts.

KJV translates here: "For that which befalleth the sons of men befalleth beasts;... as the one dieth, so dieth the other; yea, they have all one breath... All go unto one place; all are of the dust, and all turn to dust again. Who knoweth the spirit of man that goeth upward, and the spirit of the beast that goeth downward to the earth?" ASV renders verse 21: "Who knoweth the spirit of man, whether it goeth upward, and the spirit of beast, whether it goeth downward to the earth?" RSV translates: "Who knows whether the spirit of man goes upward and the spirit of the beast goes down to the earth." As rendered in ASV and RSV, this verse is as though written by an agnostic (a person who thinks that it is impossible to know whether there is a God or a future life, or anything beyond material phenomena) and not by a biblical writer. This translation is, however, in conflict with the literal grammatical meaning of the Hebrew text, which is rendered correctly in KJV. The Hebrew text has nothing that corresponds to the word "whether," but it has, as KJV translates it: "Who knoweth the spirit of man..." ASV and RSV give support to the doctrine (held by Jehovah's Witnesses, etc.) that men die as animals, having no conscious life after death (until resurrection). The mentioned errorists also use the words in Eccl. 9:10: "There is no work, nor device, nor knowledge, nor wisdom, in Sheol (KJV: grave), whither thou goest." The word "Sheol" means in the OT either grave or Hades (the "underworld" where the wicked are after death). The context determines what it means in each case. Eccl. 12:5, 7 states: "Man goeth to his everlasting home... and the dust returneth to the earth as it was, and the spirit returneth unto God who gave it." The statements in Eccl. 3:21 and 12:5, 7 both teach that the **spirit of man** does not go down to the earth as the spirit of animals goes, but **to its everlasting home, to God:** the believer to dwell with God in the eternal home, the ungodly before Him for judgment, and then into the place of eternal punishment. The statements of Eccl. 3:19-20 and 9:10 speak of the state of man's body **in grave,** and what they say is true: as to his **body** the fate of man is the same as the fate of animals. There is no conscious life in grave. But the soul of man (his spirit) does not go to grave: In His story of the rich man and Lazarus Jesus shows that both the wicked and the believers have a conscious life after death as to their soul, their real self, while their bodies are in grave and turn to "dust." In speaking of his own death Paul wrote that he expected after death to be "absent (away) from the body at home with the Lord" (2 Cor. 5:8). In death he was to "depart and be with Christ" (Phil. 1:23). Christ certainly is not in grave, and "at home with the Lord" cannot be in grave. The teachings of the Bible on these matters are quite clear and consistent if we let Scripture interpret itself and have it translated correctly.

Heb. 9:4: **Altar of incense or censer?**

The Old Testament tabernacle and temple had two parts, the first of them being the "Holy place," and the second one "Holy of holies." The former had among its utensils an altar of incense. The latter contained the ark of covenant with statues of cherubs on top of it. A golden censer belonged to its utensils, although it was not kept there. The high priest used it when he on the Day of Atonement went into the Holy of holies. Heb. 9:4 speaks of the utensils of the Holy of holies, using the Greek word **thymiaterion.** KJV translates this word **censer,** whereas both ASV and RSV render it with the word **altar of incense.** The word **thymiaterion** means both altar of incense and censer, and the context determines its meaning. In Heb. 9:4 it clearly denotes **censer.** It is hard to understand why ASV and RSV have replaced the correct rendering of KJV into one that in this context is wrong.*

---

* W. Bauer's **A Greek-English Lexicon of the New Testament** (transl. by W. F. Arndt and F. W. Ginrich, Univ. of Chicago Press, 1963), explains the word **thymiaterion:** "properly a place or vessel for the burning of incense." The commentary of Jamieson-Fausset-Brown also gives a correct interpretation of the word **thymiaterion** in Heb. 9:4.

CONCLUSION

(Prayer)

We thank and praise Thee, dear Father and Savior, for Thy holy Word, Scripture, which is the Truth that abides for ever. Work in us by Thy Holy Spirit a simple childlike faith in the truth of Thy Word and a wholehearted obedience to it. Sanctify us in Thy truth, so that our minds would be enlightened, our emotions and motives renewed and purified, and our wills and actions guided and controlled by thy Spirit into a full harmony with Thy Word.

Lord, give us strength and courage to contend earnestly for the faith that Thou hast once for all delivered to Thy saints in Thy inerrant Word. Help all thy children to be boldly outspoken against all apostasy and error, but help them also to be wise and fervent in their testimony to Thy grace and truth.

Help us all, O Lord, who are Thy children through faith in Christ, to be united in faith and love. But give us also firmness and determination to be separate in the right way and to refuse from being unequally yoked with unbelievers and apostates from Thy Word, that truth and falsehood would not be commingled and confused, but that the light of Thy grace and truth may shine through us purely and brightly among men. Help us, our Savior, by Thy Holy Spirit to avoid and overcome all the snares and cunning craftiness of the evil one and his agents by Thy blood, O Lamb of God, and by the word of our testimony, and not to love our life but to stand firm and faithful to Thee to the end.

All this we pray in Thy Name, Thou Faithful and True God, our Savior and Lord Jesus Christ. Amen.

SCRIPTURE INDEX

GENESIS
1:1	75
1:1-2:3	86
1:1-2:4a	67
1:3	168
1:3-5	167
1:6ff.	166
1:7	168
1:10	167
1:11f	167
1:14-18	168
1:20	166
1:25	168
1:26	168
1:26f	167
1:27	174
2:4ff	167
2:4	95
2:4-24	86
2:7	174
2:24	183
3:1-10	10
3:13	183
3:15	70
3:17	183
3:19	171
4:26	62, 63, 74
5:1	95
5:4	195
5 and 11	174
5:7	193
6:1	96
6:1-2	75
6:4	186
6:11	186
6:12	186
6:19f	186
7:2f	186
10:1	96
10:3	188
11	167
11:1-13	178
11:10	96
11:26-32	192
11:27	96
12:1f	193
12:4	192
12:6	84, 197
13:7	84
14:1	196
14:14	191
15:13	108, 115
	193, 194
17:1	77
17:6	85
17:19	87
18:12	87
20:11f	195
20 and 26	87
21:1	77
22:2	195
23:17f	196, 197
25:6	195
25:12	96
25:19	96
32:28	221
35:11	85
36:1	96
36:31	85
37:2	96
37:25	36
38	20
39	76
39:1	87
41:43	92
41:45	92
44:18	24
46:20	196
46:27	196
49	114, 118
49:10	85

EXODUS
2:23	94
3:6	71
3:12	75
3:13ff	62, 63, 74
6:3	63, 74
6:3ff	77
6:20	76
9:3-6	198
12:40	193
14:9	198
20	71
20:12	71
20:24	78, 79, 98
20:22-23:33	62
21:17	71
24:4	68
33:11	114

LEVITICUS
1, 4, 6, 8, 11, 13-25, 27	68
2:6f	215
13:1	71
13:49	71
14:2ff	71
18:5	72
18:9, 29	194
18:24f	98
20:9	71
20:21	195
23:5ff	89
24:13	113
23:5ff	89
25:1	113

NUMBERS
1, 2, 4-6, 8, 9, 13, 15, 17, 19	68
3:17-19, 27-28	68, 178
4:3, 38f	204
8:24	204
12:3	83
12:6-8	114
14:22	18
14:24	98
20:14ff	85
20:14-21	198
20:23	198
23:19	259f
23:24	114
25:9	190
24:7	85
26:59	76
27:17, 27ff.	98
28:16ff	89
32:19	84

DEUTERONOMY
1:1, 5	83
1:36	98
2:3-7	198
2:4	198
2:8	198
3:8, 20	84
3:8	83
3:20, 25	84
4:2	68, 105
4:41-49	83
5:15	71
6:6	259
7:2f	98
7:3f	99
8:6	20
10:1ff	105
11:29	69
12:2	79
12:4-14	77, 79

12:5-28 69	24 98	6:17f 81	15:27-31 110
12:11-14 203	24:2-10 80	7:4 114	15:30 .... 205, 208
12:31 199	24:2, 14f 178	8:3 188	16:7-9 110
12:32 68	24:25 105	8:4 189	17:1 .... 205, 207f
16:5ff 89	24:32 .... 196f	8:17 222	17:6, 24 110
16:12 245		10:18 190	18:1 .... 206ff
17:14-20 85	**JUDGES**	14:27 201	18:4 98
18:10f 114	1:20 98	18:18 201	18:9f, 13 ..... 207f
18:15 72	5:17 98	21:8 191	18:20 122
18:15-19 70	7:8 87	24 202	20:8-11 210
18:21f 98	8:24 87	24:1 .... 201f	21:8 28
20:16ff 263	11:1-3, 34 199	24:13 189	22:8ff 105
24:1-4 71	11:30-39 198	24:24 202	23:17 108
24:16 70	15:19 275		23:29 276
25:5 213	18:27-29 191	**1 KINGS**	
25:5f 195	18:31 79	2:3 .... 28, 70	**1 CHRONICLES**
25:7ff 195	21:25 103	2:4 260	3:1 161
25:17ff 90		3:2 ...... 79, 203	6:4 220
27 99	**1 SAMUEL**	3:4 204	6:7-9 178
27:2 98	1:3, 9 79	4:26 189	10:4, 13f 200
27:11-28 .... 68, 69	2:13ff, 28 81	6:1 ..... 67, 94, 194	13:9f, 12 ..... 164f
28:29 114	2:14 79	3-8 79	15:5 28
31:9ff 68, 105	3:11 114	8:9 202	16:39 ..... 79, 204
31:23-26 105	6:9f 79	8:62ff 81	21:29 204
32:4 265	10:9f 262	11:15f 190	21:1, 25 ..... 201f
32:16-18 82	10:25 105	13:1ff 79, 108	23:3, 24, 27 ... 204
32:21 73	11:15 79	15:11, 14 203	24:29 24
33 98	14:3 79	15:16 204	29:29 24
33:9 105	15 265	16:8 .... 204f	
	16:5 79	19:15 126	**2 CHRONICLES**
JOSHUA	16:14 262	21 114	1:3 ...... 79, 204
1:7 .... 28, 80	18:19 .... 191f		9:29 24
1:7, 9 68	18:27f 192	**2 KINGS**	14:2ff 203
3:7 113	18:27f 192	6:22f 208	15:17 203
3:31 28	21:1-6 222	6:25 275	16:1 205
3:33f 69	22:23 200	8:26 205	22:2 205
10:12ff 209	23:6 .... 200, 222	10:28-31 109	24:20ff 222
4:6-15 98	28:6 200	10:30 115	26:21f, 24 205
8:1, 8 79	30:11-15 243	13 114	32:32 122
2 ..... 69, 77, 203	31:3f 200	13:1ff 116	36:6, 21 145
2:5f 80	38:23 222	14:4 79	
2:9-29 77		14:4ff 204	**EZRA**
2:23, 26f, 29 .. 81	**2 SAMUEL**	15:5 205	2:1-64 191
3:6 68	1:2-10 200	15:25, 27 208	4:2 ...... 92, 110

HATH GOD SAID?

Reference	Page	Reference	Page	Reference	Page	Reference	Page
4:6f, 23	147f	**ECCLESIASTES**		37:36	122	18:6-10	113
5:5	147f			38:7f	210	18:7-9	259
6:7, 11, 17	147	3:9-20	278	39	125	18:7-11	266
6:18	28	3:19-21	277	40:1	134	22:30	212
7:1	147	3:21	278	40:9	134	25:1	114
7:3	148, 177	9:10	278	40:22	169	25:1	144, 145
7:7-14	155	12:5, 7	278	40ff	125, 126	25:11	115
8:2	161			40-48	126	25:11f	145
9:1-12	98	**ISAIAH**		40-66	123, 127	29:10	115, 145
11:2-3	148	1:1	114	40-66	131, 132	32	242
		1:4	132	41:8f	127	32:6-15	242
NEHEMIAH		1:10	70	42:1-4	127	50-51	111
7:7-66	191	1:11-15	80	43:10	126	50-51	116
8:4	142	1:11-16	82	44:1f	127	51:60	111
13:28	92	1-39, 40-66	120	45:1	130		
		2:1-5	118	45:4f	126, 127	**EZEKIEL**	
JOB		5:13	116	45:7	266	3:17-21	113
1	202	5:22	220	46:6f	265	6:1	114
26:7	169	6:8	114	49:1-6	127	13:17	257
PSALMS		7:8	110, 115	49:3	127	14:13f, 20	261
2:11f	276	7:14	116	50:4-9	127	14:14, 20	149
5:9-11	264	7:15, 18-25	120f	52:13	127	21:21	114
10:15	264	8:2	223	53	124, 127	26-28	114
14:1	172	8:9f, 19-22	120	53	128, 129	28:2f	161
17:13	264	8:16ff	101	53	130, 132	33:1-19	113
24:2	169f	9:1-7	120, 126	53:1	128	33:7-16	262
51:17	228	9:5	110, 111	53:2-3	238	33:11	261
60	190	9:6	131	53:4	127	34:26	166
90:10, 70-80	231	9:6f	212, 266	53:5	128	35-39	118
105:9f	194	10:28-32	116	53:7f	128	37:15-22	231
110:1	109f, 116	11:1-15	118, 126	53:9	128, 132	37:39	228
119:105	16	11:1-15	212	53:12	127, 128	38-39	231
119:160	45	11:11ff	116, 231	54-66	127	38-39	158
136:6	169f	13	111	55:1	221	40:1	114
137:8f	264	16:14	116	61:1-3	127		
		20:1	114	62:6	134	**DANIEL**	
PROVERBS		20:3	116	65:17-25	118	1:1	141, 145
20:1	219	21:16	116			1:1-4	144, 145
23:31ff	219	23:15	115	**JEREMIAH**		1-2	141, 162
25:21	263	25:6	221	3:6	79	1-6	140
29:1	266	25:6-8	126	7:21ff	80	2	138, 139, 159
30:5f	105	25:9	126	7:22ff	81	2	232, 233
31:4-5	219ff	27:6	126	9:24	76	2:2	144
130:5	45	29:5-8	122	18:1	114	2:2, 4	143

2:46	141	12:2f	138	14:1-9 ... 235	19:9	71
3:5, 15	143	12:7 ... 158,	159		20:29-34	239
4:4	143	12:9	159	**MALACHI**	21:33-43	228
5	146	12:11	142	1:4 ... 58	21:33, 45	157
5:11, 18	146	12:11f	159		22:7	201
5:16, 29	146	12:11ff	158	**MATTHEW**	22:24 ... 195,	213
5:31 ... 146,	147	14:13f	161	1 ... 177, 212	22:37	20
6:1ff	146	14:20	161	1:8 ... 148, 173	22:41-45	109
6:28	141			1:16 ... 213	22:41-46	116
7 ... 137, 138,	159	**HOSEA**		1:18ff ... 216	23	269
7 ... 160, 232,	235	2:19	76	1:18, 20 ... 214	23:35	222
7:8, 20ff	141	3:1	114	1:22f ... 116	24 .... 18, 116,	158
7:8, 20ff	139	4:1	76	2 ... 215	24:1-44	116
7:8, 20ff	51	12:4	221	2:1-12 ... 112	24:14	235
7:8, 20-24	163			2:5f ... 116	24:15	137
7:8, 20f, 24f	116	**JOEL**		2:22 ... 216	24:15-20	156
7:8, 24-26	160	1:1	114	4:1ff ... 218	24:30	137
7:12ff	160	3	158	5:9 ... 267	24:34 ... 230,	231
7:13f ... 137,	139	3 ... 228,	231	5:11 ... 267	24:34	235
7:13f, 27	160			5:18 ... 45, 70	25:6	235
7:25 ... 158,	159	**AMOS**		5:18 ... 28	26:17ff	245
7:25	234	3:6	265	5:18 ... 95	26:34	239
7:28	141	3:7	119	5:44 ... 264	26:64	137
7-8 ... 139,	140	5:21-25	80	5:44f ... 269	27:5-10	241
7-8 ... 152,	158	5:21-26	82	6:23 ... 42	27:9f	241
8 ... 141,	159	5:25f	81	7:15 ... 269	27:9f	242
8:3ff	152	5:25ff	82	7:16, 20 ... 269	27:16ff	276
3:9ff ... 51,	152			8:4 ... 71	27:37	243
8:25	150	**MICAH**		3:5-13 ... 221	27:44	244
9:1 ... 141,	147	3:12	114	3:17 ... 127	28:1-10	247
9:2	145	5:2	112	10 ... 224	28:1-10	251
9:24-27 ... 116,	138	5:2	116	10:9f ... 224	28:16f	**250**
9:24-27 ... 142,	151	6:6ff	80	10:34f ... 266	28:16-20	252
9:24-17 .. 152,	217			11:12 ... 227		
9:25	152	**ZECHARIAH**		12:3, 5 ... 28	**MARK**	
9:26	160			12:39-41 ... 72	1:44	71
9:27 ... 137,	155	1:1	223	12:40 ... 210, 242	2:26 ... 221,	222
9:27 ... 156,	157	3:13	232	16:19 ... 250	6:2	248
9-12 ... 141,	143	11:12f	241	16:21 ... 243	6:8f	224
10:1 ... 141,	147	11:12f	242	16:28 ... 229	7:9f	71
11:2 ... 141,	148	12 ... 158,	228	16:42 ... 28	8:31	243
11:21-45	160	12:1	232	18:18 ... 250	9:27	229
11:36ff	160	14	235	18:23-35 ... 260	10:46	276
11:45	150	14:1	235	19:4 ... 28	10:46-52	239

HATH GOD SAID? 285

12:26 ...... 58, 71	12:51ff 266	4:23f 255	20:19 246		
12:24 28	13:34 .... 261, 262	5:44 68	20:19-23 250		
13 ...... 118, 158	16:1-14 224	5:46f 70	20:19-23 252		
13:14-18 156	16:1-14 226	6:37, 39 261	20:22 253		
13:31 ..... 27, 133	16:8 225	6:45 50	20:23 53		
14:12 245	16:16 227	6:45f 28	20:24-29 252		
14:30 239	16:29ff 72	7:19 72	21 252		
14:68-74 240	18:35-43 239	7:37-39 258			
15:25 246	21 ...... 118, 158	8:13ff 34	**ACTS**		
15:25 247	21:20-23 156	8:18, 26 27	1:4, 5, 8 253		
15:26 243	21:23 230	8:28, 47 27	1:6-12 252		
15:32 244	21:24 228	8:28 230	1:8 255		
15:42 246	21:24 .... 157, 232	9:22 144	1:18ff 241		
16 256	21:29 232	10:27 32	1:23 276		
16:1-8 251	21:30f 231	10:27-29 261	2 .... 253, 254		
16:1-11 247	21:30-31 230	10:35 45	2:4 257		
16:7 250	22:3-7 240	12:38 128	2:4-8 253		
16:9-20 249	22:34 239	12:48 .... 32, 133	3:22f 72		
16:12 .... 251, 252	23:38 243	12:49 27	4:31 257		
	23:38f 244	13:27 240	4:31ff 258		
LUKE	23:54 246	13:38 239	4:36 276		
1:1ff 217	24:1-10 251	14:24 27	5:37 214		
1:1-3 215	24:12 251	15:5 21	7:2f 193		
1:26ff 216	24:13-33 252	15:19 267	7:4 192		
1:32f 212, 260	24:25 43	15:20f 267	7:14 196		
1:35 214	24:34 252	16:4-14 255	7:15f 197		
2:2 214	24:36-49 252	16:13 ..... 32, 72	7:16 197		
2:14 266	24:44f 72	17:3 76	7:23, 30 94		
2:37 128	24:44ff 31	17:7f, 17 33	7:42-43 82		
3 .... 177, 212	24:47 250	17:8 27	8:21ff 124		
3:2 ...... 217, 218	24:49 253	17:11, 17 272	8:32ff 128		
3:23 .... 213, 217	24:50-52 252	17:17 45	9:7 259		
3:35f 178		17:21-13 272	12:7 114		
3:38 182	**JOHN**	18:28 245	13:19f 18		
4:2 218	1:1 277	18:33-37 260	13:39 72		
4:18f 127	1:32 218	18:36 229	15:15 260		
6 224	2 .... 217, 221	19:14 .... 246, 247	16:29f 228		
6:35 269	2:1 218	19:19 243	22:9 259		
6:35f 264	2:10 221	19:31 246	24:14 33		
7:1-10 221	3:5f 258	20:1 247	27:23f 114		
7:36-50 227	3:22 ..... 216, 221	20:1-18 247	28:3-6 256		
9:27 229	4:1f 216, 221	20:2 247			
10:28 21	4:1-42 217	20:2-10 251	**ROMANS**		
12:32 273	4:20 93	20:11-17 252	1:3 212		

Ref	Pg	Ref	Pg	Ref	Pg	Ref	Pg
1:18	264	12:30	255	3:17	193, 194	1:1	73
2:2, 6, 8f	265	12:31	256	3:19	114	2:13f	182
2:17-21	269	12:31	257	5:4	261	4:14ff	257
3:28	267	13:1	257	5:6	268	5:23	220
5:5	257	13:6	270	5:22	255	6:17-19	226
5:12-19	183	13:9, 12	164				
5:12-19	184	13:10, 12	165	**EPHESIANS**		**2 TIMOTHY**	
6:14, 18, 22	268	14:1	257	1:13f	255	1:1f	73
8:7	35	14:5	256	1:13f	257, 258	2:24ff	270
8:13	263	14:27-29	254	2:8f	262	3:12	267
8:14	255	14:37f	34	2:8-10	268	3:13	270
8:16	255	14:39f	256	2:19f	274	3:14ff	9
8:26f	255	15:5	252	2:24	184	3:16	33, 44, 45
8:30, 38, 38	261	15:5-8	251	4:14	270		
9:5	26	15:7	252	5:18	258	**TITUS**	
9:7f	195	15:45ff	184			1:1-4	73
9:16	262	16:16	194	**PHILLIPPIANS**		3:10	269
10:5	72	18:3	188	1:21ff	238	3:10f	271
10:16	128	18:4	189	1:23	278		
11	228	18:12	189, 190	2:7	26	**HEBREWS**	
11:12, 15	232	19:18	190			1:1	33, 119
11:22	263	21:5	190	**COLOSSIANS**		1:1f	113
12:5-8	255	21:12	189	2:3	26	1:14	185
15:4	33			2:3	47	4:7	262
16:17f	269, 271	**2 CORINTHIANS**		2:17	242	4:15	26
		1:21f	255	2:23	257	4:16	47
1 CORINTHIANS		1:21f	257	3:10	184	6:4f	258
1:6	188	2:14	49			6:4-8	263
1:20	263	3:15f	73	**1 Thessalonians**		7:26	26
2:13	34, 45	5:2	26	2:13	33	8:5	242
2:14	36	5:8	278	4:15-17	236	9:4	202
3:11	28	5:18f	250	4:17	238	9:4	278, 279
4:6	46	5:21	47			10:1	242
9:26f	263	6:14ff	186	**2 Thessalonians**		10:26-30	263
10:1-12	261	6:14-18	271	2	238	11:17	195
10:8	190	9:25	189	2:1-12	118		
10:9	18	10:5	57	2:1-12	236	**JAMES**	
10:13f	200	11:3	183	2:3	45	1:18, 22	269
12	254, 256	25:4	69	2:3, 4	238	2:14-17	269
12:2, 5, 14	253			2:10-12	45	2:24	267
12:9f	255	**GALATIANS**		3:4	34		
12:11	256	1:10	68	3:15f	33	**1 PETER**	
12:13	258	1:18	34	6	34	1:2	255
12:28-30	256	2:16	268	**1 TIMOTHY**		1:5	263

1:10f	118	4:3	30, 133	11:12	234	16:12-16	234
1:12	118, 128	5:16	266	12:6, 14	159	16:13-16	160
2:5, 9	250	5:20	26, 230	12:6, 14	234	17	116, 159
2:22	26, 47			12:9	183	17	233
2:22	128	**2 JOHN**		12:15f	9	17:3-6, 14ff	159
2:24f	128	7	161	13	116, 159	17:4	234
5:12	78	9ff	269	13	232, 233	17:6	228, 234
		9:11	271	13:1ff	160	17:9	45, 238
2 PETER				13:5	159, 234	17:14	234
1:20f	49, 74	**JUDE**		13:7	234	17:16	159
1:21	33	4	30	13:7, 11f	159	17:16	228, 234
1:23	45	14	235	13:11ff	232	19:19-21	160
2:20-22	262			13:12	233	19:20f	235
		REVELATION		13, 17, 19	139	20:1-6	235
1 JOHN		2:15	270	13, 17, 19	160	22:18	105
2:18f	161	7:1-9	238	13-22	118		
3:2	238	11:3	159	14, 17-19	273		

AUTHOR, NAME AND SUBJECT INDEX

Abiathar 200, 221f
Abib (month) 206
Abomination & desolation 156, 158
Absalom 201
Absolution 53, 250, 253
Aceldama 240ff
Adam (real man) 184f
Adoption 26
Aenon 216
Age of world and mankind 177-182
Agnostic (ism) 24, 41, 277
Agradates 147
Ahaz 205-208
Ahaziah 205
Ahasuerus .... 141 147f.
Aijalon 204
Albright, W. F. 124
ALC — see TALC
Alexander the Great 148, 153, 162
Alexander, J. A. 107
Allegorical method 52-56
Allenby 231
Allis, Oswald T. .. 107, 109-113, 116,
                                  120, 126f
Alloeosis 53-55

Amenhotep III 94
Amalekites 90f
American Standard Version
   (ASV) 157, 169, 210, 245, 247f,
                                  250, 266, 275ff
Amorites 209
Amraphel 192
Ancient Church 23
Anglican Church 15
Animals in ark 186ff
Antichrist 158, 160f, 228, 232ff, 237f
Annas 217f
Antiochus IV Epiphanes .. 51, 138ff
          141f, 150, 154f, 158, 160
Apostasy 236f
Antilegomena 23
Apology of Augsburg Confession
                              161, 238
Apostolic Church 31
Aramaic, Aramean 142f, 146
Archeology 67, 93ff, 239
Archer, Gleason L. 207f
Araunah 202
Ark of covenant 202f
Ark of Noah 186ff

Armageddon, see Harmageddon
Arminians 262
Arndt, W. 211, 279
Artaxerxes I Longimanus 147, 149, 155f
Astruc, J. 62, 74
Asa 203ff
Astyages 148
Athanasian Creed 47
Augustine 17
Augustus 217
Authority, authoritative .. 9f, 12, 22, 26-35, 44
Baasha 203f
Babylon(ia) 91, 111, 116, 125, 141, 143ff, 147, 159, 162, 191
Babylon the Great 228, 232ff, 238 273
Balaam 85
Balfour Declaration 231
Barachias, Berechiah 222f
Barth, Karl, Barthian .. 24, 55, 57
Basel 54f
Bauer, W. 279
Beersheba 194
Belshazzar 145f
Ben-hadad 209
Berosos 144
Bethel 108
Bethlehem 112, 215f
Biadzein 227f
Bible-Science Association &
  Newsletter 173, 182
British 231
Brunner, Emil 55, 57
Buddhism 11
Bultmann, R. 25, 55
Burrows, Millar 30, 63
Buswell III, J. O. 176
Caesar, Julius 84
Caiaphas 136, 217f
Cain's marriage 195
Calvinists 262
Cambyses 147f

Cana 220f
Canaanites 85
Censer 278f
Census 214f
Centurion 221
Chaldean(s) 143f, 193
Charchemish 144
Christian Beacon 66, 136
Christian Century 10
Christian Life 176
Christianity Today 207
Chronology 18, 94, 204-8, 242f
Clarke, H. W. 188
Cock's crowings 239f
Codex sinaiticus 223
Computer studies 135
Confucianism 10
Cornill, C. H. 108
Creation Research Society 182
Crucifixion, date of 245f, 266f
Cyaxeres II 147
Cyrenius 214f
Cyrus 123, 125-127, 129f, 132, 141, 146, 153f
Dan 191
Darbyan dispensationalism 156, 158
Darius 141, 146ff
Darwin 61
Davidson, A. B. 106, 120f
Davidson, A. J. 66
Davidson, F. 213
Davies, L. M. 188
Dead Sea scrolls 129, 133, 150, 163
Delitzsch, Franz 125
Dictation theory 7f, 46
Demythologizing 55
Dillmann, A. 103
Diphath-Riphath 188
Divino afflante Spiritu (papal bull) 15
Docetism 46
Documentary theory 62f, 97, 99, 108
Doederlein, J. C. 120

Doublets 86ff
Dryopithecines 175
Duhm, B. 102, 124
Ecclesiasticus 148f
Ecumenism 11, 233-238
Edom(ites) 85, 189, 198
Election 261f
Elephantine 142
Ellison, John W. 135f
EL SHADDAI 74f
"Emptied Himself" (Christ) 26, 31
Enemies, attitude toward 265f
Ephron the Hittite 196f
Esarhaddon 110
Essenes 163
Eternal security, doctrine of 261ff
Ethanim (month) 206
Ethiopian eunuch 124
Evenson, C. Richard 66
Evolution 14, 61, 170-177
Fall into sin 56, 182-185
False teachers 269f
Family records 95f
Fanatics 52
Fig tree 230ff, 235
Firmament 166f
Flood, Noachic 31, 86f, 167, 174, 180, 186ff
Fluorine method 181
Fontechevade 176
Forde, Gerhard 43
Formal Principle of the Reformation 41
Formula of Concord 16, 44, 274
Frankenberg 86
Free, Joseph P. 67, 145
Froom, LeRoy Edwin 140, 152, 158
Fundamentalism 10, 37
Gad 24
Garstang, John 94
Gellius 247
Genealogies 177f
—of Jesus 212f

Generation, last 230ff
Geological methods of geochronology 178ff
Gentiles, times of 231f
Giants 185f
Gibeon 79, 209f
Gilead 208
Gilkey, Langdon 57
Ginrich, F. W. 279
Glahn, L. 123
Golden Rule of interpretation 55f
Gog 231
Gore 112
Graf, K. H. 62, 66, 81, 99
Grave 277f
Greek Orthodox 12f
Gulin, E. G. 78, 101, 141, 143, 148
Gunkel, H. 86
Habirus 94
Hadadezer-Hadarezer 183f
Haran 192f
Harlot, great 233-237
Harmageddon 160, 234f
Harrelson, W. 99, 102, 120, 140f, 145f, 148, 150-153
Hastings Dictionary of the Bible 107
Hazael 126
Heaton, E. W. 130
Hedegard, David 11
Hegel, G. W. Fr. 64
Heidegger 25
Helsinki 12, 37
Henry, Carl F. H. 52, 56f
Herod the Great 215f
Herodot 144, 146
Hezekiah 206ff, 210
High Church 13
Hippolytus 249
Holocene 181
Homo habilis 175
Holy communion 53
Holy Spirit, gift, infilling, spiritual gifts 253-258
Hordern, William 38-43, 46f, 51

Ras-esh-Shamra 161f
Rationalism 13, 58
Red beast 231ff
Red China 233
Reformation 15, 22, 38, 41-43-52, 55
Rehwinkel, Alfred 188
Repentance 259f
Restraining factors 237f
Resurrection of Jesus, events
  after it 247-252
Reu, M. 24
Revised Standard Version, RSV 26,
  155-157, 167, 169, 210, 248, 250,
                          266, 275ff
Risen Christ on Scriptures 31
Ritschl, Albrecht 13
Roman Catholics 12f, 15, 20f,
                             32, 52, 55
Ryrie, Ch. C. 57
Saarnivaara, U. 52, 136, 235
Sadducees 245f
Samaria, Samaritan
  Pentateuch 92f, 110, 208f
Sanctification 207ff
Sargon III 110
Satan 9f, 183f, 201, 240
Saul's death 200f
Scarlet beast 233ff
Schleiermacher, F. 13
Schweitzer, Albert 32
Scofield 147, 153, 159f, 168,
                   190, 196, 213, 232
Second coming of Christ 230, 232,
                             235-239
Segal, M. 97
Sellin, Ernst 103
Sennacherib 122f, 207
Septuagint, LXX 129, 151, 162f, 196
Servant Songs 127f
Shalmanezer 207
Sheol 277
Sibylla 163
Simpson, G. G. 99, 173
Sinanthropus 175

Smerdis 147f
Smith, J. M. Powis 107
Solomon 24, 87, 90, 94
Soviet Union 231ff
Species, origin of 172-177
Spinoza, Baruch 58
St. Anthony Falls, Minneapolis 181
Stephen 82, 196
Suetonius 217
Sun, creation of 167f
Sunday School material, liberal 62,
                                65-68
Sundial of Ahaz 210
Swanscomb 176
Syria 208f, 214f
Tabernacle 77, 89f, 92
Tamar 20
Tammuz 125
Targums 142
Tanganyika 175
Teigen, B. W. 25
Tell-el-Amarna 93f
Temptations of Jesus 218f
Thaddeus 224
Theodotion 151
The American Lutheran Church,
  TALC 38, 43, 66f, 73, 132, 140
Thermodynamics 170f
Thiele, E. R. 206ff
Thieves on cross 244
Thirty-nine Articles (Anglican) 15
Threshingfloor of Araunah 202
Thutmose III 94
Thymiaterion 278f
Tiberius 217
Tiglath-pileser 110
Tishri (month) 206
TORAH 27, 58, 68, 70, 124
Tongues, gift of 253-258
Torrey, C. C. 123
Torrey, R. A. 165, 197, 246
Tradition(alistic) 12-14, 32
Trivial things 19
Tyre 114

United Church of Canada 66
Unity of Christians 269-274
Universe, structure of 168ff
Ur of Chaldea 192f
"Urge Christ against Scripture" 21
Ussher, J. 177
Uzziah 24, 205
Van Til, Cornelius 57
Vedas (India) 48
Violence to God's kingdom .. 277ff
Virgin birth of Christ 213f
Voltaire 59
Water canopy 187
Wegener, Alfred 187
Wellhausen, Julius, Wellhausenian school 58,-64, 66, 78, 80f, 99
Westminster Confession 15
Westminster Study Edition of the Bible 102, 110
Wilson, R. D. 109
Wisloff, Carl Fr. 12
Wouk, Herman 58, 65
Xenophon 146f
Xerxes 141, 147f
Yahuda, A. S. 91f
Ylioppilaslehti 37
Yochebed 76
Young, Edw. J. 48, 64, 88, 134, 140, 144
Zealot 224
Zechariah son of Barachiah .. 222f
Zerrubbabel 124, 154
Zurich 54f
Zwingli, Ulrich 53

www.ingramcontent.com/pod-product-compliance
Lightning Source LLC
Chambersburg PA
CBHW071239230426
43668CB00011B/1501